A PRACTICAL
APPROACH TO
QUALITY CONTROL

Rowland Caplen

BSc, CEng, MIEE, MIProdE, MInstP, FIQA

BUSINESS BOOKS
London Sydney Auckland Johannesburg

Business Books Ltd

An imprint of Century Hutchinson Limited

Brookmount House, 62–65 Chandos Place,
Covent Garden, London WC2N 4NW

Century Hutchinson Australia Pty Ltd
89–91 Albion Street, Surry Hills, New South Wales 2010, Australia

Century Hutchinson Group (NZ) Ltd
32–34 View Road, PO Box 40–086, Glenfield, Auckland 10

Century Hutchinson Group (SA) (Pty) Ltd
PO Box 337, Bergvlei 2012, South Africa

First published 1969
Second impression 1970
Third impression 1971
Fourth impression 1972
Second edition 1972
Second impression 1975
Third impression 1977
Third edition 1978
Fourth edition 1982
Fifth edition 1988
Second impression 1988
Third impression 1989

© Rowland Henry Caplen, 1969, 1972, 1978, 1982, 1988

Photoset in Times and Univers by Deltatype, Ellesmere Port

Printed and bound in Great Britain by
Mackays of Chatham PLC, Chatham, Kent

British Library Cataloguing in Publication Data

Caplen, Rowland
 A practical approach to quality control.
 – 5th ed.
 1. Quality control
 I. Title
 658.5'62   TS156

ISBN 0–09–173581–5

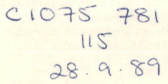

CONTENTS

Appendix

INTRODUCTION

Since the last edition was prepared, industry has become much more quality conscious, and hence quality control thinking has developed considerably. In line with this, the City and Guilds of London Institute have adopted a revised syllabus for their Certificate in Quality Control No. 743. In this 5th edition therefore I have tried to include all these developments, so that the book is once again thoroughly up to date. I have added more practical examples and techniques, so that most quality managers, quality engineers and others working in the quality field will find that it includes all the quality control they are likely to need. Hence the book can be used for reference as well as a straight text book. The most important additions this time are on vendor appraisal (chapter 4), capability studies (chapter 11), modern uses of process based quality control charts (chapter 14), u charts (chapter 15), and to quality assurance, (chapter 30), including mention of the International ISO 9000 standards.

The book continues to cover the following:

1   The complete syllabus of the Certificate in Quality Control No. 743 of the City and Guilds of London Institute. Most chapters end with questions taken from past examination papers, with the kind permission of City and Guilds. I have added a few additional problems in the same style, and provided answers to the numerical questions at the end of the book.

2   A practical introduction to quality control   The book shows how quality control can be applied to almost any practical situation, and how useful techniques can be identified and integrated into an efficient, cost conscious quality system. In doing this I have drawn on my 28 years experience both as a quality manager and as a lecturer and consultant to industry here and in Ireland. A number of original methods and techniques devised by myself have been included. For completeness the book contains essential theory.

ROWLAND CAPLEN
January 1988

PART ONE

AN INTRODUCTION TO QUALITY CONTROL AND QUALITY COSTS

CHAPTER 1

THE FIVE BASIC STAGES
OF QUALITY CONTROL

1.1   The object of quality control

The word 'quality' means different things to different people. The first car a young man buys appears to him be of superior quality, even though it is several years old and rather the worse for wear. To the company director wanting a new Rolls-Royce, however, that very same car would be merely a load of scrap. For this reason, quality is defined as 'fitness for purpose'. The second-hand car may be quite satisfactory as a runabout for our young man, but it would be a bad advertisement and insufficiently reliable for the company director. Therefore we have to consider whether the quality in question is satisfactory for the purpose for which it is intended.

Price is important too, because the quality we expect depends on how much we pay for it. When we pay £2500 for a second-hand car, we do not expect the same quality as if we were paying £15 000 for a brand new one. We shall be satisfied with a car which, in our opinion, is worth the £2500 we paid for it.

Thirdly, we shall expect our car to be delivered on time. If the manufacturer promised it in three weeks, we shall not expect to have to wait three months for it. If the delay is because the car was wrongly made in the first place, and had to be corrected before it could be delivered, we shall not have a very high opinion of that manufacturer's quality control.

The above, therefore, sets out what the customer expects, and we can rewrite it from the manufacturer's point of view, as follows.

The object of quality control is to produce a quality that:

1 Satisfies the customer.
2 Is as cheap as possible.
3 Can be achieved in time to meet delivery requirements.

Notice that our object is not to produce 'the highest possible quality', but merely to satisfy the customer. Hence the required quality level will depend on customer or market requirements, and must be related to the price the customer is prepared to pay.

1.2 Setting about quality control

Having decided our quality objectives, we must now set about achieving them in the simplest, cheapest and most practical way. Each type of production will have its own peculiar quality problems and for each, therefore, we must try to find a simple tailor-made solution. A quality control system which is a winner in one department will be an absolute failure if applied to another department where production techniques are different. Quality control offers us a large number of different quality remedies, and our problem is to select the best ones for the particular production line or job we are considering. Sometimes the methods we choose will have a statistical basis, and sometimes they will be based on down-to-earth practical ideas. We must select the most appropriate techniques, practices and routines, and blend them into an efficient quality control system, as explained in chapters 17 to 26.

The fact that every quality control system is likely to be different in detail from every other might at first sight give the impression that there is no similarity between them at all. Fortunately, this is not so. All quality control systems have basic common features, and we can illustrate this by considering a simple example.

1.3 Example of a very simple, yet efficient quality control system

Suppose we want to put up a shelf in the kitchen. This is a very simple job, and at first sight it does not appear to want any quality control at all, but in fact we shall probably employ a very efficient system. Of course we shall not call it quality control, and we shall probably never even realise that we have used it, but we shall go through exactly the same quality control stages as we should if we were dealing with a complex production line.

We shall almost certainly do the job in the following five basic stages:

1   We shall set the manufacturing specification. Thus we shall decide how long and wide the shelf is to be, in what sort of wood, and so on.
2   We shall prepare to make it. This will involve collecting together suitable tools, materials, etc.
3   We shall make the shelf, and fix it to the wall.
4   We shall correct any mistakes we have made, and we shall use the experience gained to avoid making the same mistakes in future.
5   Finally, we shall know, by how well we got on making a shelf, whether we are likely to be able to tackle something more difficult, such as a piece of household furniture.

We must now consider these steps in more detail.

1.4   Setting the quality standard

The designer decides precisely what final product quality is required. To do this he needs to know the following.

1   Exactly what quality the customer or market expects e.g.
    Physically. He needs to know the appearance, maximum weight, maximum size etc. of the product. In some cases of course, the customer will leave this entirely to us.
    Functionally. He must be quite clear what the product must do, what service it must perform etc. and for how long it is expected to work satisfactorily. Does the customer expect it to last say 2 years, 5 years or even 10 years?

2   The price at which the product can be sold in sufficient quantity.

3   Delivery date   i.e. when the product must be ready for delivery to the customer.

4   The capability of the machines, processes etc. which will manufacture it. (It's no good asking for something which cannot be made).

5   The capability of available inspection and test equipment   A quality which cannot be checked is meaningless.
    From the above information, the designer will prepare a set of manufacturing drawings and specifications, which are intended to

tell the factory precisely what quality they are required to make, and precisely what raw materials they must use.

1.5 Preparation for manufacture

Next adequate preparations must be made for manufacture as follows.

1 Decide the method of manufacture   Methods must be devised which permit the operators and processes to make the product in the quickest, easiest and most foolproof way. The people who do this may be called methods engineers, but often other terms are used, for example, planning engineers, process engineers, chemists, technicians etc.

2 Provide machines, plant, tooling and other equipment   Everything which is required for manufacture must be selected, taking care that it is capable of achieving the quality standard demanded. This will involve the plant engineer, jig and tool people etc., and they will need to work closely with those who devise the methods.

3 Obtain satisfactory raw materials   No one can make a good product from unsatisfactory raw materials. Hence every material must have a precise written buying specification, so that purchase department can buy exactly what is required, as cheaply as possible. Often they are expected to buy from suppliers who have been approved by the quality department, (this is called *vendor appraisal*), and when supplies arrive they are checked by the goods inwards inspection section, before acceptance into stores.

4 Obtain and train suitable operators   The Personnel department must obtain operators who are willing and capable of doing the work in a satisfactory manner, and they must be given whatever training they need. This may be done in the department where they work, or more formally in the training department.

5 Plan inspection and shop floor quality control   Readers may be surprised that we have put inspection and shop floor quality control as the last to be planned, but this is precisely where it should be. In an ideal world, the quality standard would be fully specified, materials would always be correct, machines, methods and operators would never go wrong, and so no shop floor inspection would be needed. Since any actual situation is never ideal, there is

6

always the risk that something will go wrong, and it is then the inspector's job to detect this as quickly as possible, so that it can be put right. Nevertheless the better the initial planning is done, the less the necessity for shop floor inspection. *Never try to cure a quality problem by putting on more inspectors.* This is only a temporary expedient whilst the true cause is found and corrected.

1.6 Manufacture

At last manufacture can begin. If we have done the planning well, we should not have too many problems. The inspectors' prime job is to monitor processes, operations etc., in order to help everyone to keep them right. They should not be placed at the end of the line sorting good from bad, except as a last resort.

1.7 Correction of quality deficiencies

In spite of all our efforts, the quality will sometimes go wrong, and we shall be faced with a pile of scrap and rework. This means that something has gone wrong with our quality planning and execution, as set out in sections 1.4, 1.5 and 1.6. We must go back, locate the reason for the trouble, and correct it permanently so that it cannot happen again. The following are obvious possibilties.
1   The shop floor had no clear idea what quality standard was required.
2   The method was such that it was very difficult to get the job right, and dead easy to get it wrong.
3   The machines and equipment were incapable of achieving the tolerances required.
4   The materials were unsatisfactory.
5   The operators were untrained or just not up to the job.
6   Shop floor quality control was either not properly planned, or not properly executed, maybe both.

1.8 Make use of the quality data collected

Any quality control system however simple, collects an enormous amount of information, which we should analyse and use for future improvement. e.g.
1   In most cases this will indicate the capabilities of the machines and processes involved.

2   We can tell which materials and which suppliers are good, and
     which bad.
3   We can identify unsatisfactory methods.
4   We can sort satisfactory operators from those which clearly
     need more help, training etc.
5   We can equally identify inspectors who need more training
     etc. We must not imagine that whilst operators make
     mistakes, inspectors are perfect. They make their share of
     mistakes like anyone else.

1.9   Keep the quality system up to date

Suppose it was possible to install a perfect quality control system
into a department. If we reviewed that system again in say 6 months
time, we would find that it was no longer perfect, because for
example, quantities have dramatically increased or decreased, or
new products have been introduced for which the existing system is
unsuitable. Hence it is necessary to check every quality system
periodically, to update as necessary and correct anything which is
not working properly. These checks are called *quality audits*.

1.10   Co-ordination

Notice that sections 1.4 to 1.9 involve just about everyone in the
company, e.g. salesmen, designers, purchase, stores, methods,
plant engineers, jig and tool people, production planning, production itself, operators, inspection and test, packing, despatch,
and maybe installation and commissioning in the customer's
premises. Indeed it is often said that 'Quality is Everybody's
Business'. Unfortunately if we are not careful, it ends up being
nobody's business. It is important therefore to ensure that everyone
is quality conscious, and that they all work together on quality
matters.

1.11   A summary of the five stages of quality control

An efficient quality control system for any type of production
should, therefore, be based on the five stages which we have just
discussed.
    If we rewrite the five stages of quality control in quality control
terms, they become:

1   Set the quality standard, or quality of design, required by the customer.
2   Plan to achieve the required quality. This will involve:
    a   Planning methods.
    b   Planning equipment.
    c   Obtaining satisfactory materials.
    d   Selecting and training operators.
    e   Planning inspection and shop floor quality control.
3   Manufacture right first time.
4   Correct any quality deficiencies, i.e. defective work such as scrap, etc.
5   Provide for long-term quality control and planning.

   Any company that can claim to carry out all five stages thoroughly, already has a very good quality control system.

1.12   The meaning of control

When we say that we have something 'under control', we mean that we know what we intend to happen, and are confident that we can see that it does. Thus, any control system has certain essential features, as follows:

1   There is a plan (in our case the quality standard).
2   We prepare to carry out that plan.
3   We carry it out, and all the time we compare what is being achieved with our plan.
4   If we begin to deviate from the plan we 'feed back' instructions, so that we return to the plan.

   The essence of any control system is this constant 'feedback' of information so as to correct any deviation from plan. Every time the control system detects that something is not going to plan, it sends instructions back up the production line to the point where the deviation is occurring and, immediately on receipt of these instructions, the fault is corrected. For example, the control system may detect that a machine has, or is about to, go out of limit, so it at once instructs the setter to reset it. Clearly, the sooner we detect any fault and correct it the less out-of-limit work we shall make. Hence, people talk about 'reducing the feedback loop'.

CHAPTER 2

THE COST OF QUALITY AND ITS EFFECT UPON THE CUSTOMER

2.1 Cost versus quality

As we saw in Section 1.1, costs are very closely linked with quality. Commercially, a product is worth what our customers are prepared to pay for it. If the quality and delivery are bad then the selling price will be correspondingly low. The days are gone when a producer could add almost any profit margin he liked to his costs of manufacture, etc. There are various reasons for this:

1   Competition is continually increasing.
2   The consumer is tending to become more knowledgeable about the goods he buys, and he has been greatly encouraged in this by organisations such as the Consumers' Association and their publication *Which?*
3   Quality standards demanded by various official bodies, and also by many commercial undertakings. Prominent amongst official regulations are the Ministry of Defence standards AQAP-1 upwards, and British Standard 5750.

More and more we find that our selling price has a ceiling and therefore, if our quality costs are higher than they need be, our profit is correspondingly reduced. In practice, quality costs often tend to be of much the same order of magnitude as the profit margin so it follows that, if these costs are excessive, the profit may be largely or even completely lost.

2.2 Analysis of quality costs

There is no precise definition of what is meant by the term 'quality costs'. Since almost everything which we do in a company has something to do with quality, we could say that almost all costs are quality costs. However, in order to clarify quality costs, it is usual to consider them under the three headings of failure, appraisal and prevention.

2.2.1 Failure costs

This is the cost of failing to design, make or provide the quality of product or service demanded by the customer. Failure costs tend to be easily the largest of the 3 quality costs, and we can divide them into internal and external costs as follows.

Internal failure costs These are the costs incurred within the manufacturing organisation, up to the moment when the product is transferred to the customer. Typically they include the following.
1   *Scrap*, i.e. work which is useless and must be thrown away.
2   *Rework, Corrective Operations.* This is the cost of correcting work which is wrong. In quality control we use the word *defective* to denote all work which is not to specification, and therefore unacceptable, regardless of whether it can or cannot be corrected.
3   *Downgrading, Seconds etc.* This is work which is still usable, even though it contains one or more *defects*, but it has to be sold at a reduced price.
4   *Associated Costs.* In addition to the cost of the defective work itself, other associated costs are usually incurred, and sometimes these are far greater than that for the work itself. Examples are as follows.
   a   Loss of production capacity and interference with production schedules.
   b   Cost of setting up again to make replacement items.
   c   Cost of investigating the cause of unsatisfactory work, and making corrections so that it will not happen again.
   d   Cost of correcting unsatisfactory designs and specifications. This is liable to have a knock on effect, because to meet the revised specification it may be necessary to modify or renew some of the production plant.

External Failure Costs These are costs incurred after the product has been handed over to the customer. For example:

11

1   Cost of products or services rejected by the customer, or recalled because of some defect.
2   Product liability, warranty costs.
3   Rushing replacement parts, engineers etc. long distances to make corrections.
4   Cost of placating irate customers, loss of future orders from that customer, and also from other potential customers who hear how inefficient we are. Bad reports in trade journals. We can never really tell how much customer displeasure has cost us, but clearly it can be very considerable.

2.2.2   Appraisal costs

These are the cost of inspection and test in its widest sense, including checks done by people who are not titled inspectors, e.g. setters, supervisors etc. We shall find it useful to divide appraisal costs into two groups.

A.   *Cost of Test and Inspection to Identify and Eliminate Defective Work*   e.g. The cost of 100% inspection or sorting to find and eliminate defective work that should not have been made in the first place. As well as in process sorting, we shall include:
   Final test and inspection before despatch, to eliminate defective work which is about to escape from the company.
   On site performance checks, checking stocks of spares etc.
In principle all of the above costs are *undesirable*, because if we succeed in making right first time, we shall have no defective work to eliminate. Hence high costs here indicate that our quality control of production is unsatisfactory.

B.   *Cost of Test and Inspection to Monitor Processes, and Keep Them Right.*
   a   1st off inspection to ensure that each production run starts off correctly.
   b   In-process checks such as patrol inspection, operator checks, monitoring by instruments etc., to ensure that production quality remains satisfactory.
   c   Goods inwards inspection to ensure that only satisfactory materials are fed into the production lines. (Note that any final inspection done by the supplier of these materials before despatch, would come under group A above, of that supplier's quality costs).
Provided that they are well planned and efficient, appraisal costs

in this group are desirable, because they assist in keeping processes running correctly.

2.2.3 Prevention costs

All that we spend to prevent defective work being made in the first place, is grouped under prevention costs. Thus they include:

a   Cost of quality management, setting up and operating quality control and quality assurance systems.
b   Providing satisfactory equipment, jigs etc.
c   Provision of foolproof methods, so that work is bound to be made correctly.
d   Supplier quality assurance, vendor appraisal etc.
e   Calibration and maintenance of measuring equipment.
f   Selection and training of operators, inspectors etc.
g   Maintenance of machines, plant and other equipment, so that they continue to produce satisfactory quality.
h   Systems etc. to ensure that designs are correct.

There is of course considerable room for discretion as to what should or should not be included in prevention costs. To make any meaningful control possible therefore, it is essential for the quality manager and the accountant to agree precisely what should and should not be included.

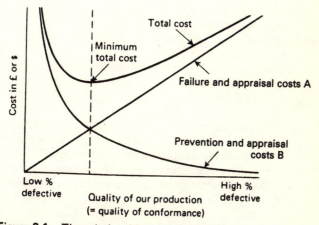

Figure 2.1   The relationship between failure, appraisal and prevention costs, and the quality of production

13

2.3 The principle of minimum overall cost

In Figure 2.1 we have plotted cost vertically against quality of production expressed as percentage defective. Conventionally quality costs are divided into 3 groups, as explained in section 2.2, but for many purposes these can be reduced to 2 groups as follows.

1 Failure costs plus appraisal costs type A The more defective work we make, the more we shall have to spend on inspection in order to sort good from bad. Hence both of these costs rise roughly linearly as the percentage defective increases, and an approximate straight line results as shown in Figure 2.1.

2 Prevention costs plus appraisal costs type B All the costs in this group are concerned with keeping machines, processes and operators working correctly. Thus provided that we spend wisely, additional expenditure will cause the percentage defective to fall, usually roughly as shown in Figure 2.1. This can be explained by the following sequence.

1   Start on the right hand side, and imagine a production shop which is completely disorganised, and makes lots of defective work. Almost any quality control effort will show a significant improvement, and so the scrap rate can be reduced with little increase in prevention costs.

2   When that shop has done all the easy things which cost almost nothing, it will have to start on the slightly more difficult and hence more costly improvements. Thus as it proceeds, each reduction of say 1% in the scrap level, costs progressively more to achieve.

3   Suppose in an extreme case, we were misguided enough to insist that our shop should never make any defective work, no matter what the cost. We should spend pounds on better machines, jigs, operators, supervisors, inspectors etc., in a futile attempt to save the odd scrap item.

Applied to Figure 2.1 this means that as we approach zero defective work, the cost of prevention shoots up, in most cases to infinity as shown. Since we want to work at *minimum overall cost*, we now add the curve for failure plus appraisal costs A to that for prevention plus appraisal costs B, to get the total cost curve shown. In most cases this curve has a minimum value *just above zero* defective work.

2.4 'Right first time' or 'zero defects'

In Section 1.11 we said that our philosophy was to be 'right first time', with no scrap or corrective operations. Under the title 'zero defects', our American friends have developed this idea into quite a cult. Everyone is expected to aim for no defective work at all.

How do we reconcile this with Figure 2.1 which shows quite clearly that in most cases minimum overall cost implies that some defective work will be made? The answer is that most production shops work well above the percentage of defectives which would yield minimum overall cost. In these days, when there is so much emphasis on quantity and when incentive schemes tend to be quantity biased, it is all too easy for those on the shop floor to become somewhat indifferent to the amount of defective work made. With a little well-directed effort they can reduce this defective work quite markedly, without any corresponding rise in prevention costs. Therefore, 'right first time' or 'zero defects' are good philosophies, which in practice assist the attainment of minimum overall cost.

2.5 Cost and the manufacturing quality

The designer is responsible for converting customer requirements into manufacturing drawings and specifications. The higher the quality standard he demands, (e.g. the tighter the tolerances), the more manufacture will tend to cost. However there is usually a critical limit represented by the capability of the machine or process. Suppose for example, that a machine is capable of producing a diameter of 20 mm to a minimum tolerance of ±0.04 mm. So long as the drawing tolerances are wider than this, it may make only a marginal difference whether they are say ±0.06 mm or ±0.12 mm. It depends on the pattern of behaviour of the machine. If however the tolerances are tighter than ±0.04 mm, out of limit work will be produced at an increasingly alarming rate. (The measurement of process capability is explained in Chapter 11).

2.6 Customer service

The value of our products to the customer will not be solely determined by their quality at the moment of delivery. The service which our customer gets from them will also be important. Depending on the type of product, it may include

15

1 Efficient installation and commissioning If we send our engineers to install and commission, then we must ensure that:

a   They go at a time convenient to the customer.

b   They are polite and considerate.

c   They are as far as possible self-sufficient, and do not have to beg odd materials from the customer.

d   They complete their work, and depart as expeditiously as possible.

2 Adequate customer training As equipment becomes more complex, so it becomes increasingly necessary to make sure that the customer is competent to get the best out of it.

a   Instruction manuals must be well written, and in the customer's native language.

b   Where necessary, the customer must be taught to use and maintain the equipment.

3 Adequate after-sales service

a   If our customer experiences a breakdown of any sort, then we must carry out repairs quickly and efficiently. Usually, the important thing is to keep the time out of service to minimum. Thus, two breakdowns which are quickly repaired may be less serious than one which takes a long while to put right.

b   Breakdowns are particularly liable to occur shortly after commissioning, for it is during this time that manufacturing weaknesses often come to light. Reliability engineers call this the early failure period, and such failures as occur at this stage should be corrected as quickly as possible, with no cost and a minimum of inconvenience to the customer. Good quality control will help to reduce the frequency of this type of failure. We shall discuss reliability more fully in Chapter 28.

2.7 Future orders

If our customers are satisfied with our quality, price and delivery, then next time they require our type of product they are likely to order it from us. Hence, as someone rather aptly put it: 'Quality makes sales; sales make jobs.'

2.8 Questions

1   Describe in detail the various items of quality costs with which a

quality manager might have to deal, and hence use a diagram to explain how he might set about minimising them. *(25 marks)*

2 Quality costs are usully divided into:
  (i) failure
  (ii) appraisal
  (iii) prevention.
Explain these terms. *(6 marks)*

2b In a small foundry the cost of each 1 per cent of scrap is approximately £350 per week. At present the scrap level is running at 7 per cent and approximately £200 per week is being spent on prevention costs. It is known that the following relation holds:

  Scrap (%) × Prevention cost = Constant

(i) Draw a graph showing cost vertically and scrap percentage horizontally, and then plot curves for:
  Prevention cost *(5 marks)*
  Scrap cost *(3 marks)*
  Total cost *(2 marks)*
(ii) Deduce the scrap percentage at which the total cost is a minimum. *(2 marks)*

3a A department has established that its quality costs per week follow roughly the relationship below.
  (Scrap percentage) × (Prevention costs, £) = 5000
Each 1 per cent of scrap costs £400 per week, including appraisal costs.
  On one pair of axes plot a curve for EACH of the following
(i) Scrap and appraisal costs *(2 marks)*
(ii) Prevention cost *(5 marks)*
(iii) Total quality costs *(4 marks)*
(iv) Identify the exact percentage of scrap at which the total cost is minimised, and state what this cost is. *(6 marks)*

3b The above calculation suggests that for minimum overall cost, the department should be operated deliberately to make the percentage of scrap at which this occurs. How can this be reconciled with the concept of 'Right First Time'? *(8 marks)*

PART TWO

PREPARING FOR SATISFACTORY QUALITY

CHAPTER 3

THE QUALITY OF DESIGN

3.1 Quality of design and quality of conformance

The quality of any manufactured article can be divided under two main headings:

1 The quality of design The quality of design is the quality specified by the designer, on behalf of the customer. In designing a book, the designer may at one extreme call for expensive leather binding, or at the other, he may only specify a paperback. Thus, a leather-bound book has a higher quality of design than the same book made as a paperback. The leather-bound book also costs more, and so is intended for a higher priced market. In the factory, we frequently refer to the quality of design as the quality standard.

2 The quality of conformance The quality of conformance is the extent to which the factory faithfully complies with the designer's specifications. Thus, a badly made leather-bound edition has a high quality of design, but a low quality of conformance, whereas a well made paperback has a low quality of design, but a high quality of conformance.

3.2 The designer's responsibility for quality

In principle, the customer sets the quality standard. He decides what he wants to buy, and he agrees with the manufacturer the price he is to pay. The customer will probably have quite set ideas about what he expects to get for his money, and the manufacturer's problem, therefore, is to make precisely this and nothing else. In some cases the customer will supply a complete set of manufacturing specifications and drawings, but more often the manufacturer will have to prepare his own.

The job of detailing the quality of design usually falls to the design department, who must prepare a complete set of specifications and drawings which:

1   Will satisfy the customer.
2   Are within the manufacturing capability of the factory.
3   Can be made within the time promised, for the price allowed for manufacture in the contract.

Notice that it is not enough merely to produce a design that will satisfy the customer. The design may be exactly what the customer wants, but if the factory cannot make it then its quality is doubtful from the start. It is also in trouble if manufacture cannot be completed either in time, or for the price allowed, because then there is always a temptation to skimp the quality in order to meet price and delivery. In fairness to the designer, however, we must remember that he is himself a link in the quality chain. If the salesman has already promised the customer an impossibly high quality, an impossibly low price or an impossibly short delivery, there may be little the designer can do to retrieve the situation. Of course, if the order is a valuable one, then it may be possible to justify the purchase of better equipment, which will have the effect of improving the manufacturing capability of the factory. Consider how the designer is expected to know the manufacturing capability of the factory. Unless the factory have told him, he is unlikely to have more than a vague idea. Fortunately, quality control can help with this, and in Chapter 11 we shall consider how to measure the capability of any machine or process, and then this information can be fed back to the designer.

The specifications and drawings produced by the designer should show the quality standard required by the customer, in clear and precise terms. Every dimension should have realistic tolerances, and every other quality should have precise limits of acceptability so that the factory can manufacture strictly to specification and drawing.

To achieve the above, the design, production and quality people should all be consulted from the sales negotiation stage onwards.

3.3   Variables and attributes

The overall quality of design of any product is made up of many individual qualities. Thus, there may be:

Dimensions, e.g. length, diameter, thickness and area.

Physical properties, e.g. weight, volume and strength.

Electrical properties, e.g. resistance, voltage, current.

Appearance, e.g. finish, colour and texture.

Functional qualities, e.g. output, or kilometres per litre.

Effect on senses, e.g. taste, feel, or noise level.

However, whatever qualities are called for, it is always possible to classify each of them as either a variable or an attribute, and this distinction is decided by the method used to observe them.

1   Variables   These include all qualities which are measured in figures. For example:

a   A length which is to be 60 ± 0.05 mm.

b   An angle which is to be 90 ± 0.75 degrees.

c   A voltage which is to be 120 ± 10 V.

d   A furnace temperature which is to be 1000 ± 50°C.

It does not matter what sort of quality it is, or how it is checked. If the results are measured in figures then we are dealing with a variable. (Sometimes variables are referred to as *measured data*).

2   Attributes are qualities which are not to be measured in figures. For example:

a   'These components to be painted red.'

b   'All components to be free of burrs.'

c   'This bearing to be well oiled.'

d   'This surface to be scratch free.'

The results of a check for an attribute can usually only be expressed as 'pass' or 'fail', or if you prefer, as 'acceptable' or 'unacceptable'. Thus, in 2a above, we can only report that the article has been painted red, or that it has not. In 2b, our surface is either scratch free, or it is scratched. There may be some argument about what is 'scratch free', but once this has been settled our surface either 'passes' or 'fails'.

Some qualities can be either variables or attributes, according to the method of test or inspection used. Thus, if we check a diameter with a micrometer, we get the result in figures, say 11.05 mm, and this will be a variable. If, however, we check the same diameter with a go/no-go gauge, we shall only find out whether it passes or fails, and so that same quality becomes an attribute.

3.4 Variables

Variables have advantages over attributes. Thus, if a drawing calls for a dimension to be 12.5 ± 0.001 mm, we may be horrified by the tightness of the tolerances, but at least we know precisely what we have got to make. Tolerances, therefore, define a variable precisely.

When the designer sets the tolerances, he must be careful to call for the *widest* limits which will be satisfactory. Thus, suppose that a dimension will be quite satisfactory provided that it is held between 12.50 and 13.00 mm. If, to be on the safe side, the designer calls for 12.65 to 12.85 mm, then:

1   The machine will have to be reset more often.
2   Any pieces which are made just outside these limits will rejected, even though they are in fact satisfactory.

The result is that manufacturing costs rise unnecessarily.

Variables have another advantage over attributes, because they tell us more about the state of the process. Suppose that a dimension is to be kept between 12.50 and 12.70 mm, and that in order to see how it is going we take a sample of five pieces and check them as attributes with a go/no-go gauge. If every piece passes, then we shall assume that production is still satisfactory within its drawing limits, but we shall know nothing more. Suppose, instead that we measure our sample of five with a micrometer, so that we are dealing with variables. The following are some of the results we might get, together with their interpretation:

Five readings in millimetres	*Inference*
12.60	This machine is very
12.60	consistent, and is correctly set
12.60	in the middle of its drawing
12.60	limits. It requires no immediate
12.60	attention.
12.70	This machine is also very
12.70	consistent, but it is running
12.70	right on top drawing limit. If
12.70	out-of-limit work is to be
12.70	avoided it must be reset
	immediately

12.65	This machine is probably too
12.50	variable to work to these limits,
12.55	and although it is correctly set
12.70	in the middle of its drawing
12.60	limits, it will want very careful
	watching if out-of-limit work is
	to be avoided

Thus, variables give us a lot more information than attributes do and so, in general, are to be preferred whenever it is reasonably practicable to use them. However:

1 Some attributes cannot be expressed in figures.
2 Some variables are much more complicated to observe than the equivalent attribute.
3 Sometimes variables have little or no advantage over attributes.

Therefore, there will always be instances where attributes will be used, and so in Section 3.7 we shall consider how to deal with them.

3.5 Accuracy and precision of measurement

No method of measurement is absolutely accurate and precise. In every case the observed reading is slightly different from the true one. When we make a measurement we assume that our errors of measurement are small compared with the variations which we are trying to observe, but this is not always justified. Thus, if the drawing calls for 19.00 to 19.01 mm, this should obviously not be checked with a micrometer which only measures to the nearest 0.01 mm, because such a micrometer might give us an error of as much as 0.005 mm. In extreme cases, our micrometer would accept work from 18.995 to 19.015 mm, and this would effectively double our drawing tolerances from 0.01 to 0.02 mm. As a rough guide, the errors of measurement should not exceed 10 per cent of the width between the two specification or drawing limits, but sometimes rather less is allowed.

There are two basic ways in which a measuring instrument may give an incorrect reading. It may be imprecise due to random errors, and it may be inaccurate due to a consistent bias.

3.5.1 Lack of precision due to random errors

Random errors will cause an instrument to give readings which are round about the correct one, being both higher and lower. When this happens, the imprecision can be reduced by taking a number of readings, and averaging them all together. For example, suppose we have to measure a voltage, whose true value is 100 V. If we take five separate observations of this same voltage, we might get:

99, 100, 102, 101, 98 V

If we average these together we get 100 V, which in this case happens to be correct, although this would not necessarily be so. All we can say is that the average is likely to be more precise than the original readings.

3.5.2   Inaccuracy due to a consistent bias

Inaccuracy, or bias, will cause all the readings on the instrument to be a fixed amount, either too high or too low. Common examples are a micrometer or a voltmeter, which has a zero error, so that it always reads say 0.01 mm or 0.1 V respectively, too high. If the magnitude of such inaccuracy or bias is known we can make a correction to our readings, but we cannot offset it by taking several readings and averaging them together. This will only result in our determining the observed reading more precisely, but this will still be equal to the true reading plus or minus the inaccuracy. For example, suppose that because our voltmeter was inaccurate, when we took five readings on a voltage with a true value of 100 V we obtained:

98, 98, 98, 98, 98 V

Averaging our readings give us 98 V, and in no way helps us to remove the inaccuracy. However, if we know from the last time it was calibrated that our voltmeter always reads 2 V low, we can add 2 V on to the 98 V and get the correct reading of 100.

Errors of precision and accuracy usually occur together in the same measuring instrument. Thus, our voltmeter might have read:

97, 98, 100, 99, 96 V

This gives an average of 98 V which is 2 V below the correct value. Notice how averaging helps to remove imprecision, but does not help at all with inaccuracy.

3.6   Routine checking of inspection and test equipment

From the above it follows that all measuring devices should be regularly checked. One convenient way of doing this is by colour coding. Thus, suppose we decide that all measuring instruments shall be checked once per month. When they are checked this month, we put a dab of one colour, say red, on them. Next month when they are checked again, we shall change the dab to another colour, say yellow. If at any time later than this an instrument with a red dab comes to light, we shall know that it has not been checked for that month. We can hang a notice in each shop which says, 'If your instrument does not bear this colour, it has not been checked this month,' and follow it by the colour chosen for this month. If an instrument or gauge is dropped, or otherwise roughly treated, it should always be rechecked before it is used again.

3.7 Attributes

Attributes tend to be difficult to use as quality standards, because they are not easy to define. A variable which has to be 12.5 ± 0.01 mm is quite clear, but a statement like 'This surface must be scratch

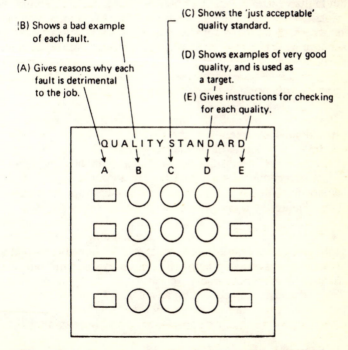

Figure 3.1 An example of a visual quality standard

27

free', is very vague. Our idea may be quite different from the designer's, and different again from that of the operator or the inspector. We must, therefore, set some sort of standard otherwise every operator and every inspector is left to use his own ideas. Often the best way is to prepare a visual quality standard, i.e. actual examples of the work concerned, showing the *lowest* quality which is just acceptable. Sometimes a visual quality standard is merely a single piece of the work concerned, suitably labelled. However, we may wish to illustrate more than one fault, and we may sometimes need to show bad examples of the fault as well as the 'just acceptable quality'. If the work is not too large, we may decide to mount all these together on a display board, along the lines shown in Figure 3.1.

Section B shows a bad example of each fault, so that both the operator and the inspector understand what the fault is. In soldering, for example, it may be desirable to show a bad instance of a 'dry joint', so that everyone knows exactly what we mean by the term. The notes in section A are used to explain why each fault shown is detrimental to the final product. It follows by implication that faults which are not illustrated are not particularly important.

Section C shows the quality standard itself, that is, the lowest quality which is just acceptable. Operators and inspectors can then compare what has been made with the standard, and if it is equal to this or better it is acceptable.

Section D shows examples of very good quality. These are not suitable as quality standards, because work of lower quality can be accepted. They may, however, be useful as 'targets'.

Finally section E of the quality standard gives any necessary instructions about the use of the standard.

Each quality standard should be prepared for shop use, and in most cases should be suitable for display. Small components are usually best mounted on a board, or in a glass case. Some sort of dust cover will be necessary if the components are on a board, in order to keep them in reasonable condition.

It is, of course, inevitable that if a standard is used in a workshop, it will deteriorate in time. On the other hand, if the standard is not used there is no point in having it. Sometimes by taking a photograph it is possible to provide secondary standards, and copies can then be given to every operator and every inspector. The operator needs a copy every bit as much as the inspector, because he/she must make the piece right in the first place.

3.8   Non-visual quality standards

So far we have assumed that our attribute is a visual quality, but this may not be so. Attributes may be recognised by any of the senses. For example:

1   *Hearing*   We may have to deal with a permitted noise level as an attribute, although in many cases it can be measured as a variable.

2   *Taste*   In the food trade, the final taste of a product is difficult to express as a variable. Furthermore, if we prepare a standard and say that everything we make 'must taste like this', then every time somebody uses the standard we lose a bite! In such cases, the easiest way is often to find someone who can recognise the taste which is required, and get him to do occasional checks, and advise those concerned.

3   *Smell*   A similar situation occurs with qualities associated with smell. If the product is sufficiently durable, then we may be able to set up a smell quality standard. Otherwise, we shall have to find someone who can recognise the particular smell required.

4   *Touch*   The 'feel' of some materials is difficult to measure, but in most cases it is possible to set up a suitable quality standard.

Where opinion enters into the assessment of a quality, as in Sections 3.7 and 3.8, then we are said to be dealing with a *subjective quality standard*, often merely referred to as a *subjective standard*.

I have found the following to be a useful guide to the suitability of a subjective standard. It should be possible to instruct the inspectors that, if an item is so near to the 'only just acceptable' quality standard that they cannot be certain whether or not it is acceptable, then it should be *accepted*. If any quality is so critical that this rule is too risky to use, then it is a sure sign that the subjective standard is inadequate for its purpose. It must be redefined, preferably as a variable.

3.9   Critical, major and minor defects

It is often possible for a single piece of production to have more than one fault or defect. Furthermore, one type of defect may be much more serious than another. In such cases it is sometimes convenient to classify the possible defects as follows:

1   *Critical defect*   A critical defect is one that is likely to result in hazardous or unsafe conditions for the people using, main-

taining or depending on the product, or one which will cause the failure of a major item. Thus, a defect which would result in the failure of the steering mechanism of a car would be classed as critical.

2   *Major defect*   A major defect is one that, although not critical, will result in failure, or will seriously reduce the utility of the product in which it is incorporated. Thus, a defect which would cause a car engine either to fail or perform badly would be classed as major.

3   *Minor defect*   A minor defect is one that, although undesirable, will not appreciably affect the use of the product concerned. Thus, paint blemishes on a car, if not too extensive, might be classed as minor.

3.10   Modifications to the quality standard

From time to time it will be necessary to modify the quality standard. Thus changes may be requested by the customer, or the designer may wish to improve or correct his design. Either way it is usually the designer who will arrange for the drawings and specifications to be altered. Strict control will then be necessary to make sure that everyone concerned gets a revised copy, when they need it. The routine might be as follows:

1   Copies of drawings and specifications are kept only in a limited number of suitably placed locations, usually drawing stores.

2   When any drawing is issued or reissued, the prescribed number of copies is sent to each. People who require a copy borrow it from the nearest store, and their name is recorded.

3   Where a reissue is concerned, all copies of the previous issue are recalled and destroyed. It is not satisfactory to let those in possession of the old issue destroy it, because they will not always do so, and then some time in the future, an obsolete issue will come to light, and work will be made to it before the mistake is discovered.

4   It is usual for the modified drawing to show clearly the alterations which have been made to it, and the date.

5   Sometimes a modified drawing contains an indication of the urgency of the changes, e.g.

    a   *Type 1 modification*   Very urgent. All partially made work to the old drawing is to be scrapped and no more produced until the modified drawing can be used.

    b   *Type 2 modification*   Partially made work which is to the old drawing can be completed, but no more is to be made to it.

c   *Type 3 modification*   Change to new issue as soon as convenient and economic. For example, when the tooling has to be renewed, or the present stocks of raw material run out.

The factory may wish to request a modification to the quality standard, to make the product easier and cheaper to produce. If the change is to be permanent, arrangements should be made with the designer to have the drawing altered and reissued. Sometimes the request is more temporary. Perhaps the material specified cannot be obtained in time, or the factory wish to use up similar material already in stock. In such cases the factory will request a *production permit*, authorising them to produce to the modified standard. Such permits are issued in advance of production, and are only valid for a limited period, or maybe production quantity. Permanent changes should be covered by a modification to the drawing.

From time to time a batch may be produced outside drawing limits, which although the inspectors will rightly reject, nevertheless could be used. The factory will then ask for a *concession*. This allows them to use the work which has already been made, but they are not permitted to produce any more like it. The term *deviation* or *quality deviation* is sometimes used to embrace both production permits and concessions.

When any change in the quality standard is authorised, care must be taken to deal with any repercussions. Thus consequential changes may be necessary to certain components, otherwise the final performance and reliability of the product may be affected.

3.11 Questions

1a Explain the following terms giving *three* examples of each, and discuss their use as quality standards:

    A variable   *(7 marks)*
    An attribute   *(7 marks)*

1b Outline the main points to be considered in revising a manufacturing specification.   *(11 marks)*

2 Explain the designer's contribution to quality, both when the initial design is prepared, and subsequently when modifications are required.

                                                (25 marks)

3a What is meant by an attribute in the context of quality control?
(2 marks)

3b State the difficulties often encountered in using attributes as quality standards, and outline practical ways of overcoming them.
(8 marks)

3c When using either attributes or variables as quality standards, explain the usual procedure for dealing with each of the following:

- *(i)* A batch of work which has been made is not quite to specification, but is thought to be usable. *(5 marks)*
- *(ii)* A batch of work if produced under existing conditions will not completely comply with specification, even though it will be usable. *(5 marks)*
- *(iii)* The material specified is no longer available, but an alternative can be obtained which is believed to be entirely satisfactory. *(5 marks)*

CHAPTER 4

CONTROL OF THE QUALITY OF INCOMING MATERIEL: VENDOR APPRAISAL

The word materiel (with an 'e' in place of the final 'a') has military origins, and denotes the baggage and equipment of an army. In industry it means everything which is supplied to the production lines, and so includes raw materials, components, sub-assemblies, liquids, powders etc. Indeed materiel is often used for work-in-progress and also for completed production.

4.1 The case for control of the quality of incoming materiel

If bad materiel is fed into our production lines, a lot of good work may be done on it, before its shortcomings are discovered. Eventually we not only have to scrap the materiel itself, but must also lose the good work we have done on it. As this is liable to be very costly, we must do our best to ensure that all materiel is satisfactory before it is issued for production.

In principle of course, if we agree with each supplier exactly what quality he has to supply, and if we pay him a fair price for it, then we have a right to expect that we shall receive consistently good quality. Our problem however, is to ensure that we do.

If we are a sufficiently large customer, we may be able to say to our suppliers: 'We expect all materiel sent to us to comply with drawing and specification, and if you fail very often we shall cease buying from you'. Provided we are a sufficiently important

33

customer, our supplier is likely to take such a threat very seriously.

However many companies are not in this strong position. If we can only buy in small quantities, the threat of losing our custom may not worry a large supplier overmuch. Single sources of supply present a particular problem, which we shall consider in section 4.4.

4.2 The principles of materiel control

Control of the quality of supplies is usually done in the following stages.

1   A buying specification is prepared, setting out exactly what quality of materiel has to be obtained.
2   Possible suppliers are checked for their ability and willingness to provide this quality. This is called *vendor appraisal.*
3   If vendor appraisal results are satisfactory, that supplier is placed on an approved list, and orders are placed.
4   When supplies are received, they are subjected to some form of goods inwards inspection.
5   The results of this inspection are used to give each supplier a numerical rating, showing how satisfactory or otherwise his supplies are. This is called *vendor rating.*
6   Results at every stage are monitored, and steps taken to improve or discontinue unsatisfactory suppliers.

4.3 The buying specification

Clearly if we expect to obtain the correct quality materiel every time, we must start by telling out supplier exactly what we want. This means that *every* materiel bought, must have a written buying specification. In most cases it will not need to be complicated; indeed the simpler the better so long as it includes everything which is required. Thus we must be careful not to include unnecessary stipulations, because this will increase the cost, and reduce the number of potential suppliers.

Best of all where appropriate, is to use a British Standard. This has the following advantages.

1   We do not have to spend time and money keeping it up to date.
2   Being a National standard, it should be familiar and acceptable to any supplier in that field. Indeed with luck he will already have it in production. This applies in particular to electronic components bought to the 9000 series of British Standards.

3   Because it is a standard materiel, it should be cheaper and more readily available than one specially prescribed by ourselves.
4   Being a well tried design, it should be more reliable than a new design with all its attendant teething troubles.

We are of course setting the materiel quality standard for our supplier, and in principle all that we said in Chapter 3 applies here.

4.4 Single sources of supply

Problems arise when a materiel can be obtained only from one supplier. Since our supplier is sure to know this, we shall be at his mercy, and a strike in his factory could shut us down as well. There is no certain panacea for this situation, but the following measures sometimes help.
1   Is it possible to make the materiel concerned in our own factory? This may not be particularly convenient or economic, but it could get us out of a jam if our single source dried up. It could also be used to put pressure on our supplier, who need not know about it being inconvenient. Let him think that we shall make the lot if he does not improve his quality.
2   Could the item be redesigned so that at least one other supplier, or ourselves could make it?
3   Could we persuade another supplier to make it at a slightly higher price, possibly combined with 2 above? At least we shall have a fall back then.
4   Is it possible to carry out some sort of remedial operation on items from a second source, to bring them up to standard?

4.5 Vendor appraisal

Vendor appraisal is a large subject which we can only summarise here. To appreciate the problem, we have to realise that what we buy as raw materiel, is our supplier's finished production. He must have bought raw materiel from his suppliers, carried out various manufacturing operations, hopefully with good quality control, and then done some sort of final test and inspection before despatch to us.

Thus vendor appraisal really involves assessing how good or otherwise, our potential or actual supplier's quality control and quality assurance is. We may need to visit him to do this, but visits take a lot of time and are expensive, and if we conclude that that particular supplier is not up to our requirements, we then have to repeat the whole investigation elsewhere. The first step therefore is to consider how much we already know, or can readily find out about a supplier. The following are possible sources of information.

1 Catalogues, booklets and similar literature from the potential supplier. Obviously these will be biased in favour of that supplier, but we can nevertheless compare what he claims to offer with what our buying specification requires. If he does not even claim to offer what we want, we may have to look elsewhere.

2 Recent goods inwards inspection results, which we have obtained by checking other purchases from that supplier. Beware if the records are old, or if the materiel concerned is quite different from what we now require.

3 Find out if the potential supplier is approved under any of the following, for the type of work we require. For example:
   a Ministry of Defence standards AQAP-1 upwards.
   b British standard 5750
   c British standards in the 9000 series for electronic components. These standards are outlined in Chapter 30.

4 Place a small order for the materiel required, and test it thoroughly. Do not tell the supplier why you are placing the order, or he may pick out all the good ones!

5 Some companies send out a questionnaire to their potential suppliers asking detailed questions about their quality assurance, and setting out the paper work etc. which they will be expected to use if they are given an order. Indeed some very large companies, typically car and computer manu-facturers, and chain stores, define the quality control system to be used by their suppliers very precisely indeed, and those who refuse to comply, do not get any orders.

Only if our potential supplier satisfies us on the above, and if the probable size and value of our purchases make it worthwhile, do we consider a visit to carry out a quality audit.

4.6 Quality audits

Make an appointment and then notice how we are received.
1 Had they forgotten that we were coming?
2 Are we received by the quality manager, or is a junior member of staff allocated to look after us?
3 Are they anxious to please?

4   Are attempts made to detain us overlong in an office, or is a time wasting lunch provided, so as to limit the time available for auditing?
5   Is the quality manager's office tucked away in some out of the way corner, or does he have a prestige office which shows that he is respected member of his company? Does he appear to have enough authority to prevent sub-standard work from leaving the factory?
6   Ask for a copy of their quality manual.
    Next inspect the company's facilities.

Research, Design and Development
1   How well are they equipped?
2   Do they keep records of all design calculations?
3   Are they informed by the factory about machine, process and test capabilities? If so, do they take any notice of this information?
4   How do they evaluate new designs? Do they sell unproved and unchecked designs to their customers, so that in effect their customers do the proving tests free of charge?

Purchased Supplies
1   Do they apply vendor appraisal to *their* suppliers?
2   What goods inwards inspection and subsequent vendor rating do they do, and is it effective?

Production
1   Are workshops well planned, adequately equipped and well maintained? Ask to see the capability study of a particular machine or process.
2   How is shop floor quality control and quality assurance operated?
    a   Examine any quality control charts, inspection records etc.
    b   Take a batch at random, and note whether the paperwork is correct and up-to-date.
    c   Observe and talk to some operators and inspectors. Do they appear to be competent, well trained and co-operative? Do they know how to tell a bad piece from a good one?
3   Notice whether safety precautions are adequate and observed.
4   Look at final test and inspection.
5   Check packaging of the final product.

Approving the supplier
Finally decide whether we can approve the supplier and inform him of our decision. Where approval is withheld, it is usual to give the

supplier a list of the things which we regard as unsatisfactory, and inform him that when he has corrected them, we will reconsider him for approval.

CHAPTER 5

GOODS INWARDS INSPECTION.
A BRIEF SURVEY OF THEORY

5.1 The principles of inspection by samples

In principle our goods inwards inspection will be simple. From each batch of materiel we take a sample, and check it for the qualities which are important to us. If the sample is satisfactory, then we infer that the batch is satisfactory, and if the sample is unsatisfactory, we likewise assume that the whole batch is unsatisfactory.

The success or otherwise of such a method will depend on:

1   Using a suitable size sample, so that we can have reasonable confidence that the quality of the sample reflects the quality of the batch.

2   Checking for the correct qualities. This means that the checks to be done must be pre-planned.

Traditionally sample sizes have often been set either by taking a fixed number of items from each batch, often 10, or by taking a fixed percentage of the batch, usually 5% or 10%. Neither method is satisfactory.

5.2 The meaning of probability

In order to explain how sample sizes should be derived, we shall need to explain the basis of probability. This is expressed on a scale from 0 to 1.0.

Thus for something which is certain to happen, (i.e. it is a 100% cert.), we write:

Probability   = 1.0

If it is a 50/50 chance, we write:

Probability   = 0.5

If it is impossible for it to happen, we write:

Probability   = 0

Hence the probability the sun will rise tomorrow   = 1.0
The probability of finding a scrap item in a batch that is 100% good   = 0
If we toss a penny

The probability of getting a head   = 0.5
The probability of getting a tail   = 0.5
The probability of getting either
a head or a tail   = certainty = 1.0

Clearly the penny is certain to come down either a head or a tail.

5.3 The addition and multiplication of probabilities

There are 2 simple rules concerning probabilities which we shall need.

1   The addition rule   Suppose that due to containers breaking in transit, we are faced with a large well mixed batch containing:

     50% bolts
     30% nuts
     20% washers.

If we now take a sample of one item:

The probability it is a bolt   = 0.5 or   50%
The probability it is a bolt
or a nut   = 0.5 + 0.3   = 0.8 or   80%
The probability it is a bolt *or*
a washer   = 0.5 + 0.2   = 0.7 or   70%
The probability it is a bolt,
nut or washer   = 0.5 + 0.3 + 0.2 = 1.0 or 100%

This is a general rule which applies where only one out of several possibilities can happen at one time. Thus our sample cannot be both a bolt and a nut at the same time – it must be one or the other. If we denote the things that can happen by A, B, C, D, etc., then the

40

probability that say either A, C or D will occur, is the *sum* of the individual probabilities of A, C and D.

2 The multiplication rule Suppose that a large batch is 20% defective, and we decide to take a sample of 2 items. Therefore:

The probability the 1st is defective   = 0.2
The probability the 2nd is defective   = 0.2
The probability they are *both* defective
                    = 0.2 × 0.2 = 0.04 or 4%

Thus where it is possible for 2 or more things to occur *together*, we get the probability they will do so by *multiplying* their individual probabilities together.

We can easily remember these rules as follows.
1   For an *either/or* type situation   *add probabilities*
2   For a *both* type situation   *multiply probabilities*

5.4 Calculation of the probability of each number of defectives in a sample, using the binomial distribution

Continue our example of a large batch which contains exactly 20% defectives. Suppose we draw a sample of 1 item from it.

The probability it is defective is 20 in 100   = 0.2
The probability it is good is 80 in 100   = 0.8
The probability it is *either* defective *or* good
                    = 0.2 + 0.8 = 1.0

It is useful to apply the addition rule here. In this simple case it is obvious that our sample must be either good or defective, but in more complicated problems, there may be a considerable number of possibilities to consider. It is then useful to check that they add up to 1.0 since, if they total less, it indicates that some possibilities have been overlooked. (If they total more than 1.0 it indicates a mistake in the calculation).

Next suppose we draw a sample of 2 items from our batch. There are now 4 possible combinations as follows.

The probability of 1 defective followed
  by 1 defective $= 0.2 \times 0.2 = 0.04$
The probability of 1 defective followed by 1 good
                                     $= 0.2 \times 0.8 = 0.16$
The probability of 1 good followed by 1 defective
                                     $= 0.8 \times 0.2 = 0.16$
The probability of 1 good followed by 1 good
                                     $= 0.8 \times 0.8 = \underline{0.64}$

Total, to check that all possibilities have been
  considered $= 1.00$

In order to work out the general case, we now assume that the batch contains a fraction p of defectives, and q good. Then for a sample of n = 2 items, we get:

The probability of 1 defective followed
  by 1 defective $= p^2$
The probability of 1 defective followed by 1 good $= pq$
The probability of 1 good followed by 1 defective $= qp$
The probability of 1 good followed by 1 good $= q^2$
Check total $= (p^2 + 2pq + q^2) = (p + q)^2$

If we repeat this calculation for any other sample size denoted by n, we shall find that the check total always reduces to $(p + q)^n$. Thus suppose we take a sample of 10 items from a batch which contains a fraction p defective and q good. To work out the probability of any particular number of defectives occurring in the sample, we must expand $(p + q)^{10}$ as follows.

$$(p + q)^{10} = q^{10} + 10pq^9 + 45p^2q^8 + 120p^3q^7 + \text{etc.}$$

Apply this to our batch which contains exactly 20% defectives, so that p = 0.2 and q = 0.8. The first term will tell us the probability of 10 good items being found in the sample.

$$\therefore q^{10} = (0.8)^{10} = 0.11$$

This means that 11% of samples of 10 taken from a batch which is really 20% defective, will contain no defectives at all. If we now want to know the probability of getting say 2 defectives and 8 good in our sample of 10, we must work out the term containing p^2 and q^8.

$$\therefore 45p^2q^8 = 45(0.2)^2(0.8)^8 = 0.30 \text{ approx.}$$

The expanded terms of the binomial theorem are known as the

binomial distribution, and we can calculate the probability that a sample will contain any chosen number of defectives denoted by r, by using the general term of this distribution, which is:

$$\frac{n!}{r!(n-r)!}\, p^r q^{(n-r)} \qquad (5.1)$$

The exclamation mark stands for *factorial* and means that the number concerned is multiplied by the next number lower, and the next again, and so on right down to 1. For example, factorial 5 = 5! $= 5 \times 4 \times 3 \times 2 \times 1 = 120$. If we put r = 2 defectives, we can repeat the above example.

$\therefore$ Probability of exactly 2 defectives =

$$= \frac{10!}{2!(10-2)!}(0.2)^2(0.8)^8 = 0.30$$

5.5 The poisson distribution

The expansion of $(p + q)^n$ becomes cumbersome if n is large, and therefore it is usual to introduce an approximation. Instead of using the binomial distribution, we use the Poisson distribution. This makes little difference so long as batches contain less than 10% defectives, which hopefully is usually the case. The general term for the Poisson distribution is:

Probability of exactly r defectives in a sample of n $\qquad$ (5.2)

$$= \frac{(np)^r}{r!e^{np}}$$

e^{np} means exponential of (np) and we get its value from mathematical tables. The term (np) is often referred to as the *expected number* of defectives, and is denoted by m. Thus if we take a sample of n = 200 from a batch which is 5% defective, we should expect 5% or 10 of our sample to be defective.

$\therefore$ m = np = 200 × 0.05 = 10

If we want to know the probability that the actual number of defectives will be say 8, we use equation (5.2).

$\therefore$ Probability of r = 8 defectives in the sample

$$= \frac{10^8}{8!e^{10}} = 0.1126$$

In practice it is not often necessary to use the Poisson distribution for sampling, because convenient tables have been prepared, such as BS6001, which we shall discuss in section 5.13. Even when special sampling plans have to be worked out, we can use tables which give the values of both the binomial and the Poisson distributions. See for example *Statistical Tables for Science, Engineering, Management and Business Studies*, by J. Murdoch and J. A. Barnes, published by Macmillan.

5.6 The risks of being wrong when inspecting with samples

When we draw a sample from a batch, we hope that the quality of the sample will be exactly the same as the quality of the batch. Due to the 'luck of the draw' this will not always be so, and therefore we take a risk that the batch will be either wrongly accepted or wrongly rejected, merely because the quality of the sample happens to be better or worse than the quality of the batch. We can reduce this risk by taking a larger sample, but we cannot eliminate it unless we do 100% inspection. Even 100% inspection is seldom completely reliable, because inspectors tend to get bored, and then make mistakes.

From this it follows that if our production line is such that we cannot risk even *one* defective item being fed into it, then effective 100% inspection is the only answer. However much of a batch we inspect without finding any defectives, we can never say with certainty, that the rest of the batch contains only good items.

5.7 The construction of the operating characteristic

Suppose that from our batch which really contains 20% defectives, we draw 100 successive samples of 10 items each. We note the number of defectives in each sample, then return it to the batch and mix well before drawing the next. Our results could be plotted as a graph as shown in Figure 5.1. The horizontal or x axis shows the numbers of defectives which could possibly be found in a sample, and the vertical or y axis shows the frequency with which each number of defectives was in fact found. Thus in our example, 11 of the 100 samples of 10 contained no defectives at all, so above 0 defectives on our graph, we plot a point at 11 in 100 = 0.11.

As we should expect, our graph shows that a sample is more likely to contain 2 defectives than any other number, but notice that this probability is only 0.30. 1 defective will be found in 0.27 or 27% of samples, and 4 or even 5 defectives will appear from time to time. Obviously if we inspected a batch containing say 40% defectives, we

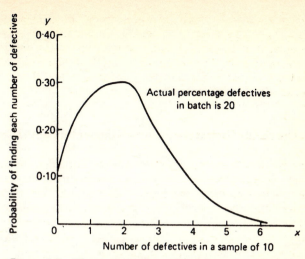

Actual percentage defectives
in batch is 20

Number of defectives in a sample of 10

Figure 4.1 The probabilities of finding each number of defectives in a sample of ten

Figure 5.1 The probabilities of finding each number of defectives in a sample of 10

should expect to get more defectives in the sample than is shown in Figure 5.1. Hence this figure only shows one of the whole family of curves, all of which can be deduced from $(p + q)^{10}$ by inserting appropriate values for p and q. Because this family of curves gets relatively complicated, we usually prefer to plot what is called an *operating characteristic*, or sometimes a *power curve*.

Each operating characteristic is associated with a particular sampling plan, and a sampling plan tells us:
1   The sample size (n), which is to be drawn.
2   The maximum number of defectives (c), which are allowed, if the batch is to be accepted.

Suppose we work out the operating characteristic for a sampling plan where $n = 10$ and $c = 2$. This means that the sample size is to be 10, and if 0, 1 or 2 defectives are found in the sample, the batch will be accepted, and if 3 or more are found, it will be rejected.

We first calculate the probabilities of finding zero, one or two defectives in samples of ten drawn from batches which actually contain a range of percentage defective, say 10, 20, 30 and 40 per cent. We shall of course utilise the expression $(p + q)^{10}$ expanded as in section 5.4, and we then get the following results:

Number of defectives found in a sample of ten	Probability of finding that number of defectives in a sample of ten, taken from a batch which actually contains the percentage of defectives given at the head of each column			
	10%	20%	30%	40%
0	0.35	0.11	0.03	0.006
1	0.39	0.27	0.12	0.04
2	0.19	0.30	0.23	0.12
Total probability of 0, 1 or 2 defectives	0.93	0.68	0.38	0.166

Since with our sampling plan the batch is to be accepted if 0, 1 or 2 defectives are found in the sample, we total each column above to find the overall probability that the batch will be accepted. Next, using the bottom total line of figures, we plot a curve showing the probability that a batch will be accepted against the actual percentage of defectives which it contains. This is shown in Figure 5.2 and it is called an operating characteristic.

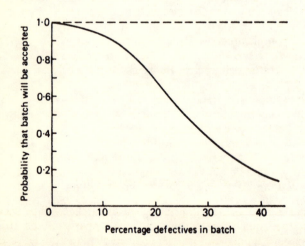

Figure 5.2   The operating characteristic for a sampling plan in which the sample size is ten. The batch may be accepted if the sample contains no more than two defectives.

5.8 The properties of the operating characteristic

Any one operating characteristic relates to a particular sampling plan. Thus, our example in Figure 5.2 relates to a plan in which the sample size is 10, and up to 2 defectives are allowed for the batch to be accepted. Now the operating characteristic tells us the probability that the sampling plan concerned will accept a batch containing any particular percentage of defectives we may care to offer it. In practice, of course, we have a batch containing an unknown percentage of defective and we have to choose a sampling plan which will:

1   Accept what we consider to be a satisfactory batch, and
2   Reject what we consider to be an unsatisfactory batch.

We can divide any operating characteristic into roughly three sections as shown in Figure 5.3.

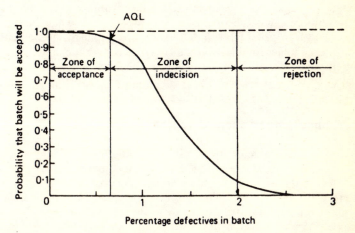

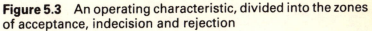

Figure 5.3 An operating characteristic, divided into the zones of acceptance, indecision and rejection

5.8.1   The zones of acceptance and rejection

Within the zone of acceptance, nearly all batches will be accepted, within the zone of rejection, they will nearly all be rejected. Therefore, we must choose our operating characteristic so that its zone of acceptance accepts what we consider to be a satisfactory batch, and its zone of rejection rejects what we consider to be an unsatisfactory batch.

47

5.8.2 Zone of indecision

Between the zones of acceptance and rejection, there is the zone of indecision. It is a region where we cannot be very certain whether any particular batch will be accepted or rejected. Indeed, roughly in the middle, there is a percentage of defectives for which the probability of acceptance is 0.5. As a batch must be either accepted or rejected, its probability of rejection is, therefore, $1.0 - 0.5 = 0.5$. Thus, the batch is just as likely to be accepted as it is to be rejected! Clearly, this point does not help us to sort satisfactory batches from those which are unsatisfactory.

Unless we are prepared to do 100 per cent inspection we cannot eliminate the zone of indecision. We can, however, reduce its width by taking a larger sample, but this will increase our inspection costs and so may or may not be justified. Fortunately, the zone of indecision is not nearly such a practical disadvantage as we might at first suppose. A batch in this zone is worse than what we have considered an acceptable batch, and better than what we have considered unacceptable. Its quality is thus borderline, and in most practical cases it will not matter much whether we finally decide to accept or reject it.

5.9 Specifying an operating characteristic

An operating characteristic is fully specified if any two points on it are fixed. By this we mean that if we specify any two points on our graph through which we want our operating characteristic to pass, there will only be one such characteristic which will do this. We cannot then add a third point through which it must also pass. It may happen to pass through the third point, but we cannot make it. Various ways of setting these two points are in use, and these give rise to many of the different sampling inspection tables which are published. Nearly all of them are derived from the same basic theory leading to the establishment of the operating characteristic, and the following are some of the methods in use.

5.9.1 Lot tolerance percentage defective

In this method we select the percentage of defectives in a batch, at and above which we wish to be almost certain it will be rejected. This is called the *lot tolerance percentage defective (LTPD)*, or nowadays the term *Rejectable Quality level (RQL)* is often used. In the example in Figure 5.4 the LTPD or RQL has a value of 3.0%. There is of course a small risk that a batch containing the LTPD will be accepted, merely because an untypically good sample happens to be drawn. We as the consumer will then feed into our production lines, a batch we intended to reject. This is therefore called the *consumer's risk*, and as a definition, it is the probability that a batch containing *exactly* the LTPD will be accepted. It is usual to set the consumer's risk at 0.1, so that the probability of rejection is $1.0 - 0.1 = 0.9$.

The second point on the operating characteristic is chosen by setting the percentage of defectives which we are prepared to accept. The idea is that this should be the normal percentage, which our producer's process makes, when it is correctly adjusted and in control. It is therefore called the *process average*, and in Figure 5.4 it has a value of 1 per cent. Again there will be a small risk that a batch containing the process average will be rejected, and returned to the producer. This is called the *producer's risk*, and it is the probability that a batch containing exactly the process average percentage of defectives, will be rejected. Like the consumer's risk, the producer's risk is usually set at 0.1. BS 5700 uses type 1 risk for the producer's risk, and type 2 risk for the consumer's risk.

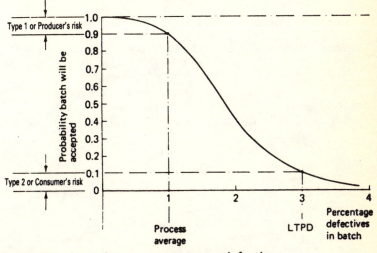

Figure 5.4   Lot tolerance percentage defective

Readers who wish to use this method should consult *Sampling Inspection Tables* by H. F. Dodge and H. G. Romig, published by John Wiley.

5.9.2 Acceptable quality level (AQL)

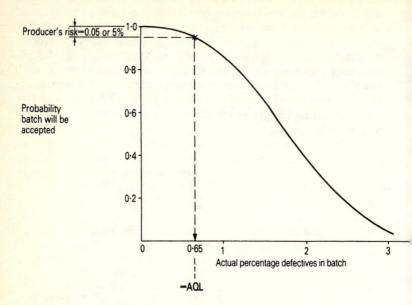

Figure 5.5 Acceptable quality level

In the example in Figure 5.5 a batch is very likely to be accepted if it contains 0.65% defectives or less. This point on the operating characteristic is, therefore, called the *Acceptable Quality Level* or AQL. The probability of a batch containing exactly the AQL percentage of defectives being accepted is often set at 0.95, but other values near this are also used. The producer's risk is thus approximately 0.05.

The AQL system has been adopted by both the United States and British Governments, and this has had the effect of making the use of AQL very common in both countries. Both Governments have issued specifications giving AQL sampling inspection tables. In the United States this is Military Standard 105D. In Great Britain it was originally Defence Specification DEF-131A, with an explanatory booklet called Defence Guide 7A, but these have since been replaced by BS 6001 and BS 6000, respectively.

5.10 Properties of the acceptable quality level

The AQL is defined as the maximum percentage of defectives

which, for the purposes of sampling inspection, can be considered satisfactory as a process average. It is thus the 'only just acceptable' quality because, in principle, any increase in the percentage of defectives above the AQL value should tend to cause the batch to be rejected. Thus, in Figure 5.5, the AQL is 0.65% defective. This means that whereas 0.65% defective will be accepted, over 0.65% will tend to cause the batch to be rejected. To reject it with certainty, however, it would be necessary for the operating characteristic to fall vertically to zero, immediately 0.65% defective was exceeded. This is not possible unless we do 100 per cent inspection.

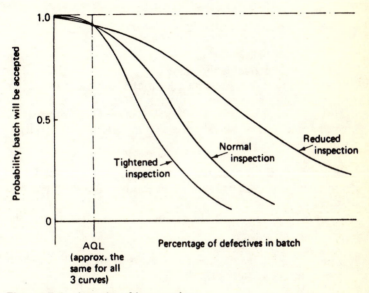

Figure 5.6 Levels of inspection

If we increase the sample size the operating characteristic will become steeper, and if we decrease it it will become flatter. Thus BS 6001 provides for three general inspection levels, as well as four special levels. The general inspection levels are referred to as *normal inspection*, *reduced inspection* and *tightened inspection*. They are illustrated in Figure 5.6. The idea is that normal inspection should be used in general cases. Tightened inpection requires a larger sample size than normal inspection, but in return we get a much steeper operating characteristic, which is more efficient in rejecting batches containing a percentage of defectives just above the AQL. Conversely reduced inspection requires the smallest of the three sample sizes, but batches must contain a percentage of defectives well above the AQL before there is any real risk of them being rejected.

5.11 Deducing the operating characteristic from the sampling plan

Starting from the sampling plan, we can construct the operating characteristic as follows. Suppose the plan is:

Sample size $= n = 100$
Allowed number defective $= c = 1$

1   In column (1) below, set out a convenient range of values of p, the fraction of defectives in incoming batches. As a rough guide the value of p where it equals c/n will occur at about the centre of the range. Thus for our example, $p = c/n = 1/100 = 0.01$ or 1 per cent defective, will be around the middle value chosen. The choice is not critical, because extra values can easily be added later, or surplus ones discarded.

2   In column (2) we put the expected or average number of defectives m, which will be found in the sample. We obviously hope that the sample will contain the same fraction defective p as does the batch. Thus for the first line of the table we have, $m = np = 100 \times 0.002 = 0.2$.

3   We now use a table of cumulative Poisson probabilities which, when we enter the value of m, will tell us the probability of r or more defectives. We want to know the probability of 1 or less defectives, so we set $r = (c + 1) = 2$. Inserting $r = 2$ and the values of m in column (2), gives us the probability of 2 or more defectives as column (3).

4   We subtract column (3) from 1.0 to get the probability of less than 2 defectives, i.e. 0 or 1.

5   To draw the operating characteristics we plot column (4) vertically, against 100p (so that we have percentages) from column (1).

(1)	(2)	(3)	(4)
p	m = np	Probability of 2 or more defectives	Probability of 0 or 1 defective
0.002	0.2	0.0175	0.9825
0.004	0.4	0.0616	0.9384
0.008	0.8	0.1912	0.8088
0.010	1.0	0.2642	0.7358
0.015	1.5	0.4422	0.5578
0.020	2.0	0.5940	0.4060
0.030	3.0	0.8009	0.1991
0.040	4.0	0.9084	0.0916

5.12 The relation between batch size and sample size

Throughout our discussion of sample size and the number of defectives to be allowed, we have made no mention of the size of the batch. So long as the batch is large, it does not have any appreciable effect on the sample size to be drawn from it. A sample of a certain size gives us a certain amount of information, and we do not have to enquire whether it came from a batch of 50,000 or 100,000.

Batch size only becomes important when it is small enough for its constitution to be appreciably changed by drawing the sample from it. In our example in Section 5.4, we had a batch which contained exactly 20 per cent defectives and we, therefore, assumed that every time we drew a sample of one our chance of getting a defective was 0.2. To take an extreme case, suppose that our batch consisted of only five pieces, so that four were good and one was defective. Further, suppose that we draw samples one at a time:

> For the 1st sample, the probability of a defective is 1 in 5
> = 0.2

If the defective in the batch is not drawn then:

> For the 2nd sample, the probability of a defective is 1 in 4
> = 0.25

If the defective is still not drawn each time, then we get successively:

> For the 3rd sample, the probability of a defective is 1 in 3
> = 0.33
> For the 4th sample, the probability of a defective is 1 in 2
> = 0.5

For the 5th sample, the probability of a defective is 1 in 1
$$= 1.0$$

Obviously if a batch of five has only one defective, and if this defective is not among the first four drawn, it absolutely must be drawn fifth, because there is then only one piece left. Thus, notice that as the sampling proceeds, the probability that a defective will be drawn progressively increases (unless, of course, it has already been drawn, in which case the probability of a defective is zero). This means that for small batches there is less chance of missing defectives than with large batches. Thus, it is possible to make some reduction in the sample size when the batch is small, but the reduction is nothing like proportional to the reduction in batch size. Sampling inspection is thus more efficient when the batch is large, in the sense that a smaller percentage of the batch has to be inspected.

5.13 AQL sampling inspection tables

BS 6001 provides a complete range of AQL sampling inspection tables. It is in the nature of a reference book, and in most cases will be too complicated to be given to the shop floor inspector. We shall, therefore, need to extract from it a suitable range of sampling plans for everyday use, and an example of how this can be done is given in the Appendix, Table 1. Unless the reader has some special requirements, it will probably suit his or her ordinary needs as it is.

The following points about Table 1 are of interest.

1   Any required AQL can be selected at will, and we shall consider the best way to do this in Chapter 6.

2   Provision is made for batch sizes up to over 500,000. In general, it is undesirable to sample larger batches than this, as a single batch. The economic consequences if a batch should be wrongly either accepted or rejected are usually too great and, unless the items in it are very small, it will probably be difficult to get the whole batch together at one time so that a representative sample can be taken. Further, it is very unlikely that such a large batch consists of a single production run. It is almost certainly a mixture of several production runs, and if it is practicable, these should be separated. Each production run can then be sampled as a batch in its own right.

3   We use Table 1 as follows. Suppose that we wish to inspect a batch of 1000 items, at an AQL of 1%. The table tells us to take a

representative sample of 80, and check it for the qualities which are important to our application. If we find up to and including two defectives in the sample we can accept the batch, and if we find three or more we must reject it.

4 Table 1 is arranged so that the steepness of the operating characteristics increases as the batch size increases. This reduces the risk of a wrong decision on a large batch, where such a mistake might be costly.

5.14 Double sampling plans

Although Table 1 will probably satisfy most needs, BS 6001 does nevertheless include a number of more advanced plans which we must explain. So far we have only discussed *single sampling plans*. This means that we always get a decision about our batch from a single sample. Thus, in our example in Section 5.13, we said that for a batch of 1000 items to be inspected at 1% AQL we must take a sample of 80, and accept the batch if not more than 2 defectives were found.

In a *double sampling plan*, there are two sample sizes, and two allowed numbers of defectives. Thus, the following is an example of a double sampling plan:

First sample   = 80 Accept number = 1 Reject number = 4
Second sample = 80 Accept number = 4 Reject number = 5

This means, take a sample of 80 and inspect them. If the number of defectives found does not exceed 1, accept the batch on the first sample. If the number of defectives is 4 or more, reject the batch on the first sample. If the number of defectives is more than 1, but less than 4, i.e. if it is 2 or 3, take a second sample of 80 and inspect. If the number of defectives from *both samples together* does not exceed 4, accept the batch. If it is 5 or more, reject it.

Double sampling plans have the advantage that when a batch is either very good or very bad it is accepted or rejected on the first sample, which is normally smaller than the corresponding sample for a single plan. If batches continually go to the second sample before a decision is reached there is little advantage. The saving in inspection has, in any case, to be offset against the disadvantages of a more complicated sampling plan.

5.15 Multiple sampling plans

The principle of double sampling can be extended to *multiple sampling plans*. Thus it is possible to have any desired number of stages, and the multiple plans given in BS 6001 have seven, as the following example shows.

	Sample size	Cumulative sample size	Accept number	Reject number
1st sample	50	50	*	4
2nd sample	50	100	1	5
3rd sample	50	150	2	6
4th sample	50	200	3	7
5th sample	50	250	5	8
6th sample	50	300	7	9
7th sample	50	350	9	10

The above means:
1 Inspect a random sample of 50.
2 If 4 or more defectives are found, reject batch.
3 If there are less than 4 defectives, inspect another sample of 50. (* indicates that not enough items have yet been tested to be able to accept the batch, even if there are no defectives at all.)
4 If 5 or more defectives are found in both samples together, reject the batch.
5 If 0 or 1 are found, accept it.
6 If they are between 1 and 5, i.e. 2, 3 or 4, inspect a third sample of 50.
7 Repeat steps 3 to 6, using the accept and reject numbers given, as often as is necessary to reach a decision, each time count *all* the defectives found so far.
8 A decision must be reached by the 7th sample at the latest, because up to 9 defectives then accepts the batch, and 10 or more reject it.

5.16 Sequential sampling plans

If we continue to increse the number of stages in a multiple sampling plan, the sample size at each stage becomes progressively smaller, and ultimately reduces to a sample of one. This is then called a *sequential sampling plan*.

In practice we take items from the batch one at a time. We inspect each, and then before inspecting the next, we check to see whether we have got enough information to decide the fate of the batch. BS 6001 offers a very simple method of doing this. With each plan it gives two numbers, which it calls the *handicap (H)* and the *penalty (b)*. After inspecting each item, we work out the *score*, given by:

Score = (*H* + No. of acceptable items found) −
(*b* × No. of defective items found)

We accept the batch if the score reaches twice the handicap, and reject it if the score falls to zero or less.

Clearly it is possible for a very borderline batch to continue indefinitely without reaching a decision. A maximum sample size is therefore given with each plan, and if this is reached, the corresponding multiple plan is consulted to get a decision.

Sequential sampling plans have the advantage that they reach a decision after the inspection of a smaller total number of items than is possible with the other plans. They are therefore attractive where the cost of inspection is high, and especially if the item under test is destroyed. They are however much more complicated to use than the corresponding single or double sampling plans.

5.17 Average outgoing quality limit (AOQL)

This is a special technique which only applies if batches which are rejected by sampling inspection, are then submitted to 100 per cent

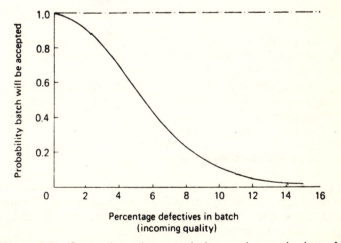

Figure 5.7 Operating characteristic used to calculate AOQ curve in Figure 5.8

57

inspection, to sort acceptable items from defectives. Thus batches which are passed to the next operation will consist of a mixture of:

1   Those which have been accepted, but which may never-the-less contain a small percentage of defectives, i.e. up to the AQL or a little more.
2   Batches which were rejected and submitted to 100 per cent inspection. Since all their defectives have been removed, they now return as 100 per cent good items.

Figures 5.7 and 5.8 illustrate how this routine will operate.

1   If the incoming batches contain zero defectives, they will all be accepted, and the outgoing quality from sampling inspection will be 100 per cent good.
2   If the incoming batches all contain say 1.5 per cent of defectives, the operating characteristic tells us that 95 per cent of them will be accepted, and 5 per cent will be rejected and then submitted to 100 per cent inspection. Our *average outgoing quality* (AOQ) expressed as percentage defectives, will therefore be:

$$\text{AOQ} = \frac{(0.95 \times 1.5)}{(0.95) + (0.05 \times 0.985)} = 1.4\%$$

3   If we continue this calculation for other values of defectives in incoming batches, we get

Defectives in batch, %	AOQ %
1.5	1.4
2.5	2.2
4.0	2.8
5.0	2.8
7.5	2.0
10.0	1.3
15.0	0.4

Notice that at the start of the above table, the AOQ increases, as the percentage of defectives in incoming batches increases, but that after a while it reaches a peak, and then begins to fall again. This is because as the operating characteristic drops, an ever-increasing proportion of batches will be rejected, submitted to 100 per cent inspection, and so return as 100 per cent good. This peak percentage of defectives in out-going batches is called the *Average Outgoing Quality Limit* or AOQL. Figure 5.8 shows that for our example, the AOQL has a value of approximately 2.9 per cent, and that it occurs for an incoming quality of approximately 4.7 per cent defectives.

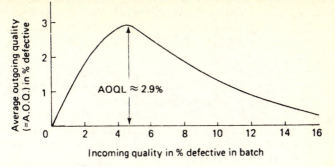

Figure 5.8 Average outgoing quality limit

Notice that we are discussing the *average* outgoing quality limit. Odd batches containing more than the AOQL percentage of defectives will, if submitted, sometimes be accepted. All that the scheme says is that the average will not exceed this.

5.18 Acceptance sampling by variables

All the sampling plans which we have so far discussed are concerned with attributes, since even where an item is actually measured in figures, we have only taken note of whether it passed or failed. It is however possible to do acceptance sampling using variables. To appreciate how it is done requires a little more quality control theory than we have so far discussed, and consideration of it has therefore been postponed until Section 13.19.

5.19 Parts per million (ppm)

Sometimes, as with complex assemblies, the use of any sort of AQL leads to difficulties. Thus suppose an assembly has 458 components, every one of which must work if the whole is to work, and suppose for simplicity, that after goods inwards inspection all batches of components are exactly 1% defective. If we draw 1 component from any batch:

$\therefore$ Probability it is defective   = 1% or 0.01
  " " " good   = 99% or 0.99

But for a completely good assembly *all* 458 components must work, so we use the multiplication rule from section 5.3.

∴ Probability of 1 good assembly
$$= (0.99)^{458} = 0.01 \text{ or } 1\% \text{ approx.}$$

Thus in theory only 1% of assemblies will contain all good components, and 99% will contain one or more defective components. For various practical reasons, the actual performance is unlikely to be quite so bad as this, but faced with this problem, companies do need to use very low AQL's, and it is then easier to express them in parts per million (ppm).

e.g. 0.0005% AQL = 5 ppm

If we could achieve 5 ppm of defective items in the component batches used in the above example, then:

Probability of 1 defective component
$$= \frac{5}{1\,000\,000} = 0.000\,005$$

"   "   1 good   "
$$= 1 - (0.000\,005) = 0.999\,995$$

Probability of one good assembly
$$= (0.999\,995)^{458} = 0.9977 = 99.8\% \text{ approx.}$$

To achieve component defective rates low enough to be expressed in ppm, the assembly company must work very closely with all of its suppliers. All must use intense and efficient quality control, and be open and honest with each other. The assembly company must reveal the precise application, circuit diagrams etc., and the component manufacturers must be open about their manufacturing methods. Components which fail on assembly are retested and returned to the supplier, with full details of the circumstances of failure. The component manufacturer examines them, reports on his findings, and improves his design/manufacture as necessary. If failure is due to unsatisfactory use conditions, then it is the assembly company that modifies its design/manufacture.

5.20   Questions

1a Samples of n components are drawn at random from a large batch which contains a fraction p that is defective and q that is satisfactory. Show by considering the possible selections that when $n = 2$ and $n = 3$, respectively, the probability of getting any particular combination of defective and satisfactory components is given by the appropriate term of a binomial distribution.

(13 marks)

1b A large batch is known to be 2 per cent defective. Using tables or otherwise, deduce
- *(i)* The probability that a random sample of 10 will contain 1 or more defectives.
- *(ii)* The probability the same sample of 10 will contain exactly 1 defective.
- *(iii)* The sample size which must be drawn if the probability of 2 or more defectives is to be approximately 90 per cent. *(12 marks)*

2a A consignment consisting of 3500 resistors, 1500 capacitors and 10,000 transistors has accidentally got thoroughly mixed. A sample of 2 is drawn at random. What are the probabilities of *each* of the following:
- *(i)* both are resistors
- *(ii)* one is a capacitor and one is a transistor
- *(iii)* both are transistors or both are capacitors
- *(iv)* neither is a resistor? *(8 marks)*

2b A consignment is to be checked by taking a sample of 350 and accepting the whole provided that not more than 2 defectives are found. Draw the operating characteristic for this plan. *(13 marks)*

2c Insert the following on the operating characteristic in (2b):
Acceptable Quality Level (AQL)
Lot Tolerance Percentage Defective (LTPD)
Producer's risk
Consumer's risk *(4 marks)*

3a Sketch a typical operating characteristic for a single sampling plan. *(5 marks)*
Mark the positions of the following:
- *(i)* Acceptable Quality Level (AQL)
- *(ii)* Lot Tolerance Percentage Defective (LTPD)
- *(iii)* Consumer's risk
- *(iv)* Producer's risk *(8 marks)*

3b The following alternative sampling plans are being considered with a view to checking the quality of a large batch:

Plan X   Sample size = $n = 100$ Acceptance number = $c = 2$
Plan Y   Sample size = $n = 175$ Acceptance number = $c = 3$

For each plan calculate (using tables or otherwise):

    (i)   The producer's risk for an AQL = 0.8%   *(4 marks)*
    (ii) The consumer's risk for an LTPD = 4.0%   *(4 marks)*

State, giving a reason for your answer, which of the two plans you would consider preferable if you were

    (iii) The producer
    (iv) The consumer   *(4 marks)*

4a Using tables or otherwise, plot 2 operating characteristics on the same axis, one for *each* of the following sampling plans:

Plan 1 Sample size (n_1) = 10 Allowed number defective (c_1)
$$= 0$$
Plan 2 Sample size (n_2) = 110 Allowed number defective (c_2)
$$= 2$$
(10 marks)

4b Mark the position of the Acceptable Quality Level (AQL) at a producer's risk of 0.10. Since both plans have almost the same value of AQL, what considerations might determine which would be used in a particular case?   *(5 marks)*

4c Explain the inspection routine with which an Average Outgoing Quality Limit (AOQL) might be used, and hence explain the meaning of the term. Sketch a typical curve showing the relation between incoming quality and average outgoing quality, and mark the position of the AOQL. [The candidate is not expected to relate this curve to the values given in parts *(a)* and *(b)* of the question.]
(10 marks)

CHAPTER 6

SETTING UP FOR THE INSPECTION OF MATERIEL

6.1 Selecting the most suitable AQL for a particular application

The best AQL in any particular case will be the one that incurs the lowest overall cost, when everything has been taken into consideration. In practice, however, we never know exactly what all the relevant costs are, and so we have to compromise between what is theoretically correct and what is practically possible. Thus, we shall now consider a method of choosing an AQL which has been developed by the author and which has been found to work well in practice. It is not absolutely exact, and any attempt to make it so would certainly render it impracticable, possibly still without achieving ultimate precision. However, readers can easily alter it to suit their own particular needs.

We must explain the method in detail although in practice a suitable AQL can be chosen by consulting Table 2 (see Appendix). There are three main costs involved in the selection of an AQL for checking a particular batch of materiel:

1 The cost of doing acceptance inspection.
2 The cost, or value, of the batch to be inspected.
3 The cost incurred if any unsatisfactory items in the batch get fed through to our production lines.

6.2 Estimating the cost of incoming inspection itself

Once we have decided what checks have to be applied to each piece, there is usually no difficulty in estimating how long these checks will take. Thus, each item checked might take one minute of the inspector's time, and our Accounts Department would tell us what this minute would cost, including overheads. Hence we can easily find the cost of checking one piece in the batch and, if the test is destructive, we must add to this the cost or value of the materiel destroyed. Suppose, for example, that it costs 6p to check each piece in the batch, and that the materiel concerned arrives in batches of 200 pieces. If we consult Table 1 of the Appendix we can read off the sample size for every value of the AQL for a batch size of 200. Now the cost of inspecting the whole sample will be equal to the cost of inspecting one piece multiplied by the number of pieces in the sample. Thus, in our example, for an AQL of say 1 per cent, the cost of inspecting the sample for one batch would be the sample size of 50, multiplied by the cost of inspecting one piece (6p), making 300p in all. This is shown plotted in Figure 6.1, where it is marked 'Inspection cost'.

6.3 The value of the materiel to be inspected

If we keep a batch which contains a proportion of defective pieces then we usually have to pay for them, whereas if we return the whole batch to the supplier as unsatisfactory, we do not. Hence, the actual purchase value of each piece in the batch must, in principle anyway, be considered when deciding which AQL to choose. If the cost of a piece is low, as is often the case, its value may not be sufficient to affect our final choice.

6.4 Reducing the cost of production scrap and rework resulting from the use of defective materiel

As explained in Section 5.6, when we use samples to inspect batches we accept the fact that, if defective items are present, some will get through in the batches which are good enough, as a whole, to pass inspection. These defective pieces will thus be fed to our production lines. How much trouble they will cause will depend partly on how far they can get before they are detected. There are three broad possibilities:
1   The defective items may be such that they are quite unusable,

64

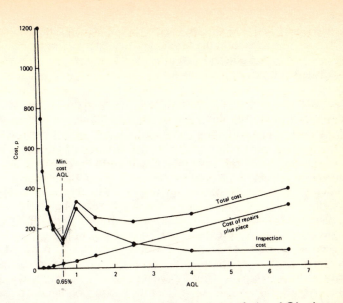

Figure 6.1 Graph showing derivation of the AQL that will achieve minimum overall cost for the example in the text.

and so are bound to be thrown out by the operator. For example, washers which have no central hole are quite unusable and so we do not have to worry about the consequences of them being used. No production effort of our own will be lost, and the nuisance value will in most cases be small. The above will not necessarily apply where an operation is fully mechanised. A machine is liable to attempt to use a defective component, possibly damaging the work or itself as a result.

2   The defective items may be usable, but the fault such that it is pretty sure to be discovered during subsequent test or inspection before the product leaves our factory. Thus, when a faulty piece is discovered it will be necessary to correct the fault or, if this is not possible, to scrap the whole piece or assembly. In a simple case, it may involve no more than removing a component from an assembly and replacing it with a good one, but in a more serious instance, it may be necessary to scrap not only the defective piece itself but also a lot of good work which has been done on it.

3   The worst case of all is when the fault is such that the item is not only likely to be used, but its fault is unlikely to be discovered by any of the tests which we apply before the finished product leaves the

factory. Thus, any faulty items which get fed to our production line are likely to be used, and the finished product containing them sold to our customers. Sooner or later they will fail, and we shall have a dissatisfied customer on our hands.

Fortunately, it is often possible to reduce the damage caused by defective items by suitable planning of the method of production. For example, suppose that we make a fairly intricate sub-assembly which we sell to a customer, who incorporates it in a large piece of equipment. Further suppose that it is important that the base of our sub-assembly does not exceed a certain size, because if it does it will not fit into the customer's equipment. Thus, if a sub-assembly is put together with an oversized base, it will have to be completely dismantled and rebuilt with a correct base. If the sub-assembly has already been sent to the customer, we shall incur the customer's displeasure as well. At first sight, we might think that it would be necessary to do very strict 100% inspection on bases when they arrive from the supplier. Clearly, we must at all costs prevent them from being used on our sub-assembly production line. In fact, however, this strict and costly 100% inspection is unlikely to be necessary. If we provide the sub-assembly operator with a jig which is so designed that it will *not accept* an oversized base, then we can be quite sure that, whatever size our supplier sends us, no oversized base can ever be used by that operator. In this way we can save ourselves the cost of 100% inspection, and be certain that we have protected our own production line at the same time. It is well worth spending a little time to consider what can be done to ensure that any defective pieces which happen to get into our production line are thrown out again, at the earliest possible moment.

6.5 Estimating the cost of scrap and rework incurred through feeding defective materiel into our own production lines

It is usually not too difficult to estimate the cost incurred if one defective piece is fed into our production lines. We merely find out how far it is likely to get before its faults are discovered, and then estimate how much it will cost to correct the damage it has done. Thus, we estimate how long it will take to get the defective item out of the product, and replace it with a good one. To this we must add the cost of any work or other materiel which is also lost. We may have done a lot of good work on the faulty item, or it may be inseparably attached, e.g. welded, to one or more good components, all of which must be scrapped with the faulty one. When we convert the repair time to money, we must allow for any overhead expenses attached to the operator who does the repairs.

We can thus estimate the cost involved if one faulty piece is fed into our production lines. Next, we need to know how many such faulty pieces will in fact be fed in, in order to calculate the total repair cost involved. This is more difficult, because it depends not only on the value of the AQL that we choose for our incoming sampling inspection, but also on what proportion of defective items the batches of materiel contain when they arrive from our supplier. Obviously, if our supplier never sent us any defectives, it would not matter at what AQL we inspected, nor indeed whether we did any incoming inspection at all. We should never get any defectives fed through to our production lines. However, in practice, we never know in advance what percentage of defectives our incoming batches of materiel are going to contain. Indeed, if we did, we should not need to do incoming inspection to find out! Of course, if the materiel is one which we have inspected before, we can get some idea of what to expect by consulting the inspection records. Very often, however, there is nothing to tell us what to expect, and a long investigation would not be justified.

Perhaps the easiest approach is to assume a suitable average level of defectives which batches passing incoming inspection are likely to contain. We do not have to worry about batches which fail incoming inspection, because they will not be fed into our production lines. Thus, all the very bad batches will be kept out and those which get through will be either of good quality or, if borderline, good enough to have passed inspection. The lower we set out AQL the more batches we shall keep out, and the higher we set it the more we shall let through. Therefore, if we assume that our supplier will send us all sorts of batches, from very good to very bad, then the average percentage of defectives in batches which pass inspection will be related to the value of AQL at which we inspect. If our suppliers are, in general, good, then the average level of defectives in batches which pass inspection will be much lower than the value of AQL at which we are inspecting. For example, if we were to inspect at 1% AQL, on batches which were, in general, very good, we might find that the average level of defectives in batches which passed is only, say, 0.1%.

So far we have considered the materiel, labour and overhead cost incurred when a defective piece is fed into our production lines, but we have said nothing about its nuisance value, although this may be quite appreciable. When a faulty item is discovered there will be production delays while it is rectified. This, in turn, may lead to late deliveries and so to customer irritation. We may have to set a machine up a second time to make replacements for work we have had to scrap and, if this happens often, factory morale will suffer. All in all, therefore, the true cost of allowing defective materiel to get into our production lines is likely to be appreciably more than the direct replacement cost. We can make some allowance for this by assuming, when we set an AQL, that the average percentage of defectives in batches which have passed incoming inspection is greater than it really is. Thus, in calculating Table 2 of the Appendix it has been assumed that the average percentage of defectives in batches which have passed inspection is equal to the value of AQL used.

We, therefore, assume that every time a defective piece is used in our production the cost incurred is equal to the cost of repairs plus the cost of the piece itself, and that the proportion of such pieces getting into our production lines is equal to the AQL at which we carry out our inspection of incoming materiel. Suppose in the example which we started in Section 6.2 that each item in the batch costs 10p and that repairs when a defective item is used cost 15p. Thus, every time we buy and use a defective item, it costs us 25p. Now the batch size is 200, and we propose that if the AQL is 1% to assume that 1% of the items in batches which pass incoming inspection will be defective. However, in order to pass a batch, the inspector must check the prescribed sample and in the process remove any defective items in it. For an AQL of 1%, the sample size is 50. Hence, after incoming inspection, only $200 - 50 = 150$ of the batch would contain the assumed 1% defectives.

Therefore, the average loss incurred per batch through using the defectives we have assumed in batches which pass inspection of 1% AQL is

$$(1.00/100) \times 150 \times 25 = 37.5p$$

As the cost is directly proportional to the AQL used, apart from the correction for the sample size inspected, the curve shown in Figure 6.1 for 'Cost of repair plus item' is nearly a straight line.

6.6 Calculating the minimum overall cost

In Figure 6.1 we have now only to add the ordinates of the two lower curves together, in order to obtain the total cost of incoming inspection, the item itself and subsequent repairs per batch. In our example, the minimum cost occurs at an AQL of 0.65%, and so this will be the best AQL in this particular case.

We can work out this same example in figures as follows:

Number of items in batch	$= N$	$= 200$
Cost of inspecting one item	$= i$	$= 6p$
Cost of one item	$= a$	$= 10p$
Cost of repairs and retest if 1 defective item is used for production	$= r$	$= 15p$
Therefore, cost of repairs plus item	$= r+a$	$= 25p$

A Available AQLs, %	B Sample size (n)	C Cost of inspection	D Number not inspected	E Cost of repairs, etc.	F Total cost = (C + E)
All	200	1200	0	0	1200
0·065	200	1200	0	0	1200
0·10	125	750	75	1·9	751·9
0·15	80	480	120	4·5	484·5
0·25	50	300	150	9·4	309·4
0·40	32	192	168	16·8	208·8
0·65	20	120	180	29·2	149·2*
1·00	50	300	150	37·5	337·5
1·5	32	192	168	63·0	255·0
2·5	20	120	180	112·5	232·5
4·0	13	78	187	187·0	265·0
6·5	13	78	187	303·9	381·9

The derivation of each of the above columns is as follows:

A *Available AQLs* Set out all the AQLs given in the top row of Table 1. Start with 'All', because in some cases 100% inspection will work out cheapest.

B *Sample size* From Table 1, copy the sample size corresponding to each AQL for the batch size concerned.

C *Cost of inspection* Multiply each sample size in column B by the cost of inspecting one item.

D *Number not inspected* Subtract each sample size from the batch size.

E *Cost of repairs, etc.* For each line work our

(Column A/100) × (Column D) × $(r + a)$

F *Total cost* Add column C to column E.

For this particular example, the minimum cost occurs in column E at 0·65%, and is marked with an asterisk.

6.7   Table 2 for choosing the most economic AQL

As we probably buy a considerable variety of material, we shall in principle need a large number of calculations to find the best AQL in each case. To avoid the work which this would involve, Table 2 has been prepared, and this does all the calculation for us.

Thus, in practice, only the following steps are required, in order to choose a suitable AQL:

1   Decide how each item in the batch is to be inspected, and what for our purpose is to be considered an acceptable item and what unacceptable. (See Section 7.3 for further details.)

2   Estimate, as accurately as is practicable, how much it costs to inspect one item in the batch ($=i$). Often, this consists only of the inspector's time plus overheads, but there may also be some materiel used. If the test is destructive, include the cost of the item itself. There may also be an allowance per item for setting up the test equipment, etc.

3   Estimate what it costs if a faulty item passes through incoming inspection and is fed into the production lines ($=r$). Add the cost of one item (a) to the cost of repair (r), to allow for the money wasted in buying a faulty item.

4   Divide the cost of repair plus the item itself, as calculated in (3) above, by the cost of inspecting one item as (2) above

$(r + a)/i$

5   Use the ratio so obtained, together with the batch size, to consult Table 2. This gives us the best AQL without further calculation.

a   If our batch sizes vary it is safest, though not necessarily cheapest, to take roughly the largest batch size which normally occurs.

b   'All' in Table 2 indicates that 100% inspection should be employed. Where 100% inspection is called for this should not be regarded as a 'failure of sampling inspection' but rather as a special case in which the best sample size equals the batch size. If inspection is fairly cheap, and the cost incurred if one single defective item gets into our production lines is large, then it may well be cheapest to inspect every one in order not to risk one defective getting through.

70

6   The AQL which we have calculated will be the most economic from our point of view. If we set our AQL higher than this then our overall costs will rise, due to increased troubles on our production lines; if we set it lower than this, our overall costs will rise, due to increased incoming inspection costs. It does not necessarily follow, however, that the AQL so chosen also represents the percentage of defectives which we expect to find in a batch of that type of materiel.

Table 2 may quote an AQL of say 2.5%, but this does not necessarily mean that we expect to find 2.5% of defectives in batches which we receive, but merely that it will not pay us to inspect more closely. If for any reason, for example nuisance value or because it will have a bad effect on morale, an AQL of 2.5% is quite unacceptable, then we must substitute a lower value.

CHAPTER 7

A PRACTICAL ROUTINE FOR THE INSPECTION OF INCOMING MATERIEL

7.1 The importance of a simple, but well defined, incoming inspection routine

Chapters 5 and 6 have been devoted to deciding the best sampling plan for a particular application. Thus, we can now select the best sample size, and state how many defective items should be allowed in that sample before the whole batch is rejected. Setting the sampling plan is only half the problem, however. It is just as important to have an efficient practical routine for the inspection of incoming materiel. In particular, we must ensure that the checks which are applied to each type of materiel are appropriate, bearing in mind the use that our production lines are going to make of it. We must also see that simple records are kept, so that suppliers who consistently send unsatisfactory materiel can be discontinued.

7.2 The incoming inspection record card

A typical incoming inspection record card is shown in Figure 7.1. One of these is used for each type of materiel, i.e. for each part number, and where one materiel is supplied by more than one supplier it is usually best to have separate cards for each supplier as well.

Part no. or code no.	INCOMING INSPECTION RECORD		Cost
B 7461 /1			55p.

Name of Item		Supplier	
RETAINING ROD		SUPER ROD CO.	
Sampling scheme	A.Q.L. = 0.65 %	Division	ENGINE

Test specification	Fault code
CHECK WITH RULE THAT OVERALL LENGTH = 40 ± 1 mm	A
" " MICROMETER, LARGE DIAMETER = 12.5 ± 0.08 mm	B
" " " , SMALL " = 6.50 ± 0.05 mm	C

Date	G.R.N. no. or works O.N.	No. in batch	No. insp.	No. faulty	% faulty.	Fault analysis									Batch			Action			Senior insp's initials
						A	B	C	D	E	F	G	H	Misc.	Pass	Fail	Insp's initials	Return to supplier	100% insp.	Rectify	
9 SEP	1241	500	80	1	1.2	1	–	–							✓		Jω				
17 "	1296	950	80	0	0	–	–	–							✓		LA				
30 "	1352	2,100	125	0	0	–	–	–							✓		LA				
2 OCT	1401	700	80	4	5	4	–	–								x	Jω	✓			RC
15 ".	1488	2,500	125	0	0	–	–	–							✓		Jω				
21 "	1564	2,500	125	1	0.8	1	–	–							✓		PSγ				
1 NOV	1621	1,500	125	3	2.4	3	–	–								x	PSγ	✓			RC
9 "	1653	1,700	–	–	100	–	–	–	WRONG TYPE SENT							x	Jω	✓			RC
17 "	1767	5,000	200	0	0	–	–	–							✓		LA				
23 "	1791	5,000	200	0	0	–	–	–							✓		LA				
4 DEC	1854	5,000	200	3	1.5	3	–	–							✓		Jω				
20 "	1923	3,500	200	0	0	–	–	–							✓		LA				
1 JAN	1969	2,500	125	0	0	–	–	–							✓		LA				
14 "	2043	2,500	125	4	3.2	4	–	–								x	PSγ	✓			RC
4 FEB	2112	2,000	125	3	2.4	3										x	Jω		✓		RC

Figure 7.1 Example of an incoming inspection record card

1 At the top of the card, there is space for the part number, the name of the part and the name of the supplier.

2 In the top right-hand corner, we put the price that we have to pay for one item. It is useful, when we are deciding what action to take about doubtful materiel, to know the amount of money with which we are dealing.

3 Below the name of the part, we put the AQL at which inspection is to be carried out. We shall have chosen this as discussed in Section 6.7.

4 Next comes the test specification. It is important that the checks to be applied should be listed by someone who is familiar with the use which will be made of the materiel in question. Otherwise it will be inevitable that our incoming inspectors will sometimes waste time checking things which do not matter, and at other times omit to check something which is vitally important. In addition to the checks themselves, the inspector should also be told the method of measurement and, where gauges are to be used, he should be told the gauge number. For electrical tests, appropriate information about meter ranges and consumption should be included.

We give each check a fault code, and these consist of successive letters of the alphabet (A, B, C, etc.). This will enable us to identify the various checks in the fault analysis, further down the incoming inspection record card.

5 The lower half of the card and the back are used for a simple record of the results on successive batches. The column headed 'GRN or Works Order No.', is used to identify the batch. Thus, we can use the number of the goods received note (GRN), if there is one, or we can use our own works order number, or we can supply a batch number.

In addition to showing the number of items inspected and the number faulty or defective, the card also indicates the type of fault. Thus, an entry of 2 under fault A would indicate that 2 items failed on check A of the test specification. This information is valuable if we have trouble with the quality of a materiel. We can then look to see what its most common faults are.

7.3 Setting up the incoming inspection routine

Before we can operate the incoming inspection routine, given in the next section, it must be set up by a responsible person who is familiar with the requirements of our production lines. For example, this person might be a production engineer or a senior inspector. The steps are as follows:

1   He prepares a separate incoming inspection record card for every different materiel which we buy. Where we buy one materiel from more than one supplier, he prepares a separate card for each supplier. It helps to colour the top left-hand corner of such cards, say red, to indicate to the incoming materiel inspector that there is more than one supplier, and so reduce the risk that he will enter his results on the wrong card.

2   He decides how each item is to be inspected, and what is to be considered acceptable, and what unacceptable. This is where his knowledge of the job is so valuable. Usually, not all qualities are equally important, and he must decide which are suficiently significant to justify the cost of checking them. Since incoming inspection is not a creative operation in its own right, its value will depend upon the extent to which it keeps out defective items which would result in costly production repairs. He must consider each check individually and ask himself, 'Will the cost of applying this check be less than the subsequent cost of production repairs if we do not apply it?' Unless the answer is yes, he should omit the check. In particular, he must examine complicated and expensive tests very carefully before he includes them.

3   He must make sure that the inspector will know what quality standard is required, in clear practical terms. All variables must have tolerances, and attributes must have visual or other quality standards, as appropriate. Unless this is done, we may well find that one inspector will accept what another will reject. Further information is given in Sections 3.7 and 3.8. Where the quality standard, or a specification, has been agreed with the supplier this agreement must obviously be the basis for incoming materiel inspection.

4   He next uses Table 2 to choose a suitable AQL, and he enters this on the card in the box provided, immediately underneath the name of the item. It is possible to have two AQLs for checking the same item. Thus, a very important quality, which would cause a lot of trouble if it went wrong, might be inspected at a very low AQL such as 0.065%, while several ordinary qualities might be checked at a higher AQL such as 1.0%. He must consider the complication of having two AQLs, and decide whether it is worth the saving in inspection achieved. He must remember that the inspector is bound

75

to take the larger sample from the batch and, having done so, the choice is merely between checking the whole sample for all the qualities involved or remembering that after the smaller sample has been checked certain tests can be omitted. Often the complication of two AQLs is not justified by the small saving in inspection achieved.

7.4 Operating the incoming inspection routine

The following is a suggestion for the routine to be operated by the incoming materiel inspector, but we can adapt it to take account of our own particular needs.

1 When a batch of materiel arrives from the supplier, the inspector takes from the file the incoming inspection record card corresponding to that part number and that supplier.

2 The card tells him the AQL at which he is to check, and he consults Table 1 to convert this into the sample size, and the number of defectives allowed.

3 He takes the prescribed sample, and carries out the prescribed checks.

4 He enters the results of his checks on the next line of the card.

5 If the batch passes inspection, it goes on to the materiel stores, and the card goes back into the file.

6 If the batch fails inspection, both it and the incoming inspection record card are put aside for the attention of the senior inspector.

7 Periodically, say once per day, the senior inspector examines the batches that have failed inspection. He first satisfies himself that the checks have been correctly carried out. (In the example card shown in Figure 7.1 we can see that every time 'L.A.' gets a batch no defectives are found in the sample. Now we know that some batches do contain defectives because J.W. and P.S.T. find them from time to time, and their results are being accepted by the senior inspector. Therefore, it is clear that inspector L.A. needs further help and instruction, etc., in the way checks are to be carried out.)

8 Next the senior inspector must decide the fate of the batch and,

in making this decision, he may need to consult his colleagues, for instance the production engineer, progress controller, foreman, etc. Ideally, if a batch fails inspection, it should be returned to the supplier complete. There are two reasons for this:

a   It puts pressure on the supplier to improve his quality.
b   It helps the supplier to understand what has gone wrong, and so improve his own quality control.

Sometimes, however, the pressure of industrial life makes it very difficult to return a batch. If our own production lines are desperately in need of the materiel in question, it may be very unwise to send back the whole batch, good as well as bad, to the supplier. In such cases, the senior inspector may decide on one of the following courses of action:

a   To carry out 100% inspection, in order to sort the good items in the batch from the bad ones. The good items can then be used for production, and only the bad ones returned to the supplier.
b   In some cases, the shortcomings of the defective items may be such that it is a practical proposition to rectify them, so that the whole batch can be used for production.

Whether the senior inspector decides to return an unsatisfactory batch or not, it is important that a suitable letter of complaint should be sent to the supplier concerned giving full details of the faults found.

7.5   Making full use of the information collected

After the routine described in Sections 7.1 to 7.4 has been in operation for some time, a lot of useful information will have been collected on the incoming inspection record cards. We should make full use of this as follows:

1   We can work out the average percentage of defectives that each supplier sends us, and we can see whether over a period he gets better or worse. An improvement might indicate that our incoming inspection is having a good effect on him. A marked deterioration would obviously have to be investigated.

2   We can compare the types of fault sent us by each supplier. Where two suppliers send the same materiel it often happens that, although they both send roughly the same percentage of defectives, they each have their own 'favourite' faults.

7.6 Vendor rating

So far, we have assumed that each of our suppliers will continue to send us batches which contain a proportion of defective pieces and that, overall, we shall be justified in assuming that the average percentage of defective pieces, in batches which pass incoming inspection, will be equal to the AQL. This is not necessarily true. Our purchasing department will no doubt do their best to buy materiel from consistently reliable suppliers. Where they succeed, we may well find that such materiel is almost always good and seldom contains any defective items at all. In such cases, it may well be a waste of time and money to carry out full incoming inspection as we have discussed, and vendor rating may be useful.

Vendor rating, also called supplier grading, takes many forms. In principle, we match the amount of incoming inspection which we do to our supplier's performance. This must be done to suit our own particular requirements, but the following is a guide.

BS 6001, discussed in Section 5.10 provides for:

a   Normal inspection.
b   Tightened inspection.
c   Reduced inspection.

We put all our suppliers into one of these grades, for each materiel they supply. The suggested routine is as follows:

1   Each supplier/materiel begins on normal inspection. If, at any time, 2 out of 5 successive batches are rejected, that supplier is demoted to tightened inspection. Then when 5 successive acceptable batches have been received, he can be returned to normal inspection. If after 10 successive batches he is still on tightened inspection, we suspend inspection and investigate.

2   Where quality is usually satisfactory, and we only need a warning if it suddenly deteriorates, we can use reduced inspection. In BS 6001 there is a gap between the accept number c and the reject number d in the reduced inspection tables. This is to be interpreted as follows.

No. of defectives found	Action
Less than or equal to c	Accept and continue on reduced inspection.
Between c and d	Accept but revert to normal inspection.
d or more	Reject and revert to normal inspection.

78

So far promotion and relegation has been based entirely on quality. Many companies, however, add additional weightings to take account of price and delivery as well. A typical method is as follows.

Starting with a maximum rating of 100 points, we divide these between quality, price and delivery, according to the importance which we attach to each. For example:

Maximum points awarded for quality	= 40
Maximum points awarded for price	= 35
Maximum points awarded for delivery	= 25
Total maximum	100

Suppose now that we have to assess the following supplier:

(a) 90% of his batches are accepted on sampling inspection.
(b) His price is £70 per batch, although the cheapest we could buy elsewhere is £60 per batch.
(c) 80% of his deliveries are on time.

We calculate like this:

$$\text{Quality rating} = 40 \times \frac{90}{100} = 36$$

$$\text{Price rating} = 35 \times \frac{60}{70} = 30$$

$$\text{Delivery rating} = 25 \times \frac{80}{100} = 20$$

Overall rating for that supplier and that materiel out of 100. $= 86$

7.7 Taking samples from a batch

Every sample which we take must be representative of the batch, because we are going to judge the quality of the batch by the quality of the sample. To get a representative sample, we usually try to take it at random. A statistically random sample is one in which every item in the batch has an equal chance of being selected for the sample. Items at the bottom of the batch have just as much chance of being chosen as those on the top. It is possible to achieve this in practice. For example, we could number each item in the batch and then, using random numbers, could decide, in a truly random and unbiased way, which were to be chosen for the sample. Clearly, however, this would take impossibly long to do for every batch of materiel which we received. We must, therefore, modify what is theoretically desirable to what is reasonable and practical. Some care and experience are necessary in doing this, and the following points will help:

1 Never take the whole sample from one part of the batch.

2 Make sure that the sample does not come entirely from the top layers of the batch. The bottom must be represented as well as the top, and one side as much as the other.

3 If a consignment consists of more than one package, then from each package we take a sample which is roughly proportional to its size. It helps to keep the sub-sample from each package separate. We never know whether a consignment received from an outside supplier is really all one production run or whether it is a mixture of two or more. If we find that of five sub-samples taken two are good and three are bad, we have an immediate indication that we have a consignment consisting of two manufacturing runs. If this is confirmed by further inspection, then only the three bad packages need to be rejected. However, the sub-sample is unlikely to be large enough to reject a package without further inspection. To make a decision on a single package, we must treat it as a batch in its own right and take the full prescribed sample from it.

4 From the above, it follows that we should never mix two small consignments together to make one large one for economy in sampling, unless we know that both consignments are from the same production run.

5 We must beware of sampling bias if we have a batch in which some items are obviously defective. For example, suppose that finish is important, and we receive a batch in which some items are obviously blemished. It will be very difficult to sample this fairly. Every time an item is drawn, there is inevitably a decision to be made: 'Shall I take a good or a bad one?' It may help not to look at the moment of taking such a sample.

6 Where something is known about the past history of the batch, a stratified sample may be useful. For example, if we know that the machine making the batch went wrong sometime during the run, we shall expect the box containing that batch to be bad at the top, and good at the bottom. If we can find the point of changeover, then we can separate the bad from the good without doing 100% inspection.

Thus, to get a stratified sample, we break the batch into sections, each of which is as homogeneous as possible within itself, although each differs in quality from the other sections. We then sample each section in proportion to its size. Depending on our results, we may keep the batch permanently in sections, if they differ sufficiently from each other, or we may reunite them. A stratified sample tends to be more representative of the whole batch than a truly random sample.

7.8 Questions

1 Explain what is involved in organising a system of goods inwards inspection, and indicate the advantages that would be expected to result from it. *(25 marks)*

2a Outline the contribution to quality which can be made by a purchasing department. *(6 marks)*

2b List the main points which should be borne in mind in preparing a specification for the purchase of incoming raw materiels and/or components. *(11 marks)*

2c What is meant by vendor rating? *(8 marks)*

3 *(In the following question, candidates were permitted to make any necessary assumptions, provided they were clearly stated.)*

(a) A manufacturing company buys considerable quantities of a particular resistor from one supplier. Inwards goods inspection records over a period show that 95% of consignments were acceptable, the remainder being returned complete to the supplier. Of his deliveries 80% arrived on time and the rest were late. The price paid was £25 per batch of 250, although they could have been bought elsewhere for as little as £20 per batch. Suggest a suitable vendor rating scheme for this product, and hence work out a rating for this vendor. *(12 marks)*

(b) When the resistors are received, inspection costs 3p per resistor, but if a defective resistor is used in the factory, its subsequent removal and replacement by a good resistor costs 35p. The inspection tables used by the company require the following number to be inspected for each Acceptable Quality Level (AQL) for a batch size of 250:

AQL, %	0.065	0.10	0.15	0.25	0.40	0.65	1.0	1.5	2.5
Sample size	200	125	80	50	32	20	50	31	20

Use economic considerations to deduce a suitable AQL.

(13 marks)

CHAPTER 8

METHODS, EQUIPMENT AND INSPECTION

8.1 Defining the method

We must now set the method by which the job is to be done, and decide the plant and equipment which will be required. If all of our production can be correctly made using satisfactory materiel, then clearly the whole of it will be good. Conversely, it must follow that, if some or all of our production is unsatisfactory, then either the materiel or the method and equipment or the way in which it is used are incorrect in some way. If, as is usually the case, some production is good and some bad, there must be a variation in one of these and we must ask ourselves, 'If we can make some of our production good, why cannot we make it all good?'

Part of the answer lies in having a consistent method for each article we make. If we leave each operator to decide his own method, we are bound to get variations in quality from one to another. Therefore, we must decide upon the correct method, and see that every operator knows what it is and adheres to it.

8.2 Assistance from method study

Method study aims to achieve the required quality and quantity in the easiest, cheapest and quickest way. Thus, at the start of a project, the methods engineer must find out precisely what quality standard his method is required to produce. He must then devise his method to achieve that quality, as well as the required quantity, in the easiest possible way. It must be such that it is as easy as possible for the operator to do the job correctly, and as difficult as possible for him to do it incorrectly. The ideal method from the quality point of view is one that cannot be done incorrectly.

One trap that the methods engineer must avoid is that of assuming that method study consists only of reducing the amount of work in an operation. This is important, of course, but if he ignores the quality requirements then the final method is unlikely to be satisfactory. He may end up with what he thinks is a very good method, e.g. 'I have cut the work by 50%', only to find that he has, at the same time, cut out one or more movements which are vital if the required quality is to be achieved. Hence, although the rate of production goes up, the scrap rate goes up with it.

It is advantageous for both the methods engineer and the quality engineer to be consulted at the design stage. The restrictions each must face, and the contribution each can make, can then be economically integrated together. The methods engineer may be able to point out that a particular quality standard would be very difficult and expensive to achieve and, therefore, propose a cheaper method producing a slightly lower quality standard. Similarly, the quality engineer may be able to make suggestions to ensure that the required quality standard is achieved as easily as possible by all concerned. Meanwhile, the designer can look after the customer's point of view, and contribute design suggestions.

8.3   Examples of how good methods can improve quality

A good example of a method which improves quality is to be found in the home. When we decide to put on the portable electric fire, we have a little assembly job to do. There are three wires on the fire, line, neutral and earth, and these must be correctly connected to the line, neutral and earth wires of the electricity supply. Failure to assemble correctly may not only result in the fire not working, but is also liable to be dangerous. Therefore, the assembly must be done correctly and, if we did not know otherwise, we might conclude that such an operation would always require at least 100% inspection. In fact, however, this is not necessary because the wires of the fire are connected to a three-pin plug, and those of the supply to a corresponding socket, and the plug and socket will only go together one way – the correct way. No inspection is necessary.

In the radial drill section of a machine shop, rejects were incurred because the operators sometimes confused drills of similar size, and so drilled a wrong-sized hole. The solution to this problem was not to dress down the operators, who were doing their best already, but to provide a very simple drill holder. Each time a job was set up the correct drills were put into the holder in the right order. The operator had only to take the drills in the sequence offered to avoid mistakes. Provision was also made at the same time to tell operators whether holes were the correct depth. The result was that errors in hole size and depth reduced considerably.

There is a wide scope for simple jigs and fixtures which will assist the operator to do the job correctly, and so make it less likely that he will do it incorrectly. Such jigs and fixtures are not confined to production lines. They can often be used to improve methods of inspection. Method study is indeed a most valuable ally of quality control.

8.4 Quality control can assist methods

We have talked about the ways in which method study can assist quality, but equally quality control can assist methods. Any quality control investigation will draw attention to the places where methods could be improved, as well as to those where quality requires attention.

Any working quality system tends to accumulate a lot of useful information. Quality control charts, inspection records, etc., will show where difficulties in production have been experienced, and what types of scrap and rework have been made as a result. Often, a change in method is the best way to improve the situation. Thus, the Pareto curve which we shall consider in Section 16.7 may well be the starting point of a method study project, as much as one in quality control.

8.5 Making the method self-proving

In the same way that we try to plan each individual operation, so that it cannot be done incorrectly, we can often link operations together so that they check each other. An example of this occurred on an assembly which had two fuses of different electrical values. They were of the same mechanical design, however, so each fuse would fit perfectly into the position intended for the other. Originally, one operator put in both fuses and from time to time became confused, so that she either put in two fuses of the same value, instead of one of each, or she put one of each but the wrong way round. A good permanent solution to this problem would be to modify the design of one fuse holder, so that the fuses were no longer interchangeable. In this particular case, however, this was not acceptable to the customer, and the solution adopted was to separate on the assembly line the insertion of the two fuses. One operator at one stage of the assembly put in one fuse, and another operator, later in the assembly, put in the other. With this arrangement, the first operator only handled one value of fuse which she put into only one position in the assembly. It was unlikely that she would accidentally put a fuse into the wrong position, because this would be inconsistent with her normal routine. Similarly, the other operator inserted her fuse into the only empty position. If the first operator had done her job correctly, the second could not possibly make a mistake. If by any chance the first operator had put her fuse in the wrong place, the second operator would be sure to notice it, and correct it before inserting her own fuse.

8.6   The effect of speed of working on quality

Speed of working is not necessarily the enemy of quality. It depends upon the type of production, the method used and the individual operator. It often happens that an operator who produces a lot of work also provides consistently good quality. This usually means that he is achieving his good output not by rushing, but because he has devised and practised a good method which yields both quality and quantity, combined with a reasonable working pace. Everyone concerned with the setting of piece work rates will have met the operator who can apparently make the rate look silly, by devising an improved method by which he can achieve a very high output. Often, the improvements involved are only details, and unless the original method has been very accurately recorded, it may be difficult to prove that a change has taken place. Such improved methods may work to the benefit of quality, as well as of quantity.

If a method is to be subjected to any form of piece work incentive, it must be possible for the operator to strive for good earnings, without his quality dropping below the acceptable level. Intricate operations which can be easily short cut, to the detriment of quality, are not usually suitable for piece work, although it may be possible to make them satisfactory by appropriate changes to the method.

86

8.7 A comparison between quality control and method study

Quality control and method study have more in common than is often realised. They collectively strive to produce the required quality and quantity as cheaply as possible, and at the time required. Even the way a project is tackled is much the same in each case. Thus, compare the following six steps for carrying out a quality control project with the corresponding steps for a method study project.

Quality control
1. Select the project.
2. Ascertain the quality standard, the quantities involved, and record the existing method of quality control.
3. Analyse the information collected.
4. Develop the improved quality control system.
5. Explain the new system to those concerned, and install it.
6. Maintain the new quality control system.

Method study
1. Select the project.
2. Ascertain the quality standard, the quantities involved, and record the existing method of production.
3. Analyse the information collected.
4. Develop the improved method.
5. Explain the new method to those concerned, and install it.
6. Maintain the improved method.

8.8 The necessity for satisfactory equipment

No one can be expected to turn out a good job with unsatisfactory equipment, e.g. tools, machines and jigs. This does not mean that every operator must have equipment of the highest quality, but it does mean that the equipment provided must be adequate to produce the quality demanded. Every typist in the company does not need the most expensive, brand new electric typewriter, because the quality of typing she is expected to produce will not always justify it. The secretary of the managing director will need a first-class machine, because the quality of the work which she produces must be first class. The girl who types records in the stores, however, will not be expected to achieve such a high quality. So long as the records are legible and can be typed quickly that is probably all that matters. A typewriter of quite modest quality may be adequate for the job.

Thus, in order to decide what sort of equipment will be satisfactory for a particular job, we need to know:

1 The quality standard which is demanded, as discussed in Chapter 3.
2 The quality of output which any prospective machine or other equipment is capable of achieving.

Fortunately, quality control will itself provide us with this latter information. Thus, the information collected on our quality control charts can often be analysed to tell us the capability of the machines, etc., concerned. If not, we may have to do a special observational run, as described in sections 11.10 and 12.1, in order to get this information.

8.9   The role of the inspector

Many production departments employ inspectors, and as we obviously want to make best use of them we must ask ourselves what their true function is. It is sometimes said that they alone are responsible for quality, but a little consideration will show that this is not correct. It is not the inspector who puts the quality into the product. This comes from a combination of the quality of the original design, the method and equipment used, the materiel, and the skill and care of the operator. If the job is then wrong, no amount of inspection will put it right.

This does not mean that the inspector cannot have any influence on the quality produced. If the rule is that nothing can leave the department until the inspector has passed it, then the production people will be forced to make everything to pass inspection. This, however, is an indirect rather than direct method of controlling quality. The control of quality remains in the hands of the production staff, and the inspector must influence them in order to improve it.

A major snag to control by rejection of defective work is that it shuts the stable door after the horse has gone. Too often with this system the inspector appears in the role of 'chief thrower-out of scrap', whose job is to do his best to find something wrong with work which production men and women have sweated to make. No wonder the inspector is sometimes unpopular.

Fortunately, with quality control, the inspector's role is not to throw the scrap out but to assist the production staff, and the operator in particular, to make everything right first time. If he can achieve this there is nothing to throw out, and only in so far as he is unable to attain what is after all an ideal will he have to resort to sorting good from bad.

8.10   The purpose of the quality schedule

By inspection we usually mean that, at certain stages in the course of production, we compare what has been made with what should have been made. Our standard of reference may be the specification, drawing or a visual quality standard. If the quality concerned is an attribute, we shall only be able to state that it is or is not acceptable. If it is a variable, observed in figures, however, we shall also know how near or far from each limit that quality is.

The checks we decide to make must be appropriate to the job, and made with suitable measuring instruments. We do not want our inspector to waste time checking things that do not matter, or to miss out an important check. Things which are unlikely to go wrong need little checking, and those which are difficult to hold within limits will need a considerable amount of attention.

The inspectors must agree among themselves what the checks are to be, but they are not the only people involved. The production engineer or method planner must plan his method so that it is compatible with the checks which are to be applied. If a dimension is important enough to be watched closely by the inspector, it must also be carefully considered when the method is drawn up. The operator needs to know what the checks are. His job is to make everything right first time which, in practical terms, means to pass inspection. If he knows what qualities will be checked, he can watch them carefully during the production run. If he does not know, he may go to a lot of trouble to make what he considers a good article, only to find that the inspector applies an unexpected check which fails it.

It will be necessary to prepare a quality schedule which lists all the checks which must be applied, together with the method by which they are to be measured or observed. In many cases, the quality schedule can conveniently form part of the planning route card or, alternatively, it may be carried on the quality control chart. Because so many people use it, the title quality schedule is preferable to that of inspection schedule.

8.11   The preparation and use of the quality schedule

The quality schedule should contain all the additional information about quality which the operator, his supervisor, the production engineer or the inspector require. Like the incoming inspection record in Section 7.3 it must be prepared by someone who is familiar with all the quality requirements of the job. This may be a senior

89

inspector or a planning engineer. While the method is being planned, it is often convenient to plan the quality control as well. At that time, the drawings will already be out, and the tolerances and other limits well in mind.

Whoever prepares it will have to see that there is no doubt about the quality standard. He will want to know the method of manufacture, because this will affect the intensity of inspection required.

The following is typical of the information which the quality schedule may contain:

1   Any information that will help to interpret the quality called for by the drawing, specification, etc.
2   A list of all the checks that the inspector is expected to apply. These will include:
     a   Each variable, converted where necessary into the actual units in which the inspector will measure. Tolerances must be given if they are not already shown on the drawing or specification.
     b   Each attribute, with a reference to the quality standard required.
     c   The method of measurement, such as micrometer, etc., and where appropriate the gauge number.
     d   How many items are to be checked, and how often.
     e   The accuracy of measurement, as discussed in Section 3.5.
3   Any information which will be required in order to draw up the quality control chart.
4   Attention can be drawn to any quality which is particularly important or which, for any reason, needs careful watching.
5   It is important to make sure that every time a drawing or specification is revised, the quality schedule is updated as well.

8.12   Initial or first-off inspection

Initial or first-off inspection is a well known and valuable aid to quality control. Whenever and wherever a production run is started, it will be prudent to check the first piece, assembly, etc., before the main run commences. Even in process work, where the first piece cannot be checked as such, it will be desirable to check the set-up itself, for example the positioning of jigs, fixtures and moulds, the temperature used and the materials which have been used, etc.

We can detect many faults by checking the first-off, and so

prevent the whole batch from being wrong. The following are some examples:

1   We can check whether the machine or other equipment is correctly set up.
2   We can discover whether the operator has fully understood his instructions.
3   In many cases, we shall be able to detect the use of incorrect materiel.
4   We may well notice any discrepancies between the drawing, the planning route card, and the quality schedule. They can then be investigated before hardly any damage has been done.

A first-off inspection is almost always worth doing, but sometimes it is more useful than at others. This will depend partly on the value of the work being produced, and partly on how far a correct first-off ensures a correct run. The more expensive the work being made, and the more it costs to put it right if it is incorrectly made, so the more it will pay us to make sure that the run starts off correctly. Sometimes a correct first-off almost ensures that the rest of the run will be correct. For example, in printing, if the type is correctly set in the first place, at least the spelling cannot be wrong during the rest of the run.

8.13   The purpose of patrol inspection

First-off inspection ensures that the job starts correctly, and the object of patrol inspection is to help the operator to make the whole run correctly. From time to time the patrol inspector will visit the machine or operator concerned and take a sample of the latest work made. He will check this to the quality schedule, and tell the operator whether it is all right or not. If the quality is wrong on any point, then this must be corrected as quickly as possible. Ideally, the machine or process should be adjusted just before it goes out of limit, so that no out-of-limit work is produced. Usually, however, this is only possible if it is practicable to measure in figures. If attributes are used, then little or no warning is given until the work is actually out-of-limit. Obviously, if something does go wrong, the sooner it is discovered and corrected the less out-of-limit work will be made. If an operator goes wrong, it is much kinder to tell him quickly, so that he can correct himself before he has made a lot of out-of-limit work. The operator should be encouraged to regard the inspector as a friend, who assists him in the task of keeping defective work to a minimum.

8.14   The use of patrol inspection

If we are to get maximum value from our patrol inspectors, we shall need a fairly set routine for them to operate, and the following is a typical example:

1   After each inspection has been made and found satisfactory, all work produced so far is cleared from the machine or operator into a container holding the whole day's production.

2   All work which is made from then to the time of the next inspection is kept in a smaller container on or near the machine, etc.

3   When the next patrol inspection is carried out:

  a   If the sample passes on all checks, the work on the machine is added to the day's production.

  b   If it fails on one or more checks, then the quality must have gone wrong since the last check was made, and so all the out-of-limit work produced will be already isolated from the bulk of the production in the smaller container holding that period's run. Therefore:

  (i)   The machine or operator is immediately stopped, so that no more out-of-limit work is produced.

  (ii)   The inspector takes possession of the last period's work, and carries out 100% inspection on it, to sort the good work from the bad.

  (iii)   The machine is reset, and the equivalent of a first-off inspection, at least on the qualities which were out of limit, is done before production recommences.

4   The frequency with which patrol inspections should be made is discussed fully in Sections 13.9–13.13, and the number of items to be checked in Section 13.8.

8.15   Taking and assessing samples on patrol inspection

The primary task of a patrol inspector is to help keep production running correctly and therefore, whatever the sample size, it should always include the last or almost the last item made because this gives the latest news of the machine's condition. It will tell the inspector and operator whether the machine is still running correctly.

In judging a sample, the inspector must ask himself not so much, 'Is this item satisfactory?' but rather, 'Is this machine all right for another period's run?' For example, if the machine has reached top drawing limit, the work itself may be just all right. However, if that machine is allowed to run for another period, it would certainly go out of limit and defective work would be made. Therefore, the machine must be reset immediately.

8.16 The last-off

At the end of the run, the last piece made should be checked to see whether the tools, etc., are still in satisfactory condition. If they need regrinding or any other attention before they will be fit for another run, this must be arranged *before* they are returned to store. Otherwise, next time those tools are required there will be a delay while they are reground and, if the job is urgent, there will be a temptation to make do with them as they are.

The last-off check can usually be combined with the last patrol inspection. It is usually desirable to do a patrol inspection at the end of a run, in order to check on work made since the last routine inspection.

8.17 Final test and inspection

The term 'final test and inspection' is usually used to denote any inspection done after manufacture has been completed, with the object of making sure that the goods concerned are satisfactory to send to the customer, or maybe to another department for the next operation. Thus, the foundry may carry out a final inspection to ensure that their castings are all right to send to the machine shop, and the machine shop may, in turn, perform a final inspection to be certain that machined castings are all right to go to the assembly department, and so on.

Now, throughout manufacture, we try to make everything right first time. If we can be sure of doing this, then the resulting batch will be 100% good and no final inspection will be necessary. The fact that final inspection is sometimes necessary indicates that we have been unable to guarantee 100% good work. There is a risk that in spite of all our efforts, some of the work may be defective. Therefore, in considering whether final inspection is necessary, we first ask ourselves if it is possible to arrange production so that every batch is bound to be satisfactory, and final inspection unnecessary.

If final inspection must be carried out, then the problem is very similar to that of the inspection of incoming materiel, which we discussed in Chapters 5, 6 and 7. Indeed, we can consider that the final inspector is, in effect, carrying out incoming acceptance inspection on behalf of the customer or the department which is about to receive the goods. Final inspection should, therefore, be regarded as a check that our production quality control is working satisfactorily, and not as the quality control system itself.

In principle, the economic considerations which we discussed in Chapter 6 still apply. The cost of any final inspection which we make, plus the cost of the trouble we shall give our customer or the next department if we let defective work get through to them, must in total be a minimum. Final inspection is often done on a 100% basis, but there is no rule about this. In suitable cases, sampling inspection using an AQL can be employed.

8.18 Questions

1a What is meant by the statement that 'The customer is the final inspector'? *(4 marks)*

1b Hence, what is the role of the inspection department? *(21 marks)*

CHAPTER 9

QUALITY AND THE OPERATOR

9.1 Be fair to the operator

The operator is a most important factor in achieving satisfactory quality. If he is not interested, then we shall be lucky if we have much success, however good in principle our quality control system is. In the first place, we must be quite fair to our operator, for unless he knows he will get a square deal he is unlikely to be very co-operative. It is no good giving him a badly planned method, poor materiel and unsatisfactory tools, and then expecting him to produce a first-class job. The care with which we have done our initial quality planning will be reflected in the quality that the operator is able to produce, and, therefore, we must be careful not to assume that, because something has gone wrong at the manu-facturing stage, it is necessarily the operator's fault.

As Figure 9.1 illustrates, every operator is entitled to:
1   A satisfactory method, as discussed in Chapter 8.
2   Satisfactory tools, machines and other equipment, as con-sidered in Section 8.8.
3   Satisfactory materiel, as discussed in Chapters 4, 5, 6 and 7.
4   Satisfactory instructions concerning:
    a   The method he is to use.
    b   The quality standard he is required to achieve, and the inspection which will be applied to help him achieve it.
The operator then does the job, and if patrol or other inspection

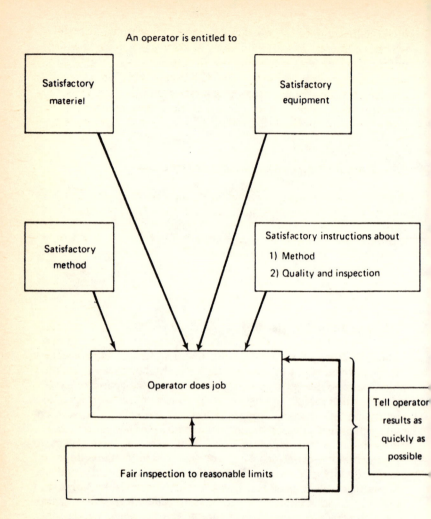

Figure 9.1 Giving the operator a fair chance to do the job correctly

is used, it must be impartial and to reasonable quality standards. As far as possible, such inspection should be done in full view of the operator but, if this is not practicable, then the operator must be told the results as quickly as possible afterwards. This will not only help to keep the operator's interest, but it will also assist him in keeping his quality right.

The word 'satisfactory' above must be interpreted in terms of the

96

final quality required. For example, a poor consignment of wood, which is quite satisfactory for making packing cases, would be quite unsatisfactory for making high-class furniture. A lathe that is quite satisfactory when working to drawing limits of ± 0.12 mm, may be completely useless when attempting limits of ± 0.012 mm. Thus, the operator must be given reasonable materiel, tools, equipment and instructions for the quality standard he is expected to produce.

9.2 The selection and training of operators

If we employ untrainable or untrained people we cannot reasonably expect to get satisfactory quality. Thus, in a factory, both the Personnel Department and the Training Department, by the selection and training of suitable operators, make a valuable contribution to the control of quality.

We must try to select people who are not only capable of doing the job but are interested in doing it well. We must check what training they have already had and, if this is insufficient, provide whatever is still required.

Because an operator has been engaged as a 'skilled' man, we must not assume that he knows everything that a skilled man should know. When an operator fault produces scrap, it is easy to fall into the trap of saying, 'He's a skilled man; he should know better than that.' Maybe he should, but if in fact he does not then he will have to be told, otherwise he will go on making the same mistake. Our quality control system will soon tell us if an operator consistently makes the same mistake, and then we must provide suitable help and instruction to cure him of it.

We must also remember that by a 'skilled' man, we usually mean a man who is skilled in one particular trade. For example, a skilled foundryman should be generally skilled in the art of foundry work. However, in our foundry, we may make a special range of castings which require a special running system or a particular method of pouring the molten metal. Obviously, we cannot expect even a skilled foundryman to know this, and so he will have to be taught it. This principle applies, of course, to both skilled and unskilled men. If the job is at all special, men will need instruction in doing it. Indeed, there can be very few cases where a man can be safely put on a new job without any instruction at all. Thus, every time he puts a different man on a particular job, the supervisor must normally give him a period of detailed instruction. This will include:

1   How to do the job.

97

2   Key points, which must be especially kept in mind (see Section 9.3).
3   The quality standard required.
4   Care of the tools and equipment, etc.

It is prudent to train men in advance of actual requirements. If two operators are required for a given job, we shall be wise to have a third man trained ready so that he can take over at short notice if either of the two regular men are ill. The spare man can be employed on other work until he is required.

	Degrease (sub assemblies)	Assemble (OP. 1)	Assemble (OP. 2)	Fit control circuit	Fit special control T.P.6	Adjust contacts		
R. Brown	3.4.79 R.H.	6.7.85 M.C.	2.1.83 R.H.					
J. Smith	5.5.81 R.H.							
P. Roberts	14.1.82 R.H.	4.12.84 R.H.	20.7.83 R.H.	13.1.85 M.C.	3.3.85 M.C.	16.5.81 M.C.		
S. Jones		14.4.83 R.H.						
K. Good		21.8.74 R.H.						
F. Long			1.11.84 R.H.					
P. Large	16.2.81 M.C.							

Figure 9.2   Example of a training schedule

It is of great assistance to prepare a simple training schedule for each department, similar to that shown in Figure 9.2. Notice how clearly the training schedule shows that only one man, P. Roberts, can undertake the three jobs concerned with the controls and the contacts. Another man will have to be trained for these jobs as quickly as possible otherwise, if P. Roberts is away, there will be no one available who knows how to do them. On the left-hand side we put the names of all the men and women in our department, and along the top we list all the jobs which have to be done. When a man is trained for a job, we write the date and the initials of the supervisor who did the training in the rectangle opposite that man's name, and under the name of the job in question.

It is then easy to see at a glance whether enough men have been trained for each job, and if not, to carry out the necessary training before an emergency arises. When an operator is ill, it is a simple matter to consult the training schedule to see who has already been taught to take his place. Even if the regular supervisor is himself away, another can immediately tell from the schedule who has been trained, and so select a competent operator to take over the job. The insertion of the date of training in the schedule permits refresher courses to be given if a long time elapses after the original date of training, during which time the man has not been called upon to do the job. The training schedule can be displayed in the regular supervisor's office.

9.3 Key points

In any work there are some points which must be especially kept in mind if the operator is to do a good job. These are usually called 'key points', and it is obviously necessary for the operator to understand them fully, and to observe them.

It is often convenient to divide the key points into two groups, as follows:

1 Standard key points which apply to every job the operator does.
2 Special key points, which apply only to one particular job, or maybe a limited group of jobs.

If the operator always does the same job, or is on very long runs, then he only requires the standard key points. In the more general case, however, although he may do only one class of work he will do a variety of jobs or part numbers within that class. He will, therefore, need standard key points to cover the general class of work, and special key points for each particular job or part number. Suppose, for example, that our operator is a painter. He will need standard key points about brush sizes, and how to apply the paint to his general class of work. He will also need special key points to tell him what colour paint to put on each individual job, and whether any areas are to be left unpainted.

As standard key points are always required, it is often convenient to summarise them on a card which can be permanently displayed at each place of work. Such a card needs protection, for example with glass or clear PVC, otherwise it soon becomes very dirty and, even if it can still be read, it then looks unimportant and so does not have the right psychological effect. The letters printed on the standard key-point card need to be large enough to be read while the operator is doing his work. If he has to deliberately stop and consult it, he may not bother. An example is shown in Figure 9.3. When the operator is first put on a job, we must explain the standard key points to him and make sure that he understands them.

Special key points change with each different type of work, and so must be fed to him as a matter of routine every time he receives a new job. He must not be expected to remember the special key points of a job from the last time he did it.

A common yet effective method of dealing with special key points is to use the ordinary planning route card, or maybe the job ticket. This is usually issued with every job, and it tells the operator the

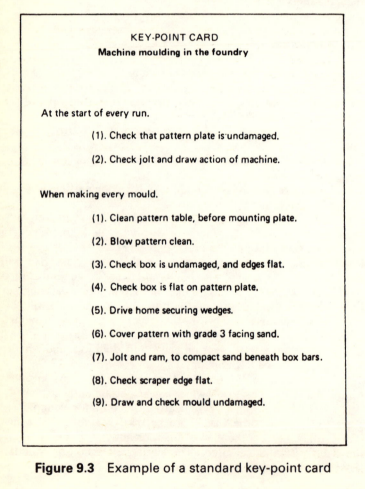

Figure 9.3 Example of a standard key-point card

method he is to use, and possibly how many he has to make. A quality schedule should be added, so that the operator knows precisely what final quality is expected and what inspection will be applied. The preparation of a quality schedule is described in Sections 8.10 and 8.11. A planning route card is frequently used in conjunction with machine shop work, but its equivalent can usefully be extended to many types of work.

9.4 How does the operator know if he is going wrong?

We have so far:
1 Chosen and trained our operator.
2 Made sure that he understands the standard and special key points which apply to each job which he does.
3 Given him a quality schedule, and ensured that he knows what quality standard is required.

The above, together with our planning of methods, materiel and equipment, should ensure that our operator has every chance of

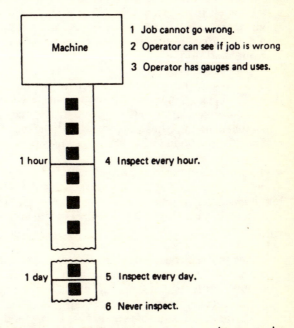

1 Job cannot go wrong.
2 Operator can see if job is wrong
3 Operator has gauges and uses.

4 Inspect every hour.

5 Inspect every day.

6 Never inspect.

Figure 9.4 The ways in which an operator may know or be told when the quality goes wrong

starting off each job correctly. We shall probably use a first-off check to make sure that this does in fact happen, and then we shall be faced with the problem of seeing that the whole batch or production run is correctly made. Primarily, this is a matter of making sure that the operator knows as quickly as possible when anything goes wrong, and that he then corrects himself, or maybe informs someone such as the setter or his supervisor.

We must, therefore, ask ourselves how the operator will know if anything goes wrong. In Figure 9.4, purely in order to make this argument clear, imagine that the work made by our operator travels on a very long conveyor belt down the shop. We now list, in order of preference, the possibilities which may be open to us in ensuring that the operator knows as quickly as possible when the quality of his work goes wrong.

1   The ideal case is where the method is so designed that the operator cannot go wrong. Thus an assembly may be arranged so that it will only go together the correct way.

2   Next best is the situation where the operator can see, feel, hear, taste or smell at once if anything goes wrong, and so correct himself. If our operator is painting letter boxes, and finds that he has been issued with green instead of red paint, he will know at once that this is wrong, and stop.

3   Next in sequence is the case where the operator is given gauges, or other checking equipment, and taught how to use them. This method is only inferior to (2) above, because the operator will not know that something has gone wrong until he makes his check, and this may be only done with, say, every fifth item.

4   Patrol inspection comes only fourth in the list. In this case, an inspector checks the operator's work at regular intervals, and tells him *immediately* whether it is satisfactory or not. The operator can then quickly correct anything which is wrong and, when nothing is wrong, have the satisfaction of knowing that his job is still all right. If this method is used:
a   See that the checks are done on a regular basis; not so regular that the operator can guess which item will be checked, but sufficiently regular that if the check is 'once per hour', it does not degenerate into 'once per day'.
b   As far as is practicable see that the inspector does his checks in full view of the operator. It is not enough to ensure that the checks are correctly done; the operator must be satisfied that

102

this is so. Try to interest him in the tests, and get him to realise that the inspector is there to help him make good work, not to catch him out after he has done something wrong.

5   Moving now into situations which cannot be considered entirely satisfactory, we have the case where the operator is not told the results of inspection on his work until the next day. This situation is most likely to arise on processes where long time cycles, or maybe several operations, must be completed before inspection can be carried out. The risk is very real that a whole day's production may be wrongly made before the fault is discovered. Chapter 21, therefore, considers ways of reducing this risk.

6   Finally, we have the case where the operator is never told whether his work is right or wrong. Do not assume that this state of affairs cannot exist. It can easily establish itself if not guarded against, even though it may not be an intended part of the routine. For example, the operator may always leave an unacceptable burr on his work, and the inspector may obligingly remove it when he inspects, without saying anything about it to the operator or his supervisor.

If the operator goes wrong, he will make defective work until he is told or finds out for himself. The longer he takes to find out, the more defective work he will make. If, therefore, we can ensure that he finds out at once, he need hardly make any defective work at all.

Thus, any method which waits for the inspector to discover that the operator has gone out of limit will be, other things being equal, inferior to getting the operator to control himself. If the inspector checks every hour, it is possible for the operator to be out of limit for almost an hour before this fact is discovered. On average, every time he goes out of limit, he will make half an hour's defective work before the fault is discovered.

We must, therefore, work down the list given above, and choose the very first method which is practicable, i.e. (1) in preference to (2), (2) in preference to (3), and so on. Possibilities (5) and (6) are added for completeness, but should not be regarded as satisfactory choices.

9.5   Helping the operator, and being helped by him

Try to establish an atmosphere of mutual trust and co-operation between the operators and their supervisors. We have already agreed that, when an operator is given a job to do, he has a right to expect satisfactory materiel methods and equipment, to be told what quality standards are required and, if inspection is necessary, for this to be carried out fairly and the results fed back to him as quickly as possible. We must encourage our operators to report to their supervisor immediately one of these features is unsatisfactory. Operators are often shy about doing this, because they regard it as 'complaining'. Unless they do, however, the supervisor may be completely unaware of their difficulties, and therefore do nothing about them. When such a difficulty is raised, make sure that action is taken as quickly as possible or, if action is impossible, explain this to the operator concerned. Do not let him think you have not bothered about the point he has raised.

9.6   Interesting the operator in quality

An operator is unlikely to produce his best quality unless we interest him in doing so. The following points will help to build up the right atmosphere in a department:

1   See that the operator clearly understands the use to which the work he is doing will be put, and that he realises the trouble and cost that will be incurred if his work is wrong. Particularly in the early stages of manufacture, it is possible for an operator to make the same component for years, without ever knowing its precise use or importance in the final assembly. Similarly, he may not realise the cost which the company incurs every time one is scrapped.

2   Where appropriate, use quality control charts as described in Chapters 11, 12, 13, 14 and 15, in order to show the operator how well he is doing. It is not uncommon to find that an operator does not really know how good or bad his work is. This is especially so if, for practical reasons, inspection cannot be carried out either by him, or in front of him. Many operators depend entirely on the feedback of inspection results to tell them how things are going, and this feedback is unlikely to be really effective unless the operator has his results recorded on a quality control chart or its equivalent.

3   Plan the work so that each operator gets what he considers an interesting share of it. If a job is broken down into very small work elements, each operator may have to repeat his element several thousand times a day, and he may find this so monotonous that he loses interest in his quality. Thus, a balance has to be struck

between what seems to be the best method, purely from the point of view of getting maximum output, and the method which will achieve the best quality. Of course, some operators do not mind monotony, especially if they have someone to talk to while they work, and such people do a very useful job.

4   Operator control, which is discussed in Sections 9.7, 9.8 and 9.9 below, helps considerably in interesting an operator in his work.

9.7   Operator control

When an operator checks his own work, as was described in (2) and (3) of Section 9.4, this is called *operator control*, and it can be a most effective way of reducing the amount of defective work. It must, however, be very carefully planned and introduced, and the following points must be emphasised:

1   Checks which we expect the operator to do must be both simple and quick. They must be simple, because we cannot expect the operator to suddenly become a skilled inspector, and they must be quick because otherwise production will be appreciably held up while the operator performs his checks.

2   A particularly attractive application is that of a machine operator who is able to check one piece while his machine is working on the next. In this case, no production time is lost at all, and we are able to make use of time when the operator would otherwise be idle.

3   We must be absolutely fair to the operator. If he is on piece work, any inspection we expect him to do must be taken into account when the rate is set. If, of course, we are using idle time during the machine cycle the time allowed is unlikely to be affected.

4   If gauges or other checking equipment are to be employed, then the operator must be taught how to use them and what checks he is to make. For this reason, operator control tends to work better on long-run production than on short runs.

5   Operator control must be carefully explained to the operators concerned. They must want to work it. If the operators suspect that we are not being fair with them, or are trying to use them to put the inspector out of work, then they will not be likely to co-operate, and

operator control will be a failure. Even if they only *think* that they are being unjustly treated they will not co-operate, in spite of the fact that we may be trying to be absolutely fair. Therefore careful explanation is essential.

9.8 A typical operator control routine

As with all quality control, it is essential to design the operator control routine to suit the type of production concerned. The following, therefore, is typical of the sort of routine which can be used, but we should not be afraid to modify it to suit our individual requirements:

1   Each time the operator is told to set up for a different production run, he receives a planning route card or method card (see Section 8.10) for that job. This tells him all the key points which will require attention, and it includes a quality schedule showing what inspection is necessary.

2   The operator or setter sets up the job to pass the required inspection and, when he is satisfied, he submits his first-off to the inspector. It usually pays to have an independent check to make sure that the job starts off correctly for, if it is wrong at the start, the whole batch is likely to be wrong.

3   When the inspector checks the first-off he does so to the quality schedule, and therefore no 'surprises' are sprung on the operator. Unless the latter has overlooked something, the first-off should pass and, if it does, then the operator is given the go ahead to commence production. If something is wrong, this must be corrected and another first-off submitted.

4   The operator then carries on with production, checking in accordance with his quality schedule. This may call for every piece to be checked or it may, for example, only call for checks, say, on every fifth piece. If the checks are quick and cheap and the cost incurred every time a piece is wrong is high, then we shall call for every piece to be checked. On the other hand, if the checks are relatively expensive, if they take so long that they appreciably hold up production or if the cost incurred when a piece is scrapped is low, then we shall call for checks at relatively infrequent intervals. The frequency of inspection is more fully discussed in Sections 13.9, 13.10, 13.11, 13.12 and 13.13.

5   So long as the work he is making is satisfactory, the operator carries on producing. If a piece fails his inspection, he puts it aside from the good ones, and considers how it happened. If he simply 'made a mistake' he corrects himself, and carries on producing. If the fault is caused by the machine then, depending on the instructions which we have given him, he may either reset it, or call the setter or supervisor. If the materiel is at fault, he will probably have to raise it with his supervisor, to whom he will certainly go if he is in any doubt about the reason for his pieces failing inspection.

6   When the operator is not inspecting every piece, he will not be certain, when he finds a faulty piece, whether that is the first wrong one he has made or not. He will, therefore, have to check all those which have been made since his last routine check, and remove those which are faulty.

7   Thus, regardless of the frequency of inspection, the operator finishes up with a set of good pieces, plus maybe a few faulty pieces, which have been kept separate. There is thus no need for the inspector to do full inspection which would have been necessary if operator control had not been used.

8   However, from time to time, the inspector will carry out a *quality audit*, in order to check that operator control is working satisfactorily. This will probably be a sample check, which may be made during a long run or at the end of a short run. Full 100% inspection will only be carried out if the quality audit gives unsatisfactory results.

9   Operator control can be most successful, but it requires mutual confidence and trust between ourselves and our operator. If we cannot trust him, we certainly will not be able to work operator control successfully. However, it is only fair to trust him in the first place. If he does not do his inspection properly, or tries to slip faulty pieces through in the good ones, the quality audit will soon catch him out.

9.9   Operator control and piece work

If our operator is on piece work, the time he will be expected to spend on inspection must be counted when assessing his rate. In addition to this, however, he must be allowed some sort of payment for any faulty pieces he declares. On ordinary piece work, the operator is usually only allowed to count for payment the good pieces that he makes. Faulty pieces are not included. If we try this with operator control, we shall in effect be saying to our operator, 'Here are the gauges; you are to carry out the checks you have been told to, and put the faulty ones aside, so that we do not have to pay you for them.'

Faced with an offer like that, no operator is likely to carry out his checks conscientiously. The temptation to try to slip any bad ones in with the good, and hope that the inspector will not find them, will be too great.

There are several methods of getting round this difficulty, but they all depend on making some sort of payment for defective work which the operator declares. The most common method is to pay the operator in full for the defective work which he declares, up to some limit such as 2%. A limit is obviously necessary, as otherwise it would be possible for the operator to work all day making everything completely wrong and then, at the end of the day, to declare it all to be scrap and claim full payment for it! The limit should be set so that any reasonably careful operator can work inside it, declare such scrap as he makes and get paid for it. Once an operator has exceeded his limit, there is no incentive whatever for him to declare any additional scrap. The limit is only intended to affect the careless worker.

Another method is to make the payment for faulty work less than that for good work. For example, the operator might be offered full payment for good work, half payment for faulty work which is declared, and no payment for faulty work which is not declared, and is found subsequently by the inspector. In this case, the operator has an incentive to make good work if he can, because at the best, he only gets paid half for faulty work. On the other hand, if he accidentally makes a mistake he has an incentive to declare it, because he then gets paid half instead of nothing. If these methods of payment are used, they must only be applied to faulty pieces which are due to operator errors. Machine, materiel and other scrap, which is outside the control of the operator, must be paid in full if declared.

9.10   The role of the inspector when operator control is used

We might think that the use of operator control was detrimental to the status of the inspector, but this is not so at all. The inspector is relieved of simple, quick, repetitive checks, and can concentrate on the more difficult inspection tasks which the operator cannot be expected to do. The operator is self-contained and, within clearly determined limits, can get on with the job unhindered. Hence, the operator and the inspector are usually on better terms with each other, and the inspector's status in the factory increases.

The Inspection Department still have the following responsibilities:

1 They must teach the operators to use the inspection equipment, e.g. gauges, which is issued to them.

2 They must continue to carry out difficult and time-consuming checks. As we said in (1) of Section 9.7, we cannot expect the operator to be a skilled inspector able to undertake complicated tests. We equally cannot expect him to make lengthy checks, because these would hold up production unduly. Checks which cannot be made at the workplace itself are similarly usually ruled out.

3 Inspectors must calibrate all the inspection equipment which is used to ensure that its accuracy is satisfactory. Gauges, etc., used by the operator should be as accurate as those used by the inspector. The gauges used by the operator should not be set to a tighter limit than those used by the inspector. One of the important jobs of operator control is to encourage mutual trust and confidence between the operator, the inspector and the supervisor. This may be shattered if the operator finds out that he is not trusted to work to the same limits as the inspector.

4 The inspectors must carry out quality audit checks, in order to ensure that operator control is running smoothly.

9.11 Work structuring, job enrichment and job enlargement

A number of attempts have been made to make industrial work more interesting, using terms such as *work structuring*, *job enrichment* and *job enlargement*. Although various companies have used the technique in a variety of forms, most of them are broadly as follows.

An operator is given a reasonable section of the work to do, and is made responsible for both manufacture and ensuring that its quality is correct. Thus he or she might be given say a complete heater to build, test and pack. It would carry their identity marks, and so would be easily traced back if it later proved to be wrong. According to the type of work, etc., some form of quality audit might be imposed. This technique is thus a development of operator control, in which operator control of method has been included.

Sometimes the operators work in small groups. They will be made responsible for say the assembly of a television chassis, or a recognisable part of a car but will be allowed to share the work amongst themselves as they please. They may elect to build the whole thing complete individually, or they may share it in a more normal way, but change jobs from time to time to avoid monotony. The type of work may of course impose some restraints.

9.12 The craftsmanship theory

According to the *craftsmanship theory*, all people have an inherent desire to take a pride in their work. Suitably encouraged they will work well, check their work, and make suggestions for improving quality. They will understand that they have a personal responsibility to make work correctly in the first place, and that no amount of inspection can correct it later. Thus, throughout this chapter, we have been discussing the craftsmanship theory.

9.13 The indifference theory

This theory propounds that operators are not interested in their work, and that the most effective way to increase output is by the extensive use of piecework and similar incentive schemes. To ensure the necessary quality, we must use inspectors and penalties for poor work. Operators treated in this way are unlikely to make suggestions, and indeed their relations with management will probably be poor.

Throughout this book we have rejected the indifference theory. No doubt operators do exist who have no intention of co-operating in the general quality effort, and as a last resort, tougher measures may have to be applied. Certainly however, everyone should be assumed to be co-operative, until he has proved the contrary.

9.14 Questions

1 Discuss the measures which can be taken to encourage and, as far as possible, ensure that an operator produces satisfactory quality. *(25 marks)*

2a Compare the contribution to quality made by the operator, with that made by the shop floor inspector. *(10 marks)*

2b Discuss the techniques and conditions under which it is possible for the operator to become his own inspector. *(15 marks)*

3a Discuss the meaning of
(i) the craftsmanship theory
(ii) the indifference theory *(10 marks)*

3b What precautions and preparations should be used in order to introduce operator control to a department? *(15 marks)*

CHAPTER 10

QUALITY CIRCLES

10.1   The origin of quality circles

In the UK industrial organisation is usually based on a suitably updated version of the ideas of F. W. Taylor (1856–1915). Thus we can nearly always identify top management who decide overall policy, middle management who execute it, i.e. the executives, and specialists such as quality engineers who provide advice in their own field. All this results in detailed instructions which the work force are expected to carry out, and at one time more or less blind obedience was demanded. Although this is no longer true, no great mental contribution is usually expected from operators.

Industrial organisation in the USA has tended to be similar, and after Japan capitulated in 1945, it too adopted American ideas, even though its problems were rather different. Before the war Japan had a reputation for being able to copy any Western idea, but always produced a version which, whilst cheaper, was very inferior in quality. Somehow this image needed to be changed, but by the end of the 1950s little progress had been made. No doubt Japanese quality had improved, but not nearly enough to erase her bad image. Her exports generally were very low and car exports were almost non-existant.

Over a long period during both the 1940s and 1950s Professor Ishikawa, amongst others, studied the situation and concluded that much of the trouble originated from the gulf between management and shop floor, i.e. from what is often referred to as the 'them and us' attitude. Operators were frequently well aware of the cause of quality problems and, with modern standards of education, often knew how to cure them. The trouble was that they were not usually asked. The solution, he concluded, was to introduce quality circles. The first of these began around 1962, and were so successful that today Japan is reputed to have over 1,000,000 circles, involving some 10,000,000 workers. The reputation for quality and reliability which Japan now enjoys, seem to stem largely from its use of quality circles.

10.2 Definition

A quality circle is a group of employees doing similar work, under one supervisor, who meet voluntarily for say an hour each week, to discuss their quality problems, recommend solutions and, with management approval, implement them.

10.3 The principle of quality circles

Most companies have an organisational structure based on the family tree. Everyone reports to a superior who is one status level higher than himself, and all but the lowest rank control subordinates who are one status level lower. Quality circles are built into this structure, as shown in Figure 10.1.

A circle consists of a team leader plus 5 to 10 members, all doing similar work. The majority of circles operate at shop floor or office floor level. Typically the foreman is the team leader, and most or all of the circle members are his subordinates. The circle will have a maximum of, say, 10 members, even though the foreman may have more people under him. People who do not report to the foreman will only be invited when they can contribute something, and then only for a limited period. Thus the quality engineer, production engineer, safety oficer, etc., will not have a permanent seat, since their presence would be liable to inhibit discussion amongst shop floor members. When needed they will be co-opted just for the advice they can give on some particular problem, and will then disappear from the circle again. Since members must be interested in the work of the circle, it is essential for them to be volunteers rather than conscripts.

Typically a circle meets once a week, for an hour or an hour and a half, to consider quality problems in their own area. Mostly they

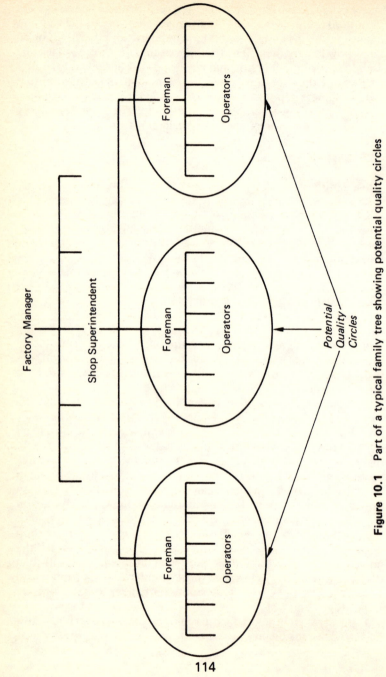

Figure 10.1 Part of a typical family tree showing potential quality circles

will tackle down-to-earth practical problems; the sort they understand only too well. They will make suggestions for solving them, which the circle leader will record. Later the best ideas will be selected, and integrated into a set of proposals. The circle members will explain these to management, and assist in implementing them.

Terminology varies a bit from one company to another. We have used the usual term quality circles, but they are also called QC circles, and quality groups.

10.4   Making a start

Since quality circles are essentially voluntary, they cannot be started simply by the managing director issuing a directive that they will henceforth be formed throughout the company. Indeed, the first step is usually to persuade the top management that quality circles would be beneficial. To this end the quality manager will probably have to prepare and give some sort of presentation, talk, etc., specifically for them. Lip service approval is not enough; top management must be seen to be actively interested in quality problems, and ways of overcoming them.

Once approval has been obtained, planning of the whole quality circle organisation can begin. Obviously this will be done to suit the type of work and organisation concerned, but usually there is a *steering committee* and a *co-ordinator*, in addition to the circles themselves.

10.5   The steering committee

The steering committee looks after the overall planning, development and continuity of the circles. It must not be so large that it is slow and cumbersome, yet all sections of the company should be represented, and members should be drawn from all status levels from top management to trade union representatives. Typically it meets once a month, and its primary job is to provide overall surveillance. It effectively brings the circles into the general company organisation, and provides links from the top right down to shop floor level. It will decide overall circle policy. Thus from its knowledge of where interest, need, etc., are, it will decide which sections of the company should be next to be brought into the circle structure.

The steering committee will also provide support and back-up wherever required. Many circles' proposals will probably be cheap and easy to implement, but occasionally considerable expenditure, expertise, reorganisation, etc., may be involved. Cost and other experts will then have to work out the proposals in detail, so that the steering committee can consider them. Once the latter is convinced that the proposition will be beneficial and viable, it must use its influence to obtain top management approval. Since the steering committee always includes senior management representatives, it will be in a much better position to do this than the quality circle which first thought up the idea.

10.6   The co-ordinator

The co-ordinator is the link man between the steering committee and the quality circles. He must report to a senior member of management, often the managing director himself, and he must be a member of the steering committee. The steering committee will determine overall policy and provide the necessary back-up, but as they only meet periodically, it is the co-ordinator who must provide day-to-day continuity. He is in continuous and direct contact with the circles. Initially he will be instrumental in setting them up, and later he will provide day-to-day help, advice, encouragement, co-ordination, etc. In a large company where circles prosper, he will eventually require a small staff to assist him.

The Americans use the term 'facilitator' for what in the UK is usually called the co-ordinator.

10.6.1   Selection of the co-ordinator

The co-ordinator has a key role and it is essential to ensure that the right person is chosen in the first place. He/she must be:

1   *Acceptable to other employees*   People must be prepared to trust and respect him. Someone with a reputation for being sly or crafty will be of no use, even if that reputation is undeserved.

2   *Enthusiastic and energetic*   If the co-ordinator is not himself convinced about the value of quality circles, he is not going to persuade anyone else that they are worthwhile. A lot of detailed work will be required, and he must be prepared to work hard and painstakingly.

3   *Not easily discouraged*   Some people who are not convinced

about the value of quality circles may tell him so bluntly. For example, there may be a shop steward who retorts: 'The moment you set foot in my shop, I shall lead the men out through the factory gate'. There will inevitably be some set-backs, although hopefully they will be small, and everything must be done to minimise them. Again there will be peaks when the demands of several circles at once will tend to overwhelm him. The man or woman chosen must be able to withstand all these pressures without going to pieces.

4 Suitably experienced and skilled The co-ordinator must be familiar with his company's organisation, and with how its administrative system, works. Frequently he is going to need to get something done, e.g. a new jig may be requested by a circle, and he must know his company's routine for doing this. In particular, he must not upset someone by inadvertently taking action within their sphere of control, without consulting them.

He will need enough technical knowledge to talk sensibly to almost anyone, but he must not pretend to understand the technical basis of every process in the factory. He merely asks the advice of the people in the department concerned. Obviously he needs to be familiar with the most commonly used quality control techniques, but again he can consult the quality engineers as necessary. He must be able to talk to circle members and explain to them the techniques they require to use. It will probably be helpful to send him on one of the courses which are offered for quality circle co-ordinators.

10.6.2 Work of the co-ordinator

The co-ordinator is responsible for the introduction of quality circles and for their efficient day-to-day operation. He is the link man who unites the circles one to another, and links the circles collectively to the management, the latter being formally through the steering committee, and less formally through contact with the departmental managers.

The requirements of industry change constantly. New products are introduced, old ones disappear, quantities increase and decrease. To cope with these, new departments are created and old ones are merged or discontinued. The structure of quality circles must be continually modified to match. Hence the servicing of existing circles will soon become an important part of a co-ordinator's work.

The status of a co-ordinator is a curious one. As the number of circles grows, he will gather a lot of responsibilities, and because he reports to someone high up, he will tend to be regarded highly. Nevertheless because he works largely by persuasion, he will have little direct authority. If as a last resort someone has to be 'instructed' to do something, he will ask that person's own supervisor to do it. He will not instruct that person himself.

10.7   Launching quality circles

The quality manager may decide to launch the first few circles himself, since this will give him a clear and first-hand understanding of the problems involved. Almost immediately, however, a co-ordinator must be chosen and trained.

Next, two or three potential circle leaders must be chosen with care. The following are guidelines:

1   Choose any area of the company which has obvious practical quality problems, i.e. problems which shop floor experience will probably be able to solve. Initially avoid problems which are technically complicated.

2   Earmark potential leaders who are likely to be interested and co-operative.

3   A single circle will probably find it difficult to exist by itself, yet if too many circles are started at the same time, the co-ordinator may be unable to cope. Hence start with about three circles, but try to get them in related areas, e.g. two machine shop circles and an assembly circle, all concerned with the same product. Thus the assembly circle will be able to refer problems concerned with components back to the machine shop circles, and *vice versa*.

4   The foremen invited to become circle leaders must be keen to accept. This is particularly important for the first few circles.

In parallel with the above, an adequate amount of publicity from management will be required, and this needs careful co-ordination. Areas where circles are to be started need to be fully informed in advance. However, it is bad for a department to receive a lot of publicity and then no action for a long time. Hence the publicity should be timed to just precede the actual formation of circles.

The circle leaders must be trained. Do not rush this. People who have not studied for some while need time to adjust to it again. One to one and a half hours a week is enough, and it must be in company's time. According to their background, they may need help in running a small meeting, putting ideas across, dealing with a dissenter, etc. Certainly they will need help with quality circle techniques, although these should be kept as simple as possible.

The following are typical of those which circles commonly find useful:

The quality standard (Sections 3.3 to 3.8).

Pareto analysis and measles charts (Sections 16.7 and 16.8).

Fishbone diagrams (Section 16.9).

Tally charts and other simple frequency distribution curves (Section 11.2).

Simple quality control charts, such as the pre-control (Section 13.17).

10.8   The structure of a quality circle

The circle members should be a representative cross-section of the work supervised by the leader. They can be elected by their colleagues, but probably the initial membership for the first few circles will be invited. They must accept the task voluntarily, although some gentle persuasion is permissible. If more people are interested than can be accommodated, so much the better. Let them rotate from time to time, so that all who are willing to serve have a chance to do so. Circle members must anyway keep their colleagues informed about their activities.

Find a suitable meeting place, preferably near the workshop, but ensure that meetings will not be disturbed by shop floor queries. For many meetings only a table and chairs will be required, but for some a marker board and/or an overhead projector will be needed.

The co-ordinator must attend initial meetings, to explain in detail what is intended, provide circle members with instruction, etc. However, he must be conscious from the start that the circle leader is the person in charge. At the earliest opportunity the co-ordinator must fade into the background, and let the leader take over. As soon as the circle is self-supporting, he should stop attending meetings. No doubt he will look in on a meeting from time to time, to see if he can help, and he will always be available to provide advice and assistance in any way he can.

10.9   The operation of a quality circle

From the first meeting it will be necessary to discuss with members what problems should be tackled and in what order. In Section 10.7 we said that circles should be started where suitable problems exist, and it may be that members will need some guidance about where to start. As far as possible, however, they should be allowed to decide for themselves. It may be that a job which really niggles them, e.g. because it is dirty or tiring, is not regarded as serious by management, in the sense that no large loss of money is involved. Nevertheless it is good for morale if such irritations are removed, and money should not be regarded as the only objective, particularly in the early stages. Overall quality circles will reduce costs considerably.

Steer the circle away from technically complicated problems, and from those solutions which are likely to be expensive to implement. Top management may be reluctant to spend a lot on a circle idea in the early stages, when it is still not fully convinced that circles are of value, whilst the shop floor will soon lose interest if their ideas are rejected. Similarly, avoid problems whose solutions can only be implemented on a long-term basis. We need a quick success which members can feel they have achieved themselves. Introduce members to quality control techniques as they are ready to use them on an actual problem. This helps them to see the relevance of what they learn.

Brief notes should be kept of decisions, etc., taken by the circle.

10.10 Dealing with a problem

Once circle members have agreed on a problem, they must start the process of solving it. The steps will be similar to the way in which any quality problem is solved, but it usually also includes the brainstorming technique of value analysis. Typically the steps will be as follows:

1   Set out clearly the required quality standard in variables and standards, etc. (Sections 3.3 to 3.8). The members must be quite clear about what is acceptable quality. However, many problems are not clear-cut. For example,

'It is difficult to get the casting firmly in the hoist sling. If it slips it's dangerous, as well as getting chipped or cracked, which means it's scrap.'

'It's almost impossible to solder that inaccessible joint neatly, without bits of solder dropping onto the PCB below.'

Methods often have to be considered as well as quality. It may help if members return to the shop floor to see for themselves what the difficulties are, unless of course it is a job all of them do. The circle leader must keep asking questions until he and other members are quite clear what the problem is.

2   Often it will be necessary to collect data, which will then be analysed. If actual measurements have been recorded, a tally chart may be used (Section 11.2); if it is in attribute form, such as numbers scrap, a Pareto chart will be useful (Section 16.7). If the position of the fault on the work is important, a measles chart may be used (Section 16.8). If it is necessary to investigate possible sources of difficulty, a fishbone diagram will be appropriate (Section 16.9). The circle must have access to whatever data it needs, e.g. drawings, planning sheets, method study records and costs. It must also be able to co-opt expertise as required, e.g. production engineer, quality engineer and safety officer. Probably the leader will have to gently restrain his members so that they consider all possibilities and do not jump to premature conclusions.

3   When all or most of the facts are known, possible solutions can be considered; this will be done by a brainstorming session. As far as practicable, all the data plus an example of the work itself will be on view at this meeting. Everyone is invited to make suggestions and these are recorded. Often the leader will write them on a marker board or even better an overhead projector, so that everyone can see them. The 'rule' is that no discussion or criticism is permitted at this stage, because this may impede the flow of ideas. Thus if someone says, 'Let's turn it upside down, it will make it much easier to machine', someone else is not permitted to retort: 'Don't be daft, it weighs half a ton'. They may however say: 'If we do it on the other machine, we can use the hoist above it'. The point is that wild ideas are often precisely those which form a bridgehead onto more practical suggestions. If we stop them, the practical ideas just don't come, and the meeting dissolves into silence. The leader must keep the flow of ideas going. When a lull comes, he can draw attention to an aspect of the problem for which no suggestions have yet been made, or he may recapitulate, by reading back the suggestions made so far. At the end of the brainstorming session he will let ideas incubate for a day or two.

4   Next the ideas must be sorted out. A lot will be discarded, but this should not be done too hastily. Beware of discarding an idea, merely because it has an unusual approach, or because it has an obvious snag, even though it is basically sound. Perhaps the snag can be overcome quite easily. From what is left the best will be selected, combined together, rearranged, simplified, etc., until they are as simple, cheap and practicable as possible. The circle members must first agree amongst themselves about what should be

done, and then explain it to, and get the agreement of, other members of the section concerned.

5 Now the proposals must be sold to management. As far as possible let the circle members explain them themselves. Usually several members each explain one section of the proposals, and use the marker board, diagrams and maybe the overhead projector to do it.

6 Once approval has been given, the proposals can be implemented. Make sure that before and after results are recorded, so that the improvement achieved can be clearly demonstrated, and then ensure that circle members get credit for it.

10.11 Enlargement

As the initial circles become self-supporting, so the co-ordinator will move on to start others. The principles discussed in Section 10.7 still apply. A solid area of committed circles is usually better than a scatter across the company. However, once interest has been aroused, it is likely that other sections will ask to be allowed to form a circle. Such requests should be granted if at all possible. Indeed they may pinpoint a second area in which a group of circles should be encouraged. Do no forget the nightshift; they need circles too.

We have discussed quality circles in terms of the production shop floor, because it is there that they have already been so successful. However, they are by no means limited to manual work, or to the lowest status levels. Office work could benefit, and so could the design departments. There are also possibilities outside the manufacturing industry, for example in government offices and colleges.

10.12 Questions

1a Outline the principle of quality circles. *(13 marks)*

1b Explain how circles could be, or have been, used in a department with which you are familiar. *(12 marks)*

2 Compare the contribution to quality which can be made by operator control, with that made by quality circles. *(25 marks)*

PART THREE

QUALITY CONTROL OF THE ACTUAL PRODUCTION OPERATIONS

CHAPTER 11

FREQUENCY DISTRIBUTION CURVES

11.1 Recapitulation

In Section 1.11, we set out the five basic stages of any quality control system, and in the subsequent chapters we have considered the first two stages in detail. Thus, in Chapter 3, we discussed the first stage, that of setting our quality standard in clear practical terms. Next, in Chapters 4 to 10, we elaborated upon the second stage, which was how to plan to achieve the required quality.

Now we must carry out our plan. We must attempt to make everything right first time and the better we have planned our quality the easier this will be.

11.2 The concept of machine or process variability

We may wonder why we are so often plagued with a small percentage of defective work, say 5%. After all, if operators can make 95% of their work correctly, why does the other 5% have to be wrong?

To try to understand this problem, suppose we have a close look at the output from any machine or process which happens to be making a quality which we can observe as a variable, i.e. in figures. It need not be a machine, but to make the example clear, suppose that a lathe is producing a diameter, whose nominal size is 10.75

mm. However, all the pieces produced will not be exactly 10.75 mm. They will vary a little, depending on various factors, for example:

1   How good the machine is.
2   How skilled the operator is.
3   Whether the materiel is easy or difficult to work, etc.

Suppose we take fifty successive pieces, just as they come off the machine, and measure them. We might get the following readings in millimetres:

10.77	10.76	10.73	10.75	10.78
10.76	10.79	10.75	10.75	10.76
10.77	10.78	10.76	10.78	10.75
10.80	10.77	10.74	10.79	10.74
10.72	10.75	10.82	10.76	10.73
10.76	10.77	10.79	10.76	10.77
10.75	10.76	10.77	10.78	10.75
10.81	10.74	10.81	10.74	10.73
10.75	10.78	10.76	10.80	10.77
10.74	10.79	10.78	10.77	10.80

What can we make of these figures? Probably not very much as they stand. We can see that the diameter varies a bit, but we can say little about how. Suppose that instead of putting the figures down as they come, we collect all the 10.75 mm readings together, then all the 10.76 mm and so on. If we put an X for each piece, we would get what is called a *tally chart* as shown in Figure 11.1. Alternatively we can draw our results as shown in Figure 11.2, in which case it would be called a *histogram*.

We can now begin to see some sort of pattern. Thus:

1   Although the nominal diameter is 10.75 mm the most numerous observation is 10.76 mm and, in fact, far more pieces are larger than nominal than are smaller.
2   Above 10.80 mm, the histogram has a tail marked CD. Although diameters are seldom more than 0.03 mm below nominal, a proportion are appreciably greater than this above nominal.

Thus, we have now got some idea how our lathe varies, and therefore of what sort of precision it is capable of achieving. Whether or not this is good enough will depend on the limits called for on the drawing. Suppose it says that all diameters must be between 10.70 and 10.80 mm. We therefore draw two vertical lines at these values, as is shown in Figures 11.1 and 11.2.

We can now see that our lathe is keeping well inside its bottom drawing limit of 10.70 mm, but that some of its work exceeds the top

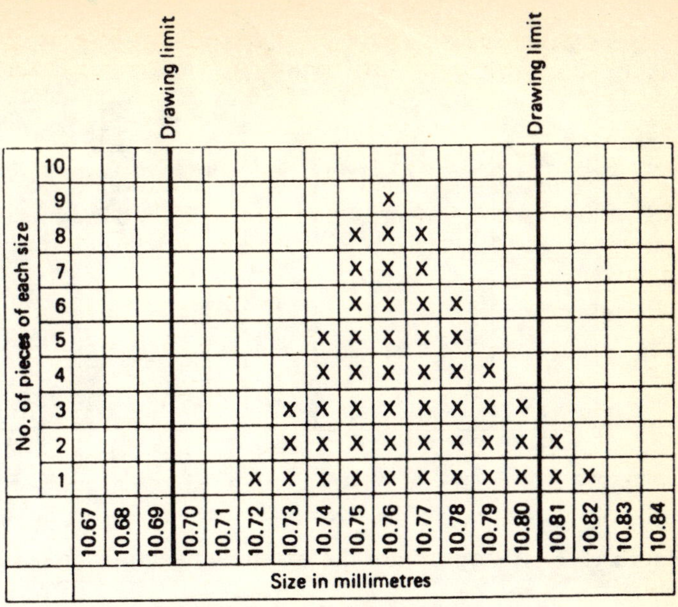

No. of pieces of each size	10.67	10.68	10.69	10.70	10.71	10.72	10.73	10.74	10.75	10.76	10.77	10.78	10.79	10.80	10.81	10.82	10.83	10.84
10																		
9										X								
8									X	X	X							
7									X	X	X							
6									X	X	X	X						
5								X	X	X	X	X						
4								X	X	X	X	X	X					
3							X	X	X	X	X	X	X	X				
2							X	X	X	X	X	X	X	X	X			
1						X	X	X	X	X	X	X	X	X	X	X		

Size in millimetres

Figure 11.1 Example of a tally chart

limit of 10.80 mm. Indeed, we can infer that:

1   Most of the work would be within limits, if the operator was asked to centre his work just below 10.75 mm rather than at 10.75 mm.

2   As 3 pieces (those reading 10.81, 10.81 and 10.82 mm) are over top limit, out of 50 pieces, we can estimate that 3 in 50 or 6% of the whole production is over top limit. This may not be an accurate deduction, because our sample of 50 may not be truly representative of production as a whole, but it gives us a first indication.

11.3   Frequency distribution curves

In Figure 11.2 we drew the variations in diameter from our lathe as a series of steps usually called either cells or intervals each 0.01 mm wide. If we had had more observations we could have decided to make the interval smaller. Thus the shape of a histogram depends partly on personal decisions and partly on the amount of data available. In general it is convenient to think of a smooth curve, called a frequency distribution curve. Strictly speaking it now

127

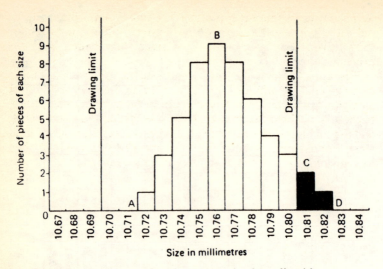

Figure 11.2 Histogram for the example described in text

relates to an infinitely large sample, and shows the probability that any given observation will occur. The following are examples of what we might find in practice.

In Figure 11.3 the specification or drawing limits are much wider than our frequency distribution curve marked ABC. Therefore, we should expect this process to give us very little trouble on the shop floor. The setting can drift as far as XYZ in either direction before

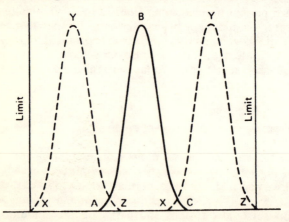

Figure 11.3 Frequency distribution curve for a process that is able to do much better than the specification demands

128

we need worry about the risk of making out-of-limit work. Indeed, our curve indicates that the machine or process is really too good for the job in question, and we should consider whether there is a more exacting job which it could do.

Figure 11.4 shows the case where the frequency distribution curve just fills the whole of the drawing limits. At first sight it is just all right, but in practice it is unlikely to be entirely satisfactory, because it will be difficult to keep the process centred exactly at B, and the slightest drift one way or the other will result in out-of-limit work. For example, if the peak of the curve drifts from B to Y, then the part of the curve shown in black will be out of limit.

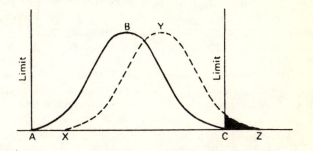

Figure 11.4 Frequency distribution curve for a process whose variability just equals the specification limits

In Figure 11.5 we have an incorrectly set process. The frequency distribution curve shows that the variability is from A to C. If we reset the process so that the peak of the curve is in the centre of the drawing limits at Y, then the whole production is within limits, as shown at XYZ.

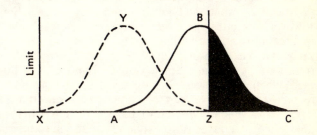

Figure 11.5 This frequency distribution curve indicates that the process is incorrectly set

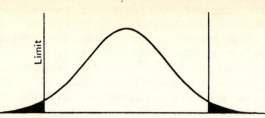

Figure 11.6 Frequency distribution curve indicating that the process is too variable to achieve the limits demanded

Finally in Figure 11.6 we have a frequency distribution curve which is actually wider than the width between the drawing limits. Clearly, no matter where we set our process, some of the work produced is bound to be out-of-limit. This means that our present combination of machine, materiel, operator, etc., is just not good enough to achieve the drawing or specification limits required. If we carry on with production, some of the work made is bound to be outside limit. In principle, therefore, there are two lines of action open to us:

1   We can improve the process or machine, etc., so that the frequency distribution curve is narrower. We might do this by moving the job to a more precise machine, giving it to a more skilled operator, or using better quality materiel, etc.

2   Alternatively, if (1) is difficult or expensive, we may approach the designer or customer with a request that the drawing or specification limits should be widened.

Meanwhile, if production is urgent, we might be forced to produce with the conditions shown in Figure 11.6, and then carry out 100 per cent inspection of the work produced, in order to remove those which are outside limit. If our sole object is to keep out-of-limit work to a minimum, then we shall centre the curve symmetrically, so that equal tails protrude beyond each limit.

However, it often happens that, whereas work outside one limit is scrap, that outside the other limit can be corrected. In such a case, it may pay us to bias the process in favour of more correctable rejects, in return for less scrap. Some caution is necessary, however, because when the process is moved off centre the increase in correctable rejects will exceed the reduction in scrap. If it is moved too far, it is possible to find that we have let ourselves in for a huge number of corrections, just to avoid a few, and in some cases not very expensive, scrap pieces.

11.4 Normal and non-Normal frequency distribution curves

So far we have assumed that our frequency distribution curve will have a regular bell shape, as shown in the figures in Section 11.3. Indeed this bell shape is very common in practice, so much so that it is called a Normal frequency distribution curve or sometimes a Gaussian curve. Its shape can be deduced mathematically, if we make two assumptions:

1   All the variables in our process are very small.
2   They are all just as likely to be positive as negative about the mean.

The first condition implies that there must be no single source of variation which is much larger than all the others. For example, the output from a machine may vary in, say, diameter because there is very slight play in all its bearings. Our condition, however, implies that there is no *one* bearing with a *lot* of play in it giving rise to a single large source of variation.

The second condition, applied to our example, would mean that the play in each bearing was just as likely to make the diameter a little larger as to make it a little smaller.

To us, as quality engineers, the importance of these two conditions lies in their converse. Suppose that when we plot an actual frequency distribution curve we find that it is nowhere near Normal in shape. This tells us that our process must be breaking one, or both, of these two conditions. Either it contains one or more large variables, or there is some bias which prevents the variables from being just as likely to be positive as negative about the mean. It should not be too difficult to identify them, and then eliminate them. Thus, if one bearing has excessive play, we must renew it; if swarf occasionally gets jammed in a diecast machine, causing excessively thick diecastings, we must prevent this from happening, and so on.

Action to restore a non-Normal variable to a Normal one, will always reduce overall variability. Hence where there are two specification limits, it is always desirable to work as near as practicable to a Normal distribution. Where there is only one specification limit the situation is different, because any adjustment which moves output quality in the favourable direction away from that limit is desirable, *even if it results in a non-Normal distribution*.

Usually the shape of a non-Normal curve gives a pointer to what is wrong with the process, and the following examples illustrate this.

1 Bimodal   If our curve has two or more peaks, as shown in Figure 11.7, this means that our output is a mixture of two, probably

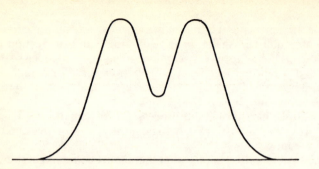

Figure 11.7   Bimodal frequency distribution curve

Normal, frequency distributions. Possible explanations for this are that:

1   The outputs of two similar machines or processes have been mixed together, or that two separate runs on the same machine have been mixed.
2   The setting of a single machine or process suddenly changed in the middle of the run.
3   The machine or process is able to take up either of two settings at will.

If the two peaks are of unequal height, then we conclude that the process has run longer at the high peak setting than it did at the other.

2   Flat-topped curve   If our curve is flat topped, as in Figure 11.8, this probably means that the setting of our process is inclined to drift. Unlike our first example, it is not limited to two fairly distinct settings but can drift through a variety of positions.

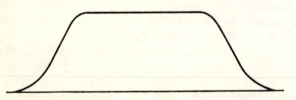

Figure 11.8   Flat-topped frequency distribution curve

3   Curve with a long tail   If our frequency distribution curve has a long tail, as shown in Figure 11.9, it is said to be *skewed*. This probably means that our process has at least one large variable,

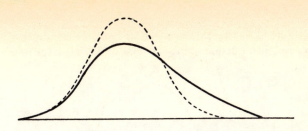

Figure 11.9   Frequency distribution curve with a long tail

which is biasing it to the right. Its elimination will probably bring the curve back to the broken line.

4   The presence of observations which do not belong to the frequency distribution curve   In Figure 11.10 the frequency distribution curve itself is Normal but in addition there are a small number of observations, marked ●, which do not belong to the curve at all. For example, in some electrical components, their resistance will in general form a Normal curve. Here and there, however, our inspector may find a near short circuit (i.e. the resistance is zero). These oddities are often very troublesome, so the best solution where possible is to refine the process, so that they are not made. Where this is not possible, then:

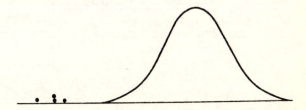

Figure 11.10   Observations that do not belong to a frequency distribution curve

1   The information given in Chapters 11 to 14, dealing with variables, will apply only to the distribution curve proper, and not to these odd observations.
2   The oddities can be treated as attributes, as discussed in Chapter 15.
3   Their complete removal will involve 100% inspection.

5   Inspection effects   In Figure 11.11, the distribution curve has an odd 'spike' just before it crosses the specification limit, and then the part of the curve which we would expect to be just outside the limit

133

does not exist. Usually, this is caused by a lenient inspector who, on finding work just outside limit, has recorded it as just within limit.

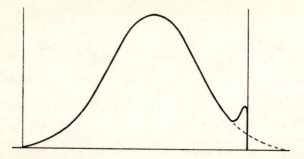

Figure 11.11 Effect of a lenient inspector on a frequency distribution curve

6 *Alternate peaks and troughs* This is usually associated with the calibration of the measuring instrument. In Figure 11.12 the weighing device was scaled in units of 0.2 g, and the inspector had to interpolate between the divisions, to read to 0.1 g. If the needle was near to 17.0 he recorded 17.0 g. Similarly if it was nearer to 17.2 he recorded 17.2 g. Only if it was so near to midway that he could not make up his mind, did he record 17.1 g. Hence peaks occurred for 17.0, 17.2, 17.4, etc., and troughs for, 17.1, 17.3, 17.5, etc. This effect will not occur if the measuring device has a digital display.

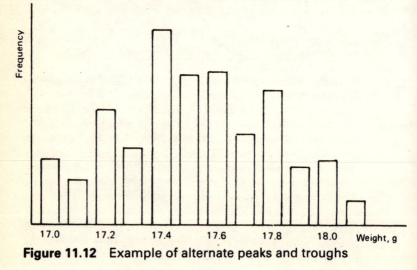

Figure 11.12 Example of alternate peaks and troughs

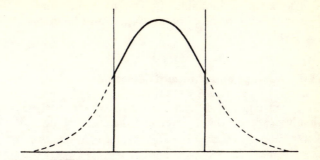

Figure 11.13 Effect of 100 per cent inspection when a process is unable to meet its limits

7 *A Normal curve with one or both tails missing* In Figure 11.13 the distribution curve has both tails missing. This can occur if the manufacturing process was much too variable to meet the specification limits and someone decided to do 100% inspection on the output to eliminate work which was outside limit. Thus, the original output included the two sections of the curve drawn in broken lines.

This effect occurs in various forms. Thus a machine with a stop which prevents the work from exceeding a specified value, may effectively give a curve with part of one tail missing. Confusion can easily be caused if the quality engineer assumes that he or she has a skewed curve, when it is really a Normal curve with a bit missing.

Plotting a frequency distribution curve Care is needed in drawing a frequency distribution curve, if information is not to be lost or bias introduced. The following are guidelines.

a   If the raw data will plot satisfactorily as it is, do not attempt to group it. In Section 11.2 it was possible to plot in the 0.01 mm steps created by the method of measurement. If measurement had been in 0.002 mm steps however, grouping into cells would have been necessary unless a large number of observations had been available. Too many cells and insufficient data result in cells being inadequately occupied. Beware of losing data by grouping. In the example in Figure 11.12, if each pair of cells had been merged into one, the alternate peak and trough effect would have been lost.

b   Aim for a minimum of about 12 cells, and a few more if possible. If the number of cells is reduced to say 4 or 5, almost any data can be made to look Normal.

c   Make all cells equal in width.
d   Choose scales carefully. A variable process can be made to look quite reasonable by cramping the horizontal scale. If two curves are to be compared, they must be drawn to the same scale.

11.5   Average and standard deviation

For each frequency distribution curve, we can work out two useful quantities, called the average and the standard deviation respectively.

11.5.1   The average

We can calculate the average, or arithmetic mean, at which our process is working in the usual way. Suppose that we have 10 observations of the weights of some pellets, as follows (in practice we should prefer more than ten observations, in order to get greater precision):

    21, 20, 20, 19, 21, 22, 20, 18, 19, 20 g

The average weight of these pellets is 200/10 = 20g.

The average tells us the machine or process setting. Thus, our pellet-making machine is set nominally at 20 g although individual pellets may vary from this value.

In Figure 11.14, frequency distribution curve A has an average value of 13 g, while B has an average value of 20 g. (If our curve is Normal, the average is at the peak of the curve.)

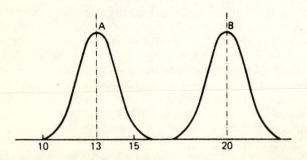

Figure 11.14 Frequency distribution curves indicating that the process average has changed

136

Thus, if we know our machine or process average, we know the value at which our frequency distribution curve is centred. If the machine or process setting moves up or down, then the whole distribution curve, including the average value, moves up or down with it.

11.5.2 The standard deviation

The standard deviation measures the variability of our observations about their mean value. In Figure 11.15 both curves have the same mean at 20 g, but A is more variable than B, and so will have a larger standard deviation. To estimate the standard deviation, the steps are as follows (the values are for the pellet example, started in Section 11.5.1):

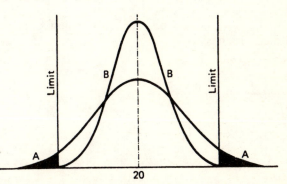

Figure 11.15 Frequency distribution curves indicating that the variability has changed

1   In column A below, set out all the observations that differ in value. Although we have 10 observations, there are only 5 different values, i.e. 18, 19, 20, 21, 22.
2   Subtract the mean of 20 g from each, giving column B.
3   Square the values in column B to give column C.
4   Allow for the fact that some values occur more than once, e.g. 19 occurs twice and 20 four times. Set out the number of times each occurs, i.e. the frequency, in column D.
5   Multiply column C by column D to give column E.
6   Total column E.
7   Divide this total by the original number of observations less one. As there are 10 observations, we divide by $(n - 1) = (10 - 1) = 9$.

8   Take the square root.

A Observations $= x_i$	B $(x_i - \bar{x})$	C $(x_i - \bar{x})^2$	D f	E $f(x_i - \bar{x})^2$
18	−2	+4	1	4
19	−1	+1	2	2
20	0	0	4	0
21	+1	+1	2	2
22	+2	+4	1	4
				12

Therefore the best estimate of the standard deviation is

$$\hat{\sigma} = \sqrt{[12/(10 - 1)]} = \sqrt{1.33} = 1.15 \text{ g}$$

The steps for estimating the standard deviation can be expressed mathematically as follows. Suppose there are n observations, so that the general term x_i takes the values $x_1, x_2, x_3 \ldots x_n$. Let the mean of the observations be $\bar{x}$. Then the best estimate of the standard deviation is

$$\hat{\sigma} = \sqrt{\left[\frac{\sum_{1}^{n} (x_i - \bar{x})^2}{(n - 1)} \right]} \qquad (11.1)$$

11.5.3   Errors in calculating the mean and standard deviation

In the above example, we attempted to estimate the mean and standard deviation of the whole process, using observations taken on a sample of 10 pellets. If we had used a sample of 25 pellets, we would have expected our estimate to be nearer to the correct value, but still not as near as if we had used a sample of 50. Thus when we calculate the mean and standard deviation from a sample, our result is only an *estimate* of the true value. We hope our estimate will be reasonably correct, but in order to distinguish it from the true value of the whole process, it is usual to use:

$\hat{\sigma}$ or $s =$ the best estimate of the process standard deviation which can be made from the sample data available.

$\sigma =$ the true standard deviation of the whole process.

This is the reason why the denominator of Eqn 11.1 is $(n - 1)$ and not (n) as we might expect. The term $(n - 1)$ is called the *number of degrees of freedom*, in which the (− 1) is a correction factor which ensures that we get an unbiased estimate of the process standard deviation. If, as often happens in quality control, we have a small sample of say 5, whether we divide by 5 or 4 makes a considerable difference. If the sample exceeds about 30, it usually makes little difference whether we divide by (n) or ($n − 1$). Nevertheless when dealing with samples, it is always correct to use ($n − 1$), however large the sample.

11.6 Properties of a Normal frequency distribution

Notice that the standard deviation is in the *same units* as the original data. Thus when we had pellet weights in grammes our standard deviation was in grammes: if we had been observing a diameter in millimetres, our standard deviation would have been in millimetres, and so on.

Figure 11.16 shows a curve of Normal distribution, and to illustrate a principle, we have scaled the horizontal axis in grammes to match our pellet example. Thus we have shown the mean of 20.0 g in the centre of the curve at 0. Starting from 0, we now measure 1 standard deviation to the right, and 1 standard deviation to the left, and draw 2 verticals at A and A'.

Thus A = (20.0 + 1.15)   = 21.15 g
    A' = (20.0 − 1.15)   = 18.85 g

Now it is a fundamental property of any Normal distribution that 34.13% of production will measure between the mean and 1 standard deviation above mean, and that another 34.13% will measure between the mean and 1 standard deviation below mean. Hence (34.13 + 34.13) = 68.26% will be within 1 standard deviation of the mean on one side or the other.

Now measure a 2nd standard deviation outwards from A and A', and draw 2 more verticals B and B' at [20 ± 2 (1.15)] = 17.70 and 22.30 g. This time as Figure 11.16 shows, each standard deviation contains 13.59% of production. Adding all our percentages so far together gives 2 (34.13 + 13.59) = 95.44%. Thus just over 95% of our production will lie within [mean ± 2 (standard deviations)]. For this reason the limits at B and B' are often referred to as *95% confidence limits*, because we have a *95% level of confidence* that any piece we care to check will lie within them.

By inserting a 3rd standard deviation on either side, we get C and C' at [20 ± 3 (1.15)] = 16.55 g and 23.45 g. The 3rd standard deviation contains 2.14% of production on each side, so we have now accounted for 2 (34.13 + 13.59 + 2.14) = 99.72% of our

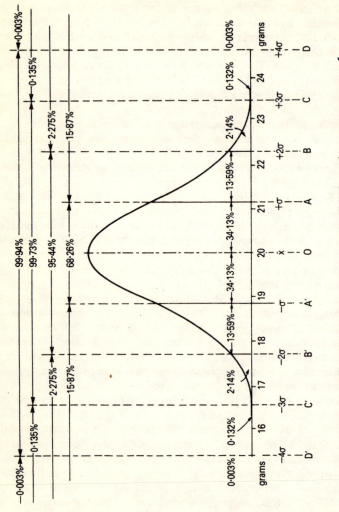

Fig 11·16 For a Normal Frequency distribution, the percentage of observations between each standard deviation are as shown

production. In theory this leaves a very small percentage beyond the [mean ± 3 (standard deviations)], but we are unlikely to observe this in practice. For all practical purposes, we usually assume that the Normal distribution ends where only 0.1% or 1 item per 1000 is beyond each tail. This occurs at [mean ± 3.09 (standard deviations)], and apart from quality control charts this is often rounded off to [mean ± 3 (standard deviations)]. In theory however the Normal distribution goes on to infinity in each direction, although beyond the 3rd standard deviation, its value is negligible.

Never-the-less in section 11.10, we show that it is often useful to be able to locate the position of the 4th standard deviation from mean, and this is therefore shown in Figure 11.16. Notice that only 0.003% of our production is theoretically beyond D or D'.

11.7 Introduction to the estimation of machine and process capability

The percentages shown in Figure 11.16 apply to any Normal frequency distribution. If a process is very variable, its standard deviation will be correspondingly large, so that almost all of it is still contained within [mean ± 3 (standard deviations)]. Suppose we have a machine producing a diameter which is nominally 18.00 mm, and for simplicity suppose that we can hold that mean absolutely constant. After many observations we have established that its standard deviation is 0.01 mm, and that its output is Normally distributed. Using Figure 11.16, we can now calculate that the tightest limits to which it can theoretically work are: [(mean) ± 3 (standard deviations)] = $(\bar{x} \pm 3\sigma)$ = 18.00 ± (3 × 0.01) = 18.00 ± 0.03 mm. In practice we could not possibly hold the mean rigidly at 18.00 mm, and therefore if a customer enquired, we would probably quote $(\bar{x} \pm 4\sigma)$ = 18.00 ± 0.04 mm for safety.

Suppose now that a valued customer wants us to produce to 18.00 ± 0.02 mm. We would like to take the job, but being prudent we wish to estimate what percentage of our production will be out of limit. Since the machine standard deviation for this operation is 0.01 mm, this request is for [mean ± 2 (standard deviations)]. This is positions B and B' in Figure 11.16, from which we read that 2.275% will be beyond each limit, making 4.55% in all.

In practice we shall be very lucky if the mean stays put. Suppose that it is incorrectly set and held at 18.01 mm. As Figure 11.17 shows, the nominal of 18.00 mm will now be at [mean − 1 (standard deviation)], and the lower limit of 17.98 mm will be at [mean − 3 (standard deviations)]. Hence on the lower side only 0.135% will

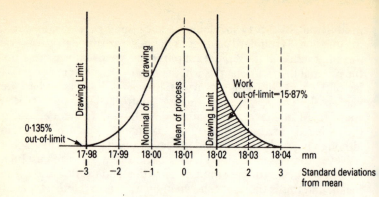

Fig 11·17 Effect of setting a process mean incorrectly, when limits are tight

now be out of limit. On the upper side however, it is a different story. 18.02 mm is now at [mean + 1 (standard deviation)], and 15.87% of our production will be over top limit.

Hence total production out of limit = (0.135 + 15.87) = 16% approx. Thus when the total tolerance permitted is of the same order as 6 standard deviations, we incur a heavy penalty in additional defective work, for failing to hold the mean centrally within the specification tolerances.

Suppose now that another customer asks us to produce to 18.00 ± 0.025 mm.

Convert tolerance to standard deviations $= \dfrac{0.025}{0.01} = 2.5.$

Since Figure 11.16 does not give percentages for fractions of a standard deviation, we consult a table giving areas in the tail of the Normal distribution, (e.g. 'Statistical Tables for Science, Engineering, Management and Business Studies' by J. Murdoch and J. A. Barnes, published by Macmillan). We insert (u) the number of standard deviations from the mean ($\bar{x}$) to the point or limit (x_i say) which interests us

$$\therefore u = \left[\frac{(x_i - \bar{x})}{\sigma}\right] = \left[\frac{(12.025 - 12.00)}{0.01}\right] = 2.5$$

If x_i is below the mean, compute $u = \left[\dfrac{(\bar{x} - x_i)}{\sigma}\right]$

Inserting u = 2.5 into the table gives:

Fraction in 1 tail = 0.00621
∴ Percentage in 1 tail = 0.621%

But our limit applies to both tails.

∴ Percentage defective from 2 tails
= 2 × 0.621 = 1.242 = 1.3% say.

If the mean is not central between the 2 specification limits, we must work out the percentage for each tail separately, and add them together.

11.8 Relative process capability

It is useful to have a simple capability index to show how capable or otherwise a process is with respect to its specification limits.

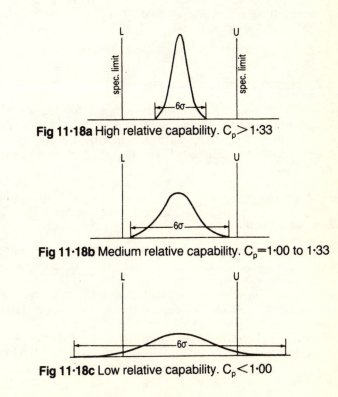

Fig 11·18a High relative capability. $C_p > 1·33$

Fig 11·18b Medium relative capability. $C_p = 1·00$ to $1·33$

Fig 11·18c Low relative capability. $C_p < 1·00$

143

The following is commonly used.

$$\text{Capability index} = C_p = \left[\frac{\text{(Total tolerance)}}{\text{(6 standard deviations)}}\right] \quad (11.2)$$

BS 5700 divides process capability into 3 classifications, where
    U = upper specificaton limit
    L = lower   "   "

11.8.1 High relative capability

If $(U - L)$ exceeds 8 standard deviations, the process is said to have a high relative capability, and corresponds to a C_p value greater than 1.33. This is illustrated in Figure 11.18a. For satisfactory production quality a C_p of 1.33 or more is desirable, and the larger it is the better, except that if it becomes too large, it can be argued that the process is too good for the job, and should be given work where tighter tolerances are demanded.

11.8.2 Medium relative capability

If $(U - L)$ is between 6σ and 8σ, corresponding to a C_p of 1.00 to 1.33, then the process is said to be of medium relative capability. This is shown in Figure 11.18b. Production quality will only be satisfactory if the mean can be held constant and central throughout the production run.

11.8.3 Low relative capability

The term low relative capability is used for the completely unsatisfactory situation where $(U - L)$ is less than 6σ, giving a C_p of less than 1.0. As shown in Figure 11.18c, the distribution curve is now too wide to fit within the specification limits, and out-of-limit work is inevitable. Section 11.3 deals with this totally unsatisfactory situation.

Where it is not possible to set the process mean midway between the specification limits, a single C_p value is misleading, and it is necessary to compute two C_{pk} values, one for each limit, and *use the lower of the two*.

144

For the upper limit $\quad C_{pk} = \left[\dfrac{U - \bar{x}}{3\sigma}\right]$

" " lower " $\quad C_{pk} = \left[\dfrac{\bar{x} - L}{3\sigma}\right]$

11.9 Cumulative frequency distribution curves

It is sometimes useful to plot a cumulative frequency distribution curve. For this purpose a sample of 50 is often used, but it is actually more correct to use a sample of 49. Thus suppose we have a machine winding resistance coils, which are required to be $100 \cdot 0 \pm 0 \cdot 8$ ohms. We take a sample of 49 *successively made* coils, and measure the resistance of each, to the nearest 0.1 ohm. This gives columns A and B in the table below.

A Observed resistance in ohms	B No. of coils with each resistance (f)	C Cumulative total $i = \Sigma f$	D Cumulative percentage $\Sigma f\%$	E Top of cell range
100·3	2	49	98	100·35
100·2	6	47	94	100·25
100·1	11	41	82	100·15
100·0	17	30	60	100·05
99·9	8	13	26	99·95
99·8	4	5	10	99·85
99·7	1	1	2	99·75

Next we cumulate the numbers of resistors, usually from the lowest value upwards, to give Σf as shown in column C. Thus opposite 99·7 ohms we write 1, for 99·8 we write $(1 + 4) = 5$, and for 99·9 we put $(5 + 8) = 13$ etc. Now we convert column C into percentages. We could do this in the usual way, but it is better to include a correction factor. The reason for this is that our data comes from a finite sample, but we would really like to know about the machine in general over a long run. For example, when we reach 100·3 ohms, we have undoubtedly accounted for 100% of our sample, but it would be wrong to infer that if we could check a long and representative run of many thousands, nothing above 100·3 would ever be found. Almost certainly a few would exceed this value. Similar arguments apply to the rest of the sample. To correct for this in an unbiased way requires the use of median ranks, but these are difficult to work out unless tables are available. It is much easier to use an excellent approximation given in BS 5700 as follows.

$$\text{Cumulative percentage} = \left[\frac{i}{n + 1}\right] \times 100\%$$

where i is the cumulative number so far as in column C, and n is the total number of observations in the sample. Thus for 99·7 ohms we have i = 1 and n = 49.

$$\therefore \text{Cumulative percentage} = \left[\frac{1}{49 + 1}\right] \times 100\% = 2\%$$

If we always take 49 observations, then (n + 1) is always 50, so to convert to percentages we merely double column C to get column D. The highest value in column D is now 98%, which means that on an unbiased basis, we estimate that in the long run, 2% of our production will exceed the 100·3 ohm cell.

Note what the above table means. It says apparently that 2% of our production measures 99.7% *or less*, 10% measures 99.8% or less, and so on. However we have measured to the nearest 0·1 ohm, so that the cell that we have called 99·7 ohms really contains all coils up to 99·75 ohms, and the 99·8 cell really contains all coils up to 99·85 etc. We have shown the top value in each cell in column E.

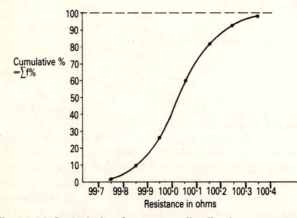

Fig 11·19 Cumulative frequency distribution curve or Ogive

We now plot column E horizontally against D vertically, to get the *cumulative frequency distribution curve* or *ogive* shown in Figure 11.19. Actually quality engineers seldom bother with Figure 11.19, and go straight on to plot the data on probability versus equal division graph paper, sometimes called arithmetic probability

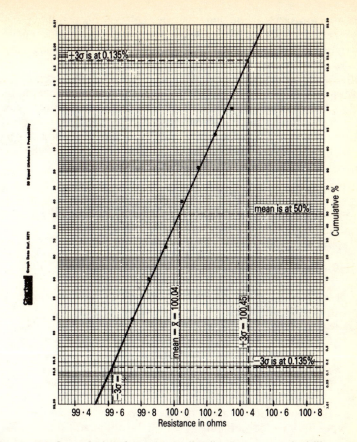

Fig 11 · 20 Cumulative frequency distribution on probability versus equal division paper

paper, as shown in Figure 11.20 or Figure 11.21. We will explain first Figure 11.20 which is drawn on Chartwell 5571 paper. Again we plot column A horizontally against column E vertically.

Notice that the vertical axis is not evenly spaced. Starting at 50% and going towards either 0% or 100%, the divisions are at first close, but progressively spaced out, and this spacing has been carefully arranged so that if the data plotted are Normally distributed, a straight line results. Since our data form a reasonably straight line, we conclude that they must be approximately Normally distributed. In drawing the best fit line, give more attention to the central points than to the outlying ones. Thus the 98% point appears to be a little adrift, but the scale shows that it is

147

only 0.7% from the line, whereas the 60% point is about 5% out.

Where the data are Normally distributed, the mean and standard deviation can be easily read from the graph. Since the Normal curve is symmetrical, the mean must correspond to 50% on the cumulative axis, which gives 100·04 ohms. Reference to Figure 11.16 shows that at C', which is 3 standard deviations below mean, the area under the curve beyond C' is 0.135%. Similarly at point C which is 3 standard deviations above mean, there is 0.135% beyond. Hence between C' and C there are 6 standard deviations. If we enter 0.135% into Figure 11.20, on first one side of the graph paper and then on the other, we read 99·63 and 100·45 ohms.

$\therefore$ Estimated standard deviation

$$= \left[\frac{(100 \cdot 45 - 99 \cdot 63)}{6}\right] = 0 \cdot 14 \text{ ohms approx.}$$

11.10   Capability study paper

In practice it is convenient to have a single capability study form which, on one side of an A4 sheet, permits the quality engineer to do the following.
1   Record the observed data for a given variable.
2   Convert that data into a tally chart.
3   Transfer it to probability versus equal division paper.
4   Check whether the data appear to be Normally distributed.
5   Estimate mean and standard deviation.
6   Estimate process capability, C_p index etc.

Paper designed as in Figure 11.21 can be obtained from Elpeeko Ltd., Wrightsway, Outer Circle Road, Lincoln. We will explain its use in detail.

1   At the top of the form we enter details as appropriate of the machine or process, the operation observed, part name and number etc.

2   The bottom left hand corner allows us to record 50 successive observations, but as explained in Section 11.9, it is better to enter 49 only, leaving space 50 blank. We must ensure that observations are taken on successively made pieces, so that any drift of process mean is minimised, and we keep strictly to the box number order, so that we can detect any change which does occur. Our example is based on the weight in grams of 49 successive components.

148

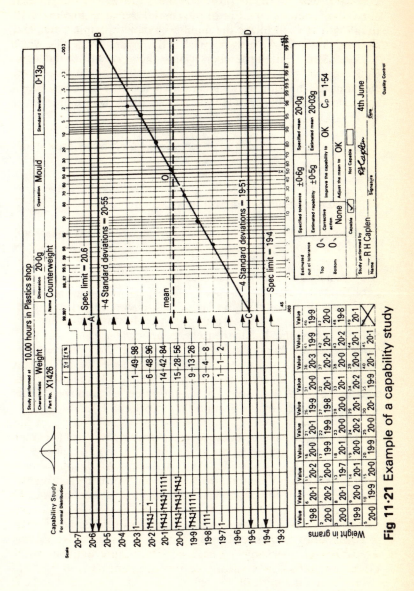

Fig 11·21 Example of a capability study

3   We put a suitable scale for the variable on the left hand side of the sheet. As a rough guide, the spread of the data should not occupy much more than a third of the total scale, and be roughly central within it. Make sure that the scale length includes all specification limits. If as in our example, the data give the mid-points of each cell, place the numbers against the thin horizontal lines as shown. If the range of each cell is given, e.g. 9·65 − 9·75, 9·75 − 9·85 etc, put the numbers against the heavy horizontal lines.

4   Transfer the data to immediately right of the scale, making a tally chart in 5 bar gate form, so that each box represents 5 observations.

5   Enter the total number of observations for each cell into column f.

6   Cumulate the data from the *lowest* value upwards, and enter in column Σf, as explained in Section 11.9.

7   Double each value in column Σf to give the cumulative percentage in column Σf%.

8   We are now ready to plot each value in column Σf% onto the probability versus equal division graph paper on the right hand side. Notice that in terms in Figure 11.20, this paper is turned on its side. The method is as follows. Starting with the lowest percentage (i.e. 2%) follow the thin line to the right, *go up with the arrow*, and put a point immediately above this percentage (i.e. 2%) on the *lower* horizontal scale. Similarly for the next percentage (i.e. 8%) follow the arrow up, and plot immediately above 8% on the lower scale, and so on. (The half step up has the effect of converting from column A of the table in Section 11.9 to column E).

9   Draw the best fit line by eye, across the whole width of the graph paper, paying most attention to the inner points, as explained in Section 11.9. If it is not possible to draw any reasonable straight line, we must conclude that the data are not Normally distributed, and we must investigate its cause as explained in Section 11.4.

10   Where our plotted line crosses the edges of the graph paper as B and C, draw 2 horizontal lines AB and CD as shown. Notice that the scale ends at 0.003% on each side. Reference to Figure 11.16 shows us that at ±4 standard deviations from mean, 0.003% of production is theoretically beyond on each side. Hence AB and CD

are at [(process mean) ± (4 standard deviations)], and so roughly represent the practical capability of the process. (In extrapolating BA and DC back to the left hand scale *do not* drop down half a cell. This is a correction factor which is not required again, once the original data have been plotted).

11 To estimate the mean we draw a horizontal line as shown at 0, where our plotted line crosses the 50% vertical. In our example this gives a mean of 20.03 grams.

12 To estimate the standard deviation we compute:

$$\text{Standard deviation} = \frac{(A - C)}{8} = \frac{(20.55 - 19.51)}{8} = 0.13 \text{ g}$$

13 Now the specification calls for 20.0 ± 0.6 g. These limits are outside our ±4σ capability limits, and the machine should therefore hold its tolerances, provided that the mean does not move excessively.

$$\therefore \text{Capability index} = C_p = \left[\frac{2 \times 0.6}{6 \times 0.13}\right] = 1.54$$

Hence the process has high relative capability.

14 If our process had been incapable, the line BC would have crossed one or both of the specification limits, within the graph paper. We could then have estimated what percentage of our production was likely to be out of limit. Thus where BC crosses the upper limit, we read the percentage immediately *above* the intersection. Where BC crosses the lower limit, we read the percentage immediately *below* the intersection. This is a general rule. For any point on BC which interests us, we can read the percentage above that measurement by going straight up, and the percentage below by going straight down. If the percentages out of top and bottom limit are not roughly equal, it indicates that the process mean is not set centrally within its specification limits.

11.11 Assignable and unassignable causes of variation

In any process there are always some large sources of variation, which we know about and do our best to control. These are called *assignable* causes, or American companies often use the term *special* causes of variation. They tend to cause non-Normal frequency distributions.

However, even when all the assignable causes of variation are under control, some unexplained variability always remains. These are called *unassignable* or *common* causes of variation, by which we mean that we do not at present understand why they occur. From time to time, the reason for an unassignable variation will be discovered and controlled, after which that particular cause will be assignable.

11.12   The mode and median

In addition to the average or *arithmetic mean*, which we explained in section 11.5.1, two other means are commonly used, and these are called the *mode* and the *median*.

11.12.1   The mode

The mode is the observation which occurs most frequently. Suppose we weighed 15 successively made items, and got the following.
19, 21, 18, 22, 21, 21, 20, 19, 20, 17, 21, 21, 20, 18, 19 g
We count how many there are of each weight.

Observation	Frequency (how many there are of each)
17	1
18	2
19	3
20	3
21	5 ←Mode
22	1

The mode is therefore 21, because this occurs more frequently (5 times) than any other value. In a frequency distribution curve, the mode is at the peak of the curve.

11.12.2   The median

When the observations are put in strict ascending or descending order, the median is the middle one. Putting our example in ascending order, we get:
17, 18, 18, 19, 19, 19, 20, _20_, 20, 21, 21, 21, 21, 21, 22 g
Hence the median is 20 g.

Since the arithmetic mean of these data is 19.8 g, we find that the mean, mode and median all have different values. This applies to any non-symmetrical curve, whereas for a Normal distribution, the mean, mode and median all have the same value. Where they do not, and we are working to two specification limits, we must investigate why. In the above example, we must find out why we get a skew towards the light weight end. There must be an assignable cause of variation which we must eliminate if possible. If of course we were given only a maximum weight, with a stipulation that items were to be as light as possible, then the above might be entirely acceptable, even desirable.

11.13   Statistical tolerances

Suppose that two parts A and B are required to fit together as shown in Figure 11.19, and that the pair will function correctly provided

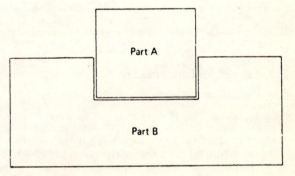

Figure 11.19

the total clearance between them is not less than 0.01 mm and not more than 0.07 mm. Traditionally half this tolerance would be allocated to each part, e.g.

Total permitted tolerance = (0.07 − 0.01) = 0.06
Tolerance on each part   =   0.03 mm

This ties the factory down unnecessarily, because the chances are remote that in practice a part A on top limit, will be mated with part B on bottom limit, or vice versa. In effect we are adding the variability of part A to that of part B, and are only concerned with their combined variability. Let

σ_o = Overall standard deviation
σ_A and σ_B = Standard deviation of each part respectively

153

Then statisticians have shown that:

$$\sigma_o^2 = \sigma_A^2 + \sigma_B^2 \qquad (11.2)$$

The square of any standard deviation is called the *variance*, so we are in effect adding the individual variances to get the overall variance.

If the frequency distribution of each part is Normal, and roughly fills the whole of the tolerance band we allocate to it, then:

$$\text{Tolerance} = T = 6 \times (\text{Standard deviation}) \qquad (11.3)$$

and Eq. (11.2) can be rewritten,

$$\left|\frac{T_O}{6}\right|^2 \quad = \left|\frac{T_A}{6}\right|^2 \quad = \left|\frac{T_B}{6}\right|^2$$

Therefore

$$T_O^2 \quad = T_A^2 \quad + T_B^2 \qquad (11.4)$$

Applying this to our problem gives,

$$(0.06)^2 \quad = T_A^2 \quad + T_B^2$$

If the tolerances are to be equally shared, therefore:

$$(0.0036) = 2 \times (\text{Tolerance on } A \text{ or } B)^2$$

Therefore

$$\text{Tolerance on } A \text{ or } B = 0.042 \text{ mm approx.}$$

If the frequency distributions are not Normal, then Eq. (11.3) is invalid. If they do not fill the whole of the tolerance band, there is no problem provided they are well centred within them. Otherwise a preponderance of extra large or extra small pieces will be made, and these will increase the risk of a mismatch between A and B.

When tolerances are based on the probabilities that certain measurements will occur, as in this example, they are said to be *statistical tolerances*.

11.14 Questions

1a Sketch frequency distribution curves to show the general shape of each of the following:

    (i)   Normal distribution   *(2 marks)*

    (ii) Skewed Normal, marking the approximate positions of the mean, mode and median.   *(5 marks)*

    (iii) Poisson or binomial distribution.   *(3 marks)*

154

1b The variability of a dimension produced by a manufacturing process is Normally distributed with a standard deviation of 0.05 mm. The mean can be held practically constant. If this dimension is to be as high as possible, provided that hardly any exceed 60 mm, at what value should the mean be set?   *(2 marks)*

1c If in the same process the components are required to be 60 ± 0.12 mm, what percentage would be out of limit:
   - *(i)*   if the mean is correctly set at 60.00 mm?   *(3 marks)*
   - *(ii)* if the mean is incorrectly set at 60.05 mm?   *(3 marks)*

1d Quality engineers sometimes use arithmetic probability paper (probability versus equal divisions).

   - *(i)*   What is the most common purpose for which they use it?   *(1 mark)*
   - *(ii)* How is the graph paper designed?   *(3 marks)*
   - *(iii)* What are the steps involved in using it?   *(3 marks)*

2 Coils from a coil winding machine are required to be 10·0 ± 0·8 ohms. To check its capability, 49 successively made coils were measured with the following results.

Resistance in ohms	No. of coils with each resistance
10·3	2
10·2	6
10·1	11
10·0	17
9·9	8
9·8	4
9·7	1

a   Plot these data on Capability Study paper as Figure 11.21 (or 11.20), and state whether they appear to be Normally distributed, and why.
b   Estimate the mean and standard deviation of this process.
c   Estimate the process capability
   - *(i)* on a basis of ±4 standard deviations,
   - *(ii)* "   "   ±3   "   "   .
d   Estimate the capability index, and comment upon its suitability for this job. (Since this is a graphical method, requiring the best fit line to be drawn, answers will vary slightly, according to the judgement of the person concerned. Readers should not therefore be worried if they do not get exactly the answer in the back of this book.)

CHAPTER 12

THE PRINCIPLES OF A TOLERANCE BASED QUALITY CONTROL CHART

A tolerance based quality control chart is one which controls the process to its drawing or specification limits.

12.1 Controlling a process over a period of time

In Section 11.5, we agreed that:
1. *The average* tells us the central value at which our machine or process is set. Our pellet machine was set at 20 g. We could, if we had wished, have set it at, say, 13 g in which case the average would have been 7 g less, but the variability would still have been much the same. (See Figure 11.14.)
2. *The standard deviation* is used to measure variability about the average. If a bearing on our machine became very worn, the variability and, therefore, the standard deviation might increase, but the average would probably stay the same. (See Figure 11.15.)

So far we have assumed that once our machine is set up it will continue to produce with the same average and standard deviation until the production run is finished. In practice, however, we can seldom rely on this and, if we wish to work within specification limits, our quality control system needs to be able to detect when a machine or process reaches these limits.

In order to do this economically, it is worth spending a little time observing its performance. Thus, suppose we choose one or two typical variables and then measure every piece made over, say, a morning or a shift. For example:

1 On a lathe we might observe a diameter.
2 On a diecast machine, the thickness of castings.
3 On a coilwinding machine, the resistance of the coils.

(For the moment, we are only dealing with variables, attributes will follow in Chapter 15.)

We plot our results as an ordinary graph, with the observed variable vertically, and successive pieces or time horizontally. We then compare our graph with the six basic possibilities described below. In many cases, we can save ourselves a lot of inspection effort, if we can identify our pattern of variation with one of these.

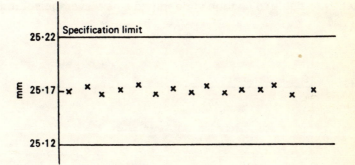

Figure 12.1 Plot of successive pieces from a machine or process that varies little compared with its specification limits – Type 1

Type 1 Figure 12.1 illustrates the ideal case, in which the machine or process goes on making piece after piece with very little variation at all. Practical examples of this are rare but, if we are lucky enough to have a very good machine or process, it would be foolish to waste money doing a lot of inspection. An occasional check to make sure that it is still all right should be sufficient.

Type 2 In Figure 12.2 our machine or process is very consistent for a time, but sooner or later at some random unpredictable moment, it suddenly goes wrong, e.g. perhaps it jams up, and after that the setting changes to a new level. Thus, the average value changes, but the variability and, therefore, the standard deviation, remain much the same. This pattern of behaviour is quite common, a typical

157

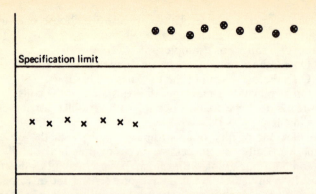

Figure 12.2 Machine or process with small variability and which is liable to change suddenly to a new average setting – Type 2

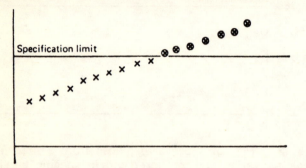

Figure 12.3 Machine or process with a small variability but a steady drift towards one limit – Type 3

example being that of automatic lathes, when they are working to reasonably wide drawing limits.

Type 3 In this type, illustrated in Figure 12.3, we have a fairly constant drift either upwards, as shown, or downwards. Successive points lie roughly in a straight line, and the moment the machine or process will go out of limit can be approximately predicted.

Type 4 The pattern of variation in Figure 12.4 is similar to that in Figure 12.2 in that the machine or process has one average setting for a time, and then at some unpredictable moment it suddenly changes to a new average. However, its variability about this

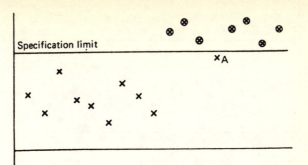

Figure 12.4 Machine or process with appreciable variability which is liable to change suddenly to a new average setting – Type 4

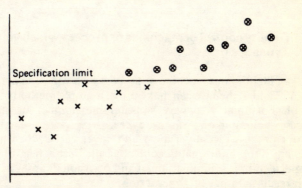

Figure 12.5 Machine or process with appreciable variability and a steady drift towards one limit – Type 5

average is much larger than before, and is now appreciable when compared with the specification limits.

Type 5 Figure 12.5 shows a corresponding variation to Figure 12.3. The average setting is gradually drifting up or down. About this average setting, however, we have a variability which is constant, but appreciable when compared with the specification limits.

Type 6 In our last example, illustrated in Figure 12.6, we have a machine or process in which the average level remains fairly constant, but at some unpredictable time the variability and, therefore, the standard deviation increases suddenly or gradually.

159

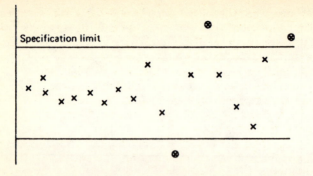

Figure 12.6 Machine or process in which the variability starts small but is liable to increase suddenly – Type 6

12.2 Quality control of machines or process which vary as Types 1, 2 or 3

If we can identify our machine or process with variation patterns of types 1, 2 and 3, then we can make use of a simple method of quality control. Fortunately, a very considerable number of industrial processes belong to one of these types.

If our process is really Type 1 and never varies, then it hardly needs any shop floor quality control at all. In practice, of course, such perfection is seldom attained and occasional lapses will occur which result in either of Types 2 or 3.

Types 2 and 3 have one very important common feature. If at any moment we wish to know how our machine or process is doing, we have only to check the last piece made, for:

1   If the last piece made is within limits, then all the pieces made so far will in general be satisfactory, and in many cases it will be unnecessary to carry out any further inspection on them.

2   If the last piece made is out-of-limit, then the work made since the last satisfactory check will consist of a mixture of good and bad, the proportions of each depending on just when the machine went wrong.

Notice that there is an implied assumption here, that once the machine has gone out of limit it will not return by itself, without assistance from someone like the operator or setter. If this assumption is not justified, then the fact that the last piece is all right is no guarantee that all the work made since the last inspection is acceptable. However, do not be put off too easily. There is always

160

the pessimist who will tell you that it will not work because, for example, 'A piece of swarf may get stuck on the stop for a short while, and then get pushed out again.' It may be *possible* for this to happen, but in many cases such an occurrence is very unlikely, and each case must be judged on fact, and not on opinions.

For machines and processes which are of Type 1, 2 or 3, therefore, we can come to several useful conclusions:

1   Each time we inspect, we only need to check a sample of one piece, the last made.
2   We can plot our results on the simplest of quality control charts, basically like any of Figures 12.1 to 12.3.

Vertically we put the variable we are plotting, and we draw two horizontal lines to represent the specification or drawing limits. Horizontally we plot successive samples which might be, say, once per hour. We do not need to use control limits, as discussed in Sections 12.3 to 12.6. Indeed, in cases where the pattern of variation is a well-defined Type 1 or 2 it may be possible to dispense with plotting variables, and plot attributes instead. Thus we merely plot √ for within limit, and ⊗ for out-of-limit, and our quality control chart will look like this:

Length 38.00 ± 0.12 mm   √√√√√√√√⊗√√√√√√√√

Attributes are not only quicker to plot, they also save a lot of space. As we may have a dozen or more qualities to check on each piece made, if we can plot them as attributes, then it will not be too difficult to get them all on to one chart by putting one row underneath the other. As a general rule, it is not convenient to put more than two, or at the most three, variables charts one under the other, since this requires a very large sheet of paper to avoid cramping them.

3   We only need to control for average. The variability is small enough compared with the specification or drawing limits to be omitted.
4   Remember that any actual quality control system must be designed to suit the production line for which it is intended. Do not be afraid to modify any of these suggestions to suit your needs.

12.3   Quality control of processes which vary as Types 4, 5 or 6

In this section, we can include not only processes that are obviously Types 4, 5 or 6, but also those which have a pattern of behaviour which does not exactly match any set type. All these have one feature in common, and that is that their variability is appreciable compared with the width between the specification or drawing limits. This means that it is not longer possible to check the last piece only and assume that, if that is all right, the rest are also acceptable. In Figure 12.4 we can see that if piece A happened to be checked as the last piece made, it would be within limits, even though practically all the pieces being made are over limit. Similar arguments apply to Figures 12.5 and 12.6. To meet this problem we need a different approach.

Now a quality control chart is rather like a frequency distribution curve turned on its side. The two specification limits are horizontal, instead of vertical, and the corresponding frequency distribution curve sits inside as shown in Figure 12.7.

If our machine or process is centred at mid-limit, the points which we plot will correspond to the frequency distribution curve marked A.

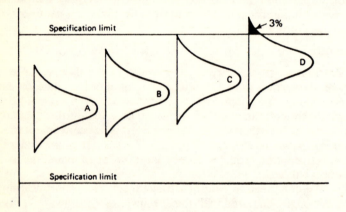

Figure 12.7 Movement of the frequency distribution curve when a process drifts towards one limit

Suppose that as manufacture proceeds the average level of production moves up. Thus, the plotted points will move up and with them the frequency distribution curve, which may now be as B in Figure 12.7.

The question is, 'How far do we dare to let this curve move up, before we stop it?' The answer must obviously be that it can move until it reaches position C, where one tail is just touching the specification limit. Thus:

162

1   If we let it drift any further, one tail of the curve will project over limit, as shown in D, and a proportion of out-of-limit work will be made.

2   If we stop the process or machine, and reset appreciably *before* the tail touches the limit, i.e. before position C is reached, then we shall waste time and money in unnecessary resetting.

This argument does, of course, apply equally to a movement of the frequency distribution curve towards the lower limit. (We have assumed here that the frequency distribution curve comes to a precise end on either side. In the mathematical sense, each tail does in fact continue to infinity, but its values become so low that for all practical purposes we can consider that it finishes at 3.09 standard deviations out from the mean. Even in theory, only 0.1% is beyond that, on each side.)

Consider now the difficulty of detecting when the tail reaches and goes over limit. Suppose that the machine or process has actually reached position D in Figure 12.7, in which case 3% of the production, i.e. the part of the curve shown black, is outside limit, and therefore 97% is within limit. Now 3% is a lot of out-of-limit work to incur on one quality, on one operation. If we have say five or six operations, and several qualities to be controlled at each operation, we shall soon approach 100% overall defectives.

However, the difficulty in detecting when 3% of production is out-of-limit is a real one, because 3% means that 3 pieces in 100 are wrong. If we tell an operator or inspector to check one piece, the chances will be only 3 in 100 that he will draw an out-of-limit piece. It is far more likely, i.e. 97 chances in 100, that he will get a satisfactory piece, and conclude that nothing is amiss. Even if we ask him to check 5 pieces, the odds are still against him finding an out-of-limit piece. Indeed, to have an average chance of finding one out-of-limit piece, he must check 33 pieces! Clearly, this is uneconomic, and we must find a more powerful method.

12.4   The effect of averaging samples

Suppose that we want to study the varying heights of men, so we decide to go down into our town centre one morning, select men at random, and assuming that they will let us, measure and record their heights. Next, we plot our observations as a frequency distribution curve, as shown in Figure 12.8. The curve we get will be Normal, because the factors which control our height obey the two conditions given in the first part of Section 11.4. Thus:

1   Our height is determined by many small variables, contributed by our parents, grandparents, upbringing, etc.
2   These variables are just as likely to make us a little taller, as a little shorter than average.

Thus, as Figure 12.8 shows, most men will be somewhere about average height, but here and there we shall find a very tall man, and his height will contribute towards tail C. Similarly, we shall come across the occasional very short man, whose height will contribute to tail A. (If we should find a deformed man only 3½ft high, his height will not be part of our curve because he has suffered some mishap which is the nature of a large variable, infringing the conditions for a Normal curve.)

Now suppose that when we go into our town centre, instead of taking men one at a time we take them 5 at a time, measure the height of each and average the 5 readings together. If we do this enough times, we shall be able to plot a new frequency distribution curve, based on *average of samples of 5* and DEF in Figure 12.8 shows the sort of curve we might get. Notice that DEF has a shorter base and steeper sides than curve ABC for men taken one at a time.

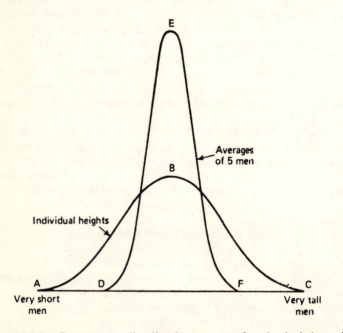

Figure 12.8 Frequency distribution curves for the heights of men

The reason for this is as follows. When we took our men one at a time, we occasionally found a very tall man who contributed to tail C. However, when we take men 5 at a time, the chances that we shall find 5 very tall men all together in the sample is so remote that it will hardly ever occur. Almost certainly, the height of each very tall man will be averaged with the heights of 4 men of more normal height. Hence, the average will be less than that of the tall man, and tail C of our original curve for men taken one at a time moves into position F. The same argument applies to very short men. The chances that we shall find 5 very short men all together in the same sample of 5 is so remote that we can dismiss them, and therefore tail A moves into D.

Clearly, the frequency distribution curve for averages of samples of five will have a smaller standard deviation than the original curve, and we can estimate its value from the following relation:

Let σ = The true standard deviation of the original samples of one, as discussed in Section 11.5.

n = the number of observations we propose to average together each time. This is 5 in the above example.

σ_n = the standard deviation of the averages of samples, taken n at a time. Statisticians call σ_n the *standard error of the mean*.

Then,

$$\sigma_n = \sigma/\sqrt{n} \tag{12.1}$$

Our new curve will still be Normal in shape. Indeed, if the original curve ABC was not quite Normal, the new curve DEF will be nearer Normal than the original one.

12.5 The use of control limits

We now return to the problem which we posed in Section 12.3, of detecting quickly when a process or machine starts to make a proportion of out-of-limit work.

In Figure 12.9 the curve marked C is the same as is marked C in Figure 12.7. Thus, it is a frequency distribution curve for individual samples of one, and its position is such that it just touches one specification or drawing limit. Inside curve C is another curve E, which would be formed by taking samples of 5, measuring each piece, and then drawing a new curve of averages of samples of 5. Because this new curve is plotted from the same information as the curve for samples of one, it must always sit inside it as shown. If the curve for samples of one moves up or down, then the curve for averages of samples of 5 moves up or down with it.

Now, when the curve is in position C, so that it just touches the specification or drawing limits, we draw a control limit as shown. Its position is just below the tip of the upper tail of curve E and it is, in fact, 1.96 standard deviations of curve E above its average value. We also draw a corresponding lower control limit, based on the lower specification or drawing limit.

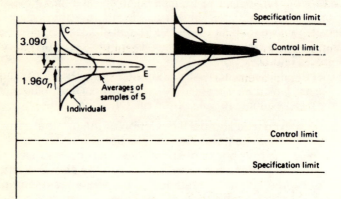

Figure 12.9   The principle of control limits

We now instruct our inspector that each time he visits the process or machine he is to take a sample of 5 pieces, measure them, average the results together and plot this average on the quality control chart, using the control limits as his limit lines. Consider now what happens:

1   If the average of the process or machine is comfortably in the middle of the specification limits, then the averages of samples of 5 will plot comfortably inside the two control limits.

2   When the process is in position C, so that the curve for samples of one just touches the specification limit, almost all the averages of samples of 5 will still be within the control limits. The only exception will be if the inspector happens to draw a sample of 5 which, when averaged, comes from the little bit of curve E, which is above the control limit. The chance that this will happen is only 1 in 40 but, if it should occur, it will be a warning that the process is just about to go out-of-limit and so should be reset.

3   Suppose now that our curve gets into position D, where 3% of individual pieces are outside limit. Notice what has happened to

166

curve F, for averages of samples of 5. Because of its short base and very steep sides, the same movement which took 3% *of curve D* outside *specification limits*, has taken some 77% *of curve F* outside *control limits*. This means that the inspector has a 77% chance, which is better than two chances to one in favour of detecting this shift on his first sample of 5. This enormous improvement over that discussed in Section 12.3 has been achieved merely by *averaging the 5 readings together, and plotting the result against control limits.*

Of course, the larger the sample which is averaged, the more curve E contracts, and the more powerful the method becomes. There are limitations, however:

1   The improvement is not proportional to the increase in sample size. Equation 12.1 shows that the square root is involved. Thus, if we use a sample of 6, instead of 5, the improvement is proportion to $\sqrt{6}$ compared with $\sqrt{5}$.
2   There are in any case objections to very large samples, and we shall discuss these in Section 13.8.

12.6   Detecting changes in variability

The quality control chart which we have just discussed will be very useful for detecting when the *average* level of our process changes. Thus, referring back to Figure 11.14, it will easily tell us when our process changes from that of curve A to that of curve B. It is, however, unlikely to tell us if the variability suddenly increases without a change of average. For example, a change from B to A in Figure 11.15 would probably go undetected, and for this we need a second chart, which we call a range chart.

In any sample, of say 5 observations, the range is the difference between the largest and the smallest. Thus, suppose we are measuring the resistance of 5 resistors. We might get:

40, 41, 38*, 42*, 39 ohms
Now range = (Largest − Smallest) = (42 − 38) = 4 ohms

Clearly, the greater the variability of the process, the greater the range will tend to be, although a single calculation of the range will give us no more than a rough indication of its variability. If, however, we observe the range of a lot of samples of say 5 each and average our results together, the mean range we shall obtain will give us a good indication of the variability. Indeed, there is a precise relation between true mean range and standard deviation. Thus to convert the mean range to the corresponding standard deviation, we divide it by the appropriate constant, depending upon the sample size.

Sample size	2	3	4	5	6	7	8
Constant	1.128	1.693	2.059	2.326	2.534	2.704	2.847

On the shop floor, range is easier to use than standard deviation.

Detailed instructions for drawing up a range chart are given in Sections 13.2 and 13.3. We need only note here that the range chart has its own control limits, similar in principle to those of the average chart.

12.7 Quality control charts using 'modified limits'

Historically, the first quality control charts to be developed were those working to process capability, as described in Chapter 14. Later this method was 'modified' to permit charts to work to specification or drawing limits. Hence, the type of quality control chart which we have described in this chapter and in the next is commonly referred to in quality control literature as charts working to 'modified' limits, even though the term is not really appropriate.

CHAPTER 13

THE PRACTICAL USE OF TOLERANCE BASED QUALITY CONTROL CHARTS

13.1 Machines and processes whose variability is small compared with the width between the specification or drawing limits

If by an observational run we can identify our process as Type 1, 2 or 3, as shown in Figures 12.1–12.3, then our whole system of control, including the quality control chart, can be simplified as explained in Section 12.2 since:

1 Only 1 piece need be checked at each inspection.
2 The quality control chart need only consist of the two specification or drawing limits, as shown in Figures 12.1–12.3.
3 No control limits are required.
4 This method can be used for short or long runs.

13.2 Machines and processes whose variability is comparable with the specification or drawing limits

If our observational run shows a pattern of variation like that in Figures 12.4–12.6, or if we are uncertain about the form it takes, then we should start off with average and range charts, even though some simplification may be possible later. We proceed as follows:

169

1   Draw outline quality control charts as shown in Figure 13.1a. At this stage our chart will only show:

a   *Average chart*   The left-hand y axis, scaling the variable to be observed, and the two specification or drawing limits.

b   *Range chart*   The left-hand y axis, and a horizontal line at zero range. Notice that all range measurements are counted upwards from zero range.

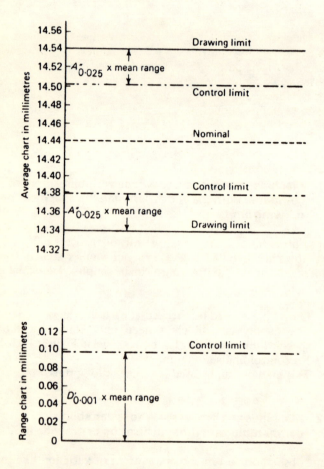

Figure 13.1a Construction of average and range charts for controlling a process or machine to specification or drawing limits

2   Instruct the inspector to start plotting points on the blank chart. Thus, if the sample size is to be 5 pieces, taken once per hour, he will, every hour:

a   Take a sample of 5 pieces, from among those most recently made.

b   Measure each piece, and calculate the sample average and the sample range.

c   Plot the average and range so obtained on the quality control chart.

3   When we have at least 10 settled points on the chart, we are ready to set the control limits. Sometimes at the start of a production run, particularly if it is a relatively new process, the variability is higher than it will be when the process has settled down. Hence, the reference to 'settled points'. Any obviously unsettled points should be discarded. Setting the control limits should not, however, be unduly delayed, because they can be useful in persuading the process to settle. In such cases it may be best to set provisional control limits early on, and then recalculate them later when the process has settled down.

4   To calculate the control limits we:

a   Work out the range of each settled sample, as 2b above.

b   Average each of these range values together to give the mean range.

c   Multiply the mean range by the constant $A''_{0.025}$ below, choosing the value which corresponds to the sample size used.

Sample size	2	3	4	5	6	7	8
$A''_{0.025}$	1.51	1.16	1.02	0.95	0.90	0.87	0.84

d   On the average chart, draw each control limit so that it is a distance $[(A''_{0.025}) \times \text{(mean range)}]$

inside each specification or drawing limit, as shown in Figure 13.1a.

e   Multiply the mean range by the constant $D'_{0.001}$ below, which corresponds to the sample size used.

Sample size	2	3	4	5	6	7	8
$D'_{0.001}$	4.12	2.98	2.57	2.34	2.21	2.11	2.04

f   On the range chart, draw the control limit a distance

$[(D'_{0.001}) \times \text{(mean range)}]$

up from zero range, as shown in Figure 13.1a.

5   Our quality control chart is now complete. The constants $A''_{0.025}$ and $D'_{0.001}$ are repeated in Table 3 at the end of the book.

13.3   Example of a tolerance based quality control chart

Suppose we have a machine which is required to make a dimension to 14.44 ± 0.10 mm, and we wish to set up tolerance based average and range charts to control it. The steps will be exactly as explained in Section 13.2, but for clarity we have summarised them below, *using the same paragraph numbers* as we used then. We shall refer to Figure 13.1b which shows the finished chart, complete with all its calculations.

1   At the start the average chart only has the left hand axis, scaled from 14.32 up to 14.56 mm, plus the two drawing limits. The range chart is scaled from 0 to 0.12 mm. The range scale *always* starts at zero range, and zero range is the datum line from which the control limits are set. Try to make each scale long enough to allow all out of limit points to be plotted.

2   We set up the machine and start production. Every hour we take a sample of 5 pieces, measure each and record those measurements, together with the sample average and range. Thus for the first hour the average was 14.438 mm, and the range was $(14.46 - 14.42) = 0.04$ mm.

3   The machine settles down at once, and so after 10 samples of 5 have been recorded, we are ready to set the control limits.

4a and b   The total of all 10 ranges is 0.41 mm, so the mean range is

$$\frac{0.41}{10} = 0.041 \text{ mm.}$$

c and d   *Average chart*. For a sample of 5, the value of $A''_{0.025}$ is 0.95. We therefore draw each control limit = $(A''_{0.025} \times \text{mean range}) = (0.95 \times 0.041) = 0.039$ mm *inside* each drawing limit as shown in Figure 13.1b.

e and f   *Range Chart*. For a sample of 5, the value of $D'_{0.001}$ is 2.34, so we set the range control limit = $(D'_{0.001} \times \text{mean range}) = (2.34 \times 0.041) = 0.096$ mm *up* from zero range.

The chart is now complete as shown in Figure 13.1b.

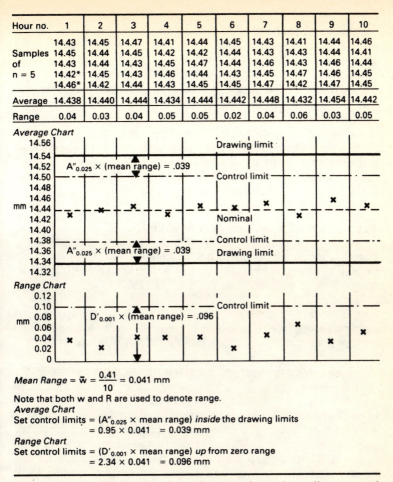

Hour no.	1	2	3	4	5	6	7	8	9	10
	14.43	14.45	14.47	14.41	14.44	14.45	14.43	14.41	14.44	14.46
Samples	14.45	14.44	14.45	14.42	14.42	14.44	14.43	14.43	14.44	14.41
of	14.43	14.44	14.43	14.45	14.47	14.44	14.46	14.43	14.46	14.44
n = 5	14.42*	14.45	14.43	14.46	14.44	14.43	14.45	14.47	14.46	14.45
	14.46*	14.42	14.44	14.43	14.45	14.45	14.47	14.42	14.47	14.45
Average	14.438	14.440	14.444	14.434	14.444	14.442	14.448	14.432	14.454	14.442
Range	0.04	0.03	0.04	0.05	0.05	0.02	0.04	0.06	0.03	0.05

Average Chart

Range Chart

Mean Range = $\bar{w} = \dfrac{0.41}{10}$ = 0.041 mm

Note that both w and R are used to denote range.
Average Chart
Set control limits = ($A''_{0.025}$ × mean range) *inside* the drawing limits
= 0.95 × 0.041 = 0.039 mm
Range Chart
Set control limits = ($D'_{0.001}$ × mean range) *up* from zero range
= 2.34 × 0.041 = 0.096 mm

Figure 13.1b Example of a tolerance based quality control chart

13.4 Making use of the quality control chart

To be of maximum use, the quality control chart must show the state of the process or machine at a glance. Therefore:

1 Provide the person who will fill in the chart with a red pen, as well as a black one. All points, etc., are entered in black but, whenever a point is out-of-limit, it is ringed in red. This makes it stand out and so encourages correction action.

173

2   Make sure that a note is made on the chart of all changes in the process settings, resets, adjustments, etc., indicating the time at which the change occurred, even if the change is not believed to affect the quality. It is not uncommon to find that some believed harmless change does in fact affect the quality and, if the change has been noted down on the chart, it is easy to relate it to the resultant change in quality.

3   Ensure that everyone concerned is clear about the action to be taken when a point plots outside limit. It is no good the chart drawing attention to unsatisfactory quality, if nothing is done about it.

13.5   Practical points about control limits

Consider the quality control chart of Figure 13.1a. The greater the variability of the process, the greater will be the value of the mean range. Now this means that:

1   On the range chart, the control limits will be higher up the chart giving us more 'room' in which to plot our points before they go outside the control limit. Clearly, this will not worry us at all.

2   However, on the average chart, the greater the mean range, the further each control limit is from its specification or drawing limit, and therefore, the *less* the room between them, within which we hope our points will plot. If the specification or drawing tolerances are very narrow, or if the variability of the process is very large, the control limits may be so close together that we cannot possibly work between them. Indeed, in extreme cases, it is possible for the control limits to cross over, and then we are completely snookered!
   Now when this happens, it does not mean that quality control has failed. It is simply the chart telling us that, with that combination of machine or process, materiel and operator, etc., we cannot possibly hold those specification or drawing limits.

13.6   The control routine

Having taken some considerable trouble to set up our quality control chart, we must be careful not to assume our job is done. The chart is not an end in itself. Our job is to produce within specification or drawing limits, as cheaply and as easily as possible. If our chart assists in doing this, it justifies its existence. If it is of no help, it should be modified or discarded. Be careful before you discard, however. Most charts have uses which are not immediately apparent.

In order to reduce inspection to a minimum, the routine already discussed in Sections 8.10 to 8.16 is most useful. Thus:

1   Prepare a quality schedule, to tell inspector, setter and operator, etc., which qualities are to be inspected.
2   When each new run has been set up, check the 'first-off', to ensure that the set-up is satisfactory, for the first period's production.
3   Periodically check samples of the work produced, to ensure that the quality is still all right. Arrange that all work made between one inspection and the next is kept separate from the bulk of the production, until the check at the end of that period has proved satisfactory. If this check should be unsatisfactory, that period's work is isolated for 100% inspection of the quality which is wrong, and the machine or process is readjusted for the quality which is out-of-limit. A further check is then made, before production recommences.
4   Check the last piece made in a production run, to check the condition of tools, etc.
5   Use final inspection only where economically justified. Consider whether operator control, as described in Sections 9.7 to 9.10, could with advantage replace some of the patrol inspection in (3) above.

13.7   Taking samples

When we require a sample of one only, we shall take the last, or almost the last, piece made. This is because we want to know the latest news about our process. We want to know whether it is all right now, and not whether it was all right some time ago.

When we take a larger sample of, say 5, we shall still include the last, or almost the last piece made, but we have a choice about the other 4. We can either take them from among the most recent work, or to be representative of the whole period's run. Our decision will depend upon what we want to know.

1   Most probably our desire will still be to get the latest news about our process, in order to keep it within specification limits, and, in this case, we shall take the whole sample from the most recent work.
2   It is just possible, however, that we may wish our sample to be representative of the whole of that period's work, so that we can use it to judge whether the period's work should be accepted without further, say 100%, inspection. In this case, we shall take our sample from the whole of that period's work.

175

13.8 Sample size

The general rule for sampling a machine or process using variables, is 'little and often'. 'Often', because if a process approaches or goes out of limit, the sooner we find out about it and make a correction, the less out-of-limit work we shall make. The sample size must be sufficient to tell us the quality condition of our process, but should be no more. Thus, if a sample of 5 tells us all we need to know, a sample of 10 merely tells us all we need to know twice over! In such a case, a sample of 5 every half hour is better than 10 every hour, because when the process goes out of limit, we catch it, on average, in half the time.

As we have already shown in Section 12.2, if the pattern of variation of our process is as Figures 12.1, 12.2 or 12.3, then a sample of one, the last off, is usually sufficient. However, if our pattern is like Figures 12.4, 12.5 or 12.6, or if we are uncertain what it is, then a sample of one is unlikely to be enough. In such cases, a sample of 2 or 3 may also be too small to tell us how the frequency distribution is varying, and we must usually consider samples of, say, 4 upwards. Now, beyond about 7 the relation which connects range and standard deviation (see Section 12.6) becomes insensitive and, therefore, we try not to go beyond this. This leaves us, in general, with a useful range of sample sizes of 4, 5, 6 and 7.

Since 5 is a convenient sample size to handle, we often settle for 5, almost as a standard. It is easier for the inspectors, etc., if the sample size is always the same. However, there is nothing magic about 5, and if another sample size is more appropriate, we should use it. For example:

1   Suppose a coilwinding machine has 3 heads. In this case, a sample of 5 has no meaning. We should either have a sample of 3 i.e. one from each head, or 6, i.e. 2 from each head.

2   On a plastics press, or a diecast machine, we may have a 6 impression tool, and again a sample of 5 has no meaning. This demands a sample of 6, one from each impression.

3   Suppose we have a multi-impression die, with say 16 impressions. We shall probably decide to take a sample from the 16 in a single load. If we know nothing about the way the impressions vary one from another, we may take a random sample of 5. Very often, however, there is some relation between the impressions. Probably the outside impressions always exhibit the largest variation from mean, and we might decide to have a sample of 4, one from each outer row.

This again emphasises the desirability of finding out the variation patterns and characteristics of each type of machine or process we use, because this so often enables us to simplify the quality control system and increase its effectiveness.

13.9   Frequency of sampling

Like so much of quality control, deciding how often to sample is essentially an economic problem, since:
1   The more often we sample, the more our inspection costs us.
2   The less often we sample, the more the cost of out-of-limit work which is made from the moment the machine or process goes out of limit until the moment that we detect that it has done so.

Our object must be to choose a frequency of inspection which will make the total of the above two costs a minimum.

Now our machine or process can go out of limit in two different ways, and we must consider them separately, as follows:
1   It can drift out, in the manner shown in Figures 12.3 and 12.5.
2   It can go suddenly out of limit, at some random and unpredictable moment, as shown in Figures 12.2 and 12.4.

13.10   Drifting out of limit

If our machine or process always drifts towards one limit, then we can increase the length of run between adjustments or resets, by making sure that it is always set as near as possible to the other limit. Thus:
1   For a sample of one used without control limits, set the machine or process so that the first point is just comfortably inside the specification limit away from which it will drift.
2   For samples larger than one used with control limits, set the machine or process so that the first average point is just comfortably inside the control limit away from which it will drift.

We must now estimate how long it is safe to leave it between inspections. Our object is clearly to catch the machine or process just before it runs out of limit. In practice, at the start of a run little information may be available, and we may have to set a provisional time between inspections. In this case, we play safe and set the frequency of inspection on the short side. As production proceeds, we can easily see whether our judgement was correct, since:

177

1   If most inspection points are near, but not over, the limit towards which the process is drifting, our estimation was probably correct.
2   If most points are well inside limit, we can afford to lengthen the interval between inspections.
3   If an appreciable proportion of the points is over the limit, we must shorten the interval between inspections.

If we decide to adjust the interval between inspections, then we must inspect the quality control chart again after a while, to see whether our change has been correct, and to adjust further as necessary. Where our sole problem is a predictable drift, it should be possible to control so that very little out-of-limit work is made and, at the same time, to ensure that inspection costs are a minimum. If an observational run has been carried out, this will of course give a first indication of what frequency of inspection will control the drift.

13.11   Going out of limit at some unpredictable moment

Where at some unpredictable moment a machine or process may jump suddenly and completely out of limit, we cannot hope to run without any defective work, and so must settle for minimum total cost. The following method of achieving this has been devised by the author. Suppose we have a machine which we operate to the patrol inspection routine given in Section 13.6, and that at the moment we carry out one inspection per hour. Consider what would happen if we decided to change this to one inspection every half hour, i.e. we decide to inspect twice as often. The effect on costs would be as follows.
1   The cost of patrol inspection would roughly double, because twice as many inspections would require twice as many inspectors.
2   The cost of defective work would roughly halve. In order to see why this should be, consider the machine when it is checked once per hour. Now the machine may go wrong at any moment, giving rise to varying amounts of defective work on each occasion, depending on how long the machine falters before the patrol inspector is due. However there are two extreme cases.
    a   The machine may go wrong just as the inspector arrives to check it. As he will catch it at once, almost no defective work will be made.
    b   The machine may go wrong immediately the inspector

178

has left it, and so make defective work for almost an hour, before the inspector returns to check it.

Balancing these two extremes and all the other possibilities together, we conclude that if we check once per hour, every time the machine jumps out of limit we shall *on average*, make half an hours defective work. If we check every half hour, we shall *on average* make a quarter of an hours defective work, every time it jumps out of limit, and so on. Hence the cost of defective work depends on how often the machine jumps out of limit, and what it costs in defective work per hour when this happens. We proceed as follows.

Start production with an assumed frequency of patrol inspection, based on experience. Over some convenient period, say one week, we note the cost of defective work, (let this be S), and the cost of the patrol inspectors with their overheads, (let this be I). Any time the inspector devotes to 100% inspection of work which has plotted out of limit on the quality control chart, should be included with the cost of defective work S, and not with the inspection cost I. Purely as an example, suppose we have a machine section where the patrol inspector visits each machine once every 4 hours. Over a typical week we notice that:

Cost of defective work, plus necessary
                    100% sorting   = S = £5120
Cost of patrol inspection with overheads   = I = £ 320

We can draw up a table to show what will happen if we change this frequency of inspection.

Check every	4 hr	2 hr	1 hr	½ hr	¼ hr
Cost of defective work, S	£5120	2560	1280	640	320
Cost of patrol inspection, I	320	640	1280	2560	5120
Total cost	£5440	3200	2560*	3200	5440

Clearly in this example, minimum cost of £2560 occurs when patrol inspection takes place once per hour. Indeed the data take the same form as the general cost curves in Figure 2.1, and again the minimum cost occurs when the cost of defective work equals the cost of patrol inspection.

Our example was of course constructed to illustrate a principle. Dividing and multiplying by 2, would be unlikely to find the exact minumum cost in practice. We work this out as follows.

1   Having assumed a suitable frequency of inspection, run for a typical period, and obtained values for S and I, we compute $f = \sqrt{\dfrac{S}{I}}$. In the above example we get:

$$f = \sqrt{\frac{S}{I}} = \sqrt{\frac{5120}{320}} = 4. \qquad (13.1)$$

2   We now increase our *assumed* frequency of inspection by factor f. Thus as we assumed patrol inspection every 4 hours, we now check 4 times as often, which is one inspection per hour. If f had been ½, we should check half as often, etc. Hence regardless of the assumed frequency with which we start, this formula will always bring us to minimum cost.

There are a few practical points about the use of $f = \sqrt{\dfrac{S}{I}}$.

1   Inevitably f often works out to an awkward quantity, and has to be rounded to something practicable on the shop floor.

2   The cheapest frequency of inspection often calls for a fraction of an inspector, and has to be rounded to the nearest whole number.

3   If a section does a variety of work then, in principle each type of work has its own best frequency of inspection. However this tends to be complicated to operate. Fortunately within a section of similar machines, the value of work produced per hour is usually roughly constant, even though the part numbers are different. It is then possible to set a single frequency applicable to the whole section.

13.12   Processes which both drift and go out of limit at random

In most processes, either drift as discussed in Section 13.10 or sudden random changes as in Section 13.11 predominate sufficiently to be able to neglect the other. Where, however, both effects are serious enough to be taken into consideration, we proceed as follows:

1   Deal first of all with drift, along the lines suggested in Section 13.10.

2   Only after out-of-limit work due to drift has been largely eliminated do we count the cost of the remaining out-of-limit work, in order to use Eq. (13.1). Unless we work in this order, our calculation for random changes will be influenced by those due to drift.

3   We now have two 'best' frequencies of inspection, and we adopt the most frequent, because this is bound to suit the other.

13.13   The effect of operator control on frequency

Where operator control is used, as described in Sections 9.7 to 9.10, that operator replaces the patrol inspector by doing some or all of the periodic checks. The principles for deciding the frequency of inspection remain the same, with the following additions:

1   Where the operator has enough idle time while the machine is working on one piece to check the previous piece, then the case for checking every piece is very strong. In terms of cost, the operator has to be paid anyway for machine cycle time, so we might just as well utilise it as leave him doing nothing.

2   Where the operator cannot do his checks during the machining or processing cycle, then production of the next piece or load is held up while he checks that which he has just made. Thus, strictly speaking, the cost of operator checks should include the value of lost production. In practice, the calaculation tends to become complicated and, therefore, unless a lot of money is involved, we shall probably decide to do it on the following basis:

a   The loss of production while the operator does his checks must be small. We therefore give time-consuming checks to a patrol inspector.
b   The routine must be simple enough for an operator to work. In one section of a department, it is usually convenient to have a fixed frequency of inspection, such as 1 item in 5 for all except perhaps special jobs.
c   Remember that the effect of operator control is to increase operator interest in quality, and this in itself reduces defective work, over and above the reduction to be expected from the routine itself.

13.14   Interpretation of a quality control chart for variables

Our quality control chart is a link in a chain. By means of various checks, we collect information about the state of our machine or process, and when we plot this information on to the chart we intend that:

1   The information shall be recorded for future use.
2   The chart shall be largely self-analysing, and show at a glance whether any corrective action is required.

However, we must ensure that this action is taken, otherwise our chart is no more than a decoration on the wall! I remember one case in particular, where three supervisors spent most of one day trying to correct some trouble they had on their production line. And the irony of it was that they already had a quality control chart which showed exactly what was wrong but, unfortunately, they had not been adequately taught to read it!

Now there are two important points about the interpretation of a quality control chart:
1   When the average chart is out of limit, this means something quite different from when the range chart is out of limit.
2   Interpretation must be related to the particular type of production, and to the way the chart itself has been designed.

13.14.1 Average chart

If the average chart goes out of limit while the range stays put, then our frequency distribution curve has moved as shown in Figure 11.14, indicating that our machine or process has moved to a new average setting.

1 Sudden changes of average   If the change is sudden, then the cause must also be sudden. Therefore, we consider possibilities like the following, which are appropriate to our type of work:
a   The machine jammed up, so altering its setting.
b   The process suddenly picked up an impurity.
c   There was an unauthorised alteration of switches, taps, valves, etc., on the control equipment.
d   There were sudden changes in the setting of a temperature controller.

There are also many other possibilities which should normally be accompanied by a note on the quality control chart, e.g.
e   The start of a new batch of materiel of quality different from usual.
f   The start of a different operator or inspector, especially if inexperienced.
g   Changes made by an engineer or supervisor for some other reason which he did not think would upset the process.

2 Drifts of the average   When the average drifts, this indicates a

182

progressive change in the setting, etc. Many processes always drift a little:

a   As the tool wears.
b   As chemical solutions become spent, etc.

We soon get to know if our process is of this type and allow for the drift as discussed in Section 13.10.

Suppose, however, that a process or machine which does not normally drift, suddenly begins to do so or, if it does normally do so, it suddenly starts to do so at a much greater rate than usual, or in the opposite direction. This must indicate a progressive change and, again, we shall seek a cause which is applicable to our type of work. For example:

a   The tool is not tight, and keeps moving a bit during each operation or cycle.
b   A batch to be treated in a chemical bath has picked up some impurity, and each time a piece goes into the bath, the impurity level in the bath increases.
c   The setting of a temperature or other controller is drifting.

Occasionally, something happens accidentally, which proves to be advantageous. Thus, a variable which causes a drift in the opposite direction from usual, might be useful in keeping the process average steady.

13.14.2   Range chart

Now the range is a measure of variability and, when it goes out of limit, it indicates that the frequency distribution has changed as shown in Figure 11.15.

On machine work, the range often indicates the general overall condition of the machine, e.g. the effect of play in its bearings, etc. It is therefore, not likely to increase suddenly unless perhaps one bearing suddenly deteriorates, or something equivalent. Where machines are well maintained, we may find that the range changes very little, and it may be possible to omit the range chart altogether and control solely on the average chart.

Sometimes the operator can affect variability, particularly if his work is not controlled by a machine to any extent. In photographic development, for example, careless timing of the immersion of the plates in the chemical baths, sometimes too long, sometimes too short, would cause the variability to increase. If, however, all times at one stage were say just two minutes too long, this would affect the average rather than the range.

Changes in the quality of materiel may affect the range. If the materiel being used suddenly becomes more variable, then the range chart may go out of limit. (If the materiel suddenly changes to a different level of quality, but is consistent within itself, this would show up on the average chart.)

13.14.3 Examples of particular applications

A quality control chart must be interpreted, having due regard for the way it and its routine were devised. The following examples illustrate this:

1   Suppose we have a multi-impression tool which we use for moulding, for example, a diecast tool or one which is making plastics components. We might decide that every time the inspector visits the machine, he is to take a sample of, say, 5 from among the various impressions of the same moulding load. Now, if we then find that our average chart goes out of limit, this suggests that all the impressions have gone out of limit together. Thus, if the sample average is too thick, this may indicate that a piece of swarf is jammed in the tool, so that it cannot close properly. However, if the range chart goes out of limit, while the average remains steady, this indicates an increase in the difference from one impression to the next. For example, if the two faces of the tool were no longer parallel, this would tend to make the impression on one side of the tool yield pieces which were too thick, while those on the other side might be too thin.

2   If we have a multi-headed machine, for example a coilwinding machine with four heads, then we might decide to take a sample of four, one coil from each head. If then the average chart goes out of limit, this would mean that the change was one which affected all four heads together. However, if the range went out of limit, this would indicate a change which affected at least one head, but not all four. Notice that a large change which affected one head, while it would affect the range considerably, would probably alter the average a little as well.

3   Suppose that we have to heat-treat batches of components in a furnace. We may decide that each time a batch comes out of the furnace, the inspector shall take a sample of 5 components, measure their hardness and plot an average and a range chart. In this case, if the average chart goes out of limit, it probably indicates one of the following:

a	Wrong temperature.
b	Wrong timing.
c	Furnace atmosphere contaminated.
d	Incorrect quality of batch submitted for treatment.

If the range chart goes out of limit, it might indicate:

a	Uneven temperature distribution within the furnace.
b	Variable quality of the original batch.

Analysis of this example is discussed more fully in Section 16.9.

Notice how relatively simple these examples tend to be. Thus, your first reaction might be that it is easy with straightforward work, but that your type of production is much more complicated. This may be true, but in general, production troubles arise from comparatively simple causes. The problem usually is to locate the precise cause of a given undesirable effect, and this is where the quality control chart is so useful. Once the cause is known, correction is straightforward. Even in instances which do appear to be somewhat involved, the complication often arises because a number of simple effects are going on together, and it is difficult to distinguish them. Thus, suppose that on our quality control chart both average and range are constantly wandering, apparently with no underlying pattern. A good approach to this problem is to control every process parameter we can, regardless of whether it is supposed to affect the quality. Later, when we have found out which parameters are important, we may be able to relax a little.

13.15 Isolating each period's work

In Section 13.6, paragraph 3, we agreed that each period's work should be kept separate until the check at the end of the period has proved satisfactory. The way that we shall do this in practice will vary with the type of work involved, and the following are examples:

1 Where the components are small, a separate container can be provided to store them temporarily until they can be added to the bulk of the production. This applies to many small parts, for example the output from lathes, drilling machines, etc. Some care may be necessary, however, to avoid damage to the components.

2 Where work stacks easily, it may be convenient to place it in separately marked piles.

3   Sometimes it is convenient to mark the component when it is checked, or to put in paper markers at the points where inspection took place. If a period's work has to be isolated, the inspector or operator goes back to the last paper or other mark. Where an inspection is satisfactory the paper marker can usually be left, and thrown out during the next operation.

4   Sometimes unusual methods are possible. In forging, for example, the fact that the most recently made forgings are hot may be sufficient indication of the last period's work.

13.16   Review of control limits

It may well be that experience gained, and the resultant improvements to the process, will have the effect of progressively reducing its variability. In such cases, it is desirable to recalculate the control limits from time to time. If variability has reduced, we shall find that the range control limit is lower, but as a compensation the average control limits have moved outwards, towards the specification or drawing limits.

Sometimes we may decide to issue instructions that control limits are to be recalculated at regular intervals. Now occasionally it happens that for some reason the variability of a process increases. If this should prove to be the case, the inspectors should be instructed to report the fact, so that the reasons for it can be investigated.

13.17   Pre-control charts

One of the drawbacks of the standard quality control chart is that control limits cannot be set until we have at least 10 reasonably settled points (see Section 13.2, paragraph 3). If these are taken at say hourly intervals, it may well be that a short production run is finished well before the control limits can be set, and even if the runs are long, 10 hours is still a long time to wait. The pre-control chart offers one possible solution to this problem.

At the start, we do not know how the variability of our process compares with the specification limits. We therefore assume that the specification limits represent ± 4 standard deviations of the process, as shown in Figure 13.2. This is probably about the worst situation which will be satisfactory, since the frequency distribution itself will require ± 3 standard deviations, and the extra standard deviation on either side allows for process drift, setting errors, etc. Next we draw two pre-control limits ± 2 standard deviations from the mid-point 0. Notice that these will fall right at the start of the steep part of the distribution curve.

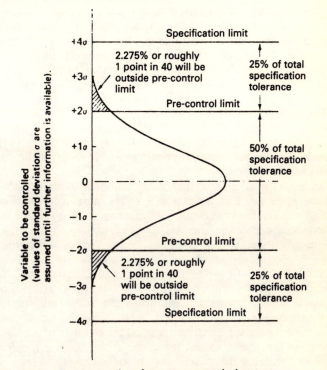

Figure 13.2 An example of a pre-control chart

We now take samples of one, and plot them on our chart.

1   As Figure 11.16 shows, approximately 2.275% of the points will plot outside each control limit. This is roughly 1 point in 40.

2   If the process average moves appreciably off-centre, the fraction of points outside the pre-control limit will increase sharply because of the steepness of the curve. If for example, it moves a whole standard deviation either way, points out of limit rise to $15.87 + 0.135 = 16.0\%$, or roughly 1 point in 6, and this is easy to detect. Thus two successive points outside the pre-control limits mean that a change has almost certainly occurred.

187

3   Suppose however that the frequency distribution curve is not as we have assumed it to be in Figure 13.2. Then: *(a)* if the process variability is less than we have assumed, almost all the plotted points should lie within the pre-control limits, and we shall have no worries, or *(b)* if its variability is greater, then more than 1 point in 40 will lie outside the pre-control limits. If the average setting can be held steady in the centre of the specification limits at 0, then in theory we can accept up to 6.7 per cent or roughly 1 point in 15 out of limit. However if we exceed 1 point in 40 out of limit, we shall be immediately warned that the process is finding the specification limits uncomfortably tight. We shall then investigate and take action as necessary.

The frequency of inspection is often set so that there are about 20 samples between each reset of the process. If the run is long enough, we shall consider changing over to a standard quality control chart, as soon as sufficient information is available to draw the control limits for it.

Where a process capability study has been done as shown in Figure 11.20 or 11.21, an estimate of the standard deviation will already be available. Pre-control limits can then be set correctly at $\pm 2\sigma$ from specification nominal, and we can note whether $\pm 4\sigma$ fall inside or outside the specification limits. If they fall inside, the process should produce satisfactorily, unless the mean is very variable. If they fall outside, the process is not capable of meeting its specification limits comfortably, although it might just do so if the mean is almost constant, and the $\pm 3\sigma$ limits fall inside the specification limits.

An alternative approach is to convert the estimate of the standard deviation into mean range, using the constants given in Section 12.6, and then use this to set conventional average and range chart control limits in the usual way. The chart can be either tolerance or process based, but in the latter case it will also be necessary to use the estimate of the process average from the capability study. Such control limits should be regarded as provisional, to be reviewed when more information becomes available.

13.18   Multi-vari charts

The multi-vari chart is useful where we have two sources of variation of the same quality. For example:

1   The diameter of machined components may vary not only from piece to piece, but also within a piece, due to say a taper along its length.

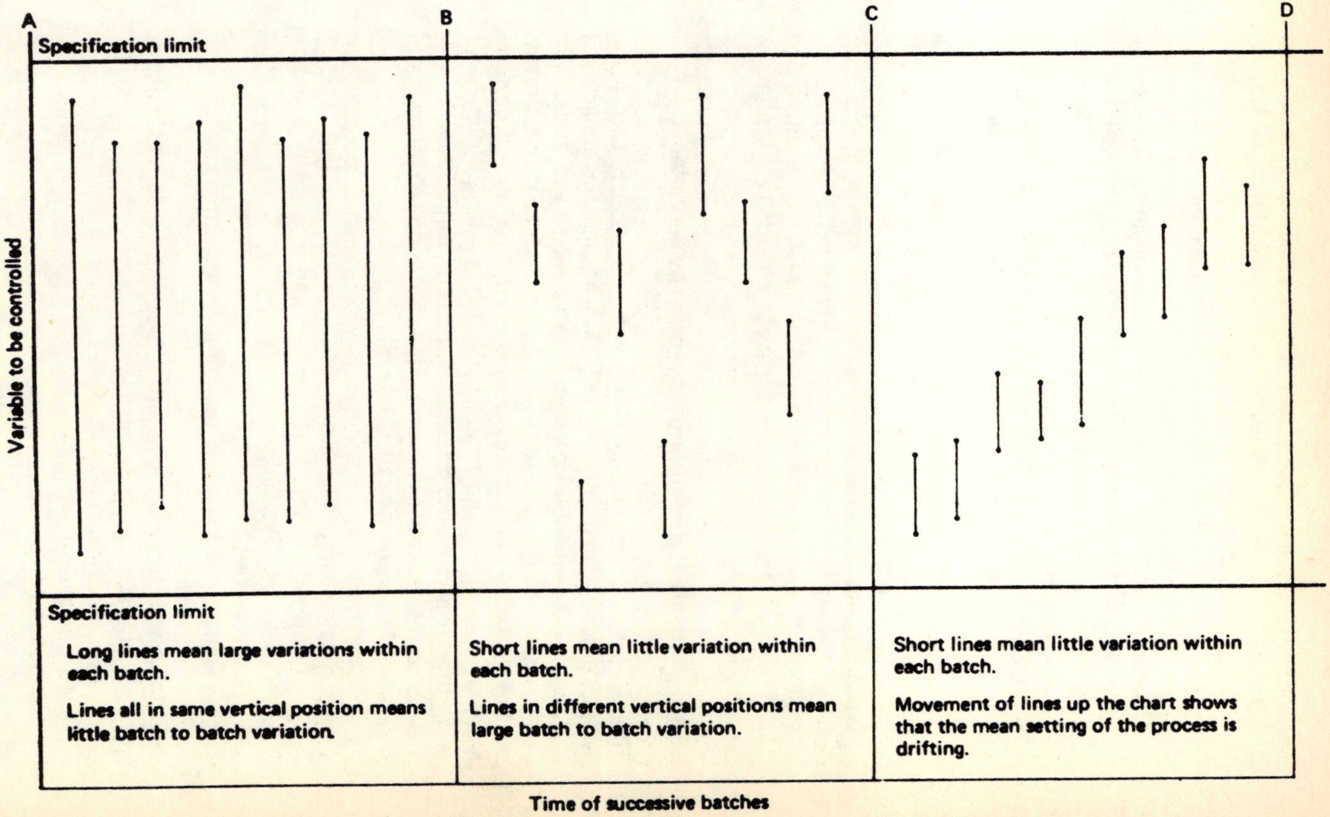

Figure 13.3 Example of a multi-vari chart

A

Specification limit

Variable to be controlled

Specification limit

Long lines mean large variations within each batch.

Lines all in same vertical position means little batch to batch variation.

B

Short lines mean little variation within each batch.

Lines in different vertical positions mean large batch to batch variation.

C

Short lines mean little variation within each batch.

Movement of lines up the chart shows that the mean setting of the process is drifting.

D

Time of successive batches

189

2   When components are heat treated in batches, we may wish to compare the hardness variations within a batch, with those from batch to batch. Suppose we ask the inspector to check the hardness of five components from each batch. He is then to plot his results as shown in Figure 13.3. Thus he plots the value of the largest and the smallest and joins them with a vertical line. Hence the longer the line, the more variable the batch. (In some cases it will be useful to plot the intermediate values as well).

The interpretation of the chart is most easily seen from Figure 13.3. Thus:

Section AB   shows excessive hardness variation within each batch, although successive batches are quite similar to each other.

Section BC   indicates that there is little variation within each batch, but an excessive variation between batches.

Section CD   shows little variation within each batch, but a considerable drift in average hardness with time.

13.19   Acceptance sampling inspection by variables

Most acceptance sampling inspection is done using attributes, in the manner described in Chapters 4 to 7. Even where items are actually measured, e.g. with a micrometer, the inspector still declares so many good and so many bad, which means that the measurements are being treated as attributes. However, it is possible to perform acceptance sampling inspection by variables and full details for doing this are given in BS 6002 and in the American MIL-STD-414. The choice between the two methods depends on the following:

1   *Sampling inspection by variables:*
     Advantages
        Smaller sample sizes.
        Information about the mean and standard deviation becomes available.
     Disadvantages
        Can only be used if the frequency distribution curve is approximately Normal.
        More calculation is required, but with modern calculators this is no great drawback.
2   *Sampling inspection by attributes*
     Advantages
        Simpler to use than variables.

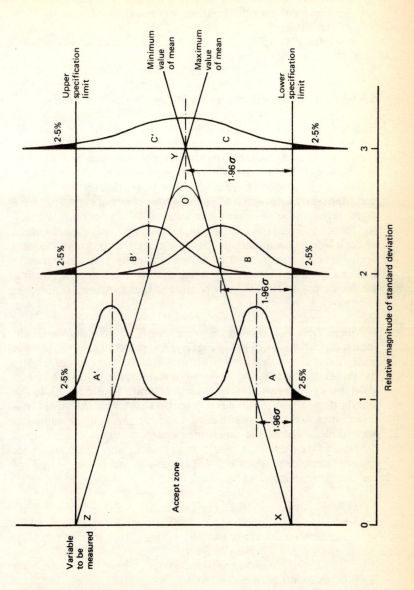

Figure 13.4 Theoretical situation when using acceptance sampling by variables

Many checks can only be done as attributes.

Several qualities can be checked and included in one AQL.

The frequency distribution curve need not be Normal.

Disadvantages

Larger samples are required, but they yield less information.

13.19.1 *Principles of sampling inspection by variables*

Various methods of sampling inspection by variables are available, but we shall confine ourselves to those given in BS 6002. So that each scheme using variables can be exactly related to its equivalent in attributes, all plans are called up by their AQL.

Suppose the AQL is to be 2.5%. This means that the batch can be accepted if no more than 2.5% of its items are out of limit, and curve A of Figure 13.4 shows a 'just acceptable' batch on this basis. Reference to Figures 11.16 and 14.1 shows that if 2.5% of the area under a Normal frequency distribution curve is outside specification limit, then the mean must be 1.96σ inside the limit, as shown in Figure 13.4. How this affects the practical situation depends on how we decide the AQL is to be applied, and there are 4 possibilities as follows.

1 Single Limit   If there is only one specification or drawing limit, for example the lower limit in Figure 13.4, then the mean must be at least $1.96\ \sigma$ above that limit, if the batch is to be accepted. Clearly the larger the value of the standard deviation, the further the mean must be kept above the specification limit. In Figure 13.4, the standard deviation of curve B is twice that of A, and for curve C it is three times A. Hence we can draw a line XY marking the minimum acceptable value of the batch mean, depending on the standard deviation. (If there is a single upper limit, the same argument applies to curves A′, B′, C′, and the maximum value of the batch mean is shown by line YZ.)

2 Double Limits   If there are two limits, we must differentiate between:

a   Separate limits where *each* limit is permitted to have the AQL value, e.g. 2.5%, out of limit.

b   Combined limits where the total out-of-limit items from *both limits* together, must not exceed the AQL.

3 Separate Double Limits   This is equivalent to applying two

192

entirely independent single limits, so that the bottom and top halves of Figure 13.4 both exist together. For a batch to be accepted, its mean must be on or above line XY, and on or below YZ. This gives accept zone XYZ. When the standard deviation is small compared with the width between the limits, as shown in position A, the frequency distribution curve cannot possibly have a tail outside more than one limit at a time. Curve C in the limiting position Y, however, has its full AQL (in this case 2.5%), outside each limit, and any larger value of standard deviation will cause the batch to be rejected. Hence any batch to the right of Y will be rejected.

4 Combined Double Limits So long as the frequency distribution curve is sufficiently small so that it is impossible for it to have a tail outside both limits at the same time, it makes no difference whether the limits are separate or combined. At the other extreme position Y is obviously unacceptable, because it has 2.5% outside each limit, making 5.0% in all. Similarly positions near to Y, where the total out of limit exceeds 2.5%, are unaccepable, and this has the effect of rounding off the accept zone from XYZ to XOZ as shown.

13.19.2 Practical use of sampling plans for variables

In order to use a variables sampling plan, we must in some form or other know or estimate the standard deviation. BS 6002 provides for three possibilities:

1   The standard deviation is already well established from previous deliveries. This is called the σ method, and it requires the smallest sample size of the three methods.
2   We estimate the standard deviation from the measurements on the sample, in principle using Eq. 11.1, although in practice the inspector would have a calculator. This is called the *s* method.
3   We estimate the mean range, which (as we said in Section 12.6) is exactly related to the standard deviation. This is called the *R* method.

BS 6002 provides tables for each of the above situations. Where there is only a single limit, or two which are to be treated separately, a decision can be reached by comparing the observed results with an acceptability constant given in the tables. Where two limits are combined, the solution must be found graphically, but again all necessary graphs are given in BS 6002.

13.20 Questions

1 Coils are wound four at a time on a four-headed coil winding machine, and are required to have an electrical resistance of 11.0 ± 0.7 ohms. A sample of four coils (one from each head) is checked for resistance value every hour, and over the first ten samples the following results (in ohms) are obtained:

Sample No.	1	2	3	4	5	6	7	8	9	10
Head A	11.2	11.0	10.9	10.9	11.2	11.0	10.9	11.2	11.1	11.2
Head B	10.8	10.9	10.8	10.9	11.0	10.8	10.9	10.8	10.8	10.9
Head C	10.8	10.7	11.0	11.1	11.1	10.5	11.1	10.9	10.8	10.9
Head D	11.1	11.0	11.3	11.2	11.3	10.9	11.5	11.1	11.2	11.1

1a Plot these results on average and range quality control charts, and insert control limits designed to control to specification limits, i.e. charts to modified limits. *(15 marks)*

Observations proceed as follows:

Sample No.	11	12	13	14	15	16	17	18	19	20
Head A	11.2	11.0	11.0	11.1	10.9	10.8	11.1	11.1	11.0	11.2
Head B	10.9	11.0	10.8	10.8	10.9	11.1	10.8	10.9	10.8	10.8
Head C	10.8	11.0	11.2	11.2	11.4	11.5	11.6	11.8	11.9	11.9
Head D	11.1	11.2	10.8	11.1	11.0	11.0	10.9	11.2	10.8	10.9

1b Plot these further observations on the charts and comment upon them. *(10 marks)*

2a For what purpose might a multi-vari chart be used? *(7 marks)*

2b Batches of raw materiel are each divided into five furnace loads which are processed and heat treated to produce electrical resistance elements. A sample of four elements is taken from each furnace load, and the resistance of each element is measured. Results from 20 successive furnace loads are given below (in ohms).

Batch	A					B				
Furnace load	1	2	3	4	5	6	7	8	9	10
	199.0	201.5	203.5	203.0	198.5	196.5	199.5	198.0	202.5	202.0
	203.0	198.0	200.0	201.5	198.0	203.0	197.0	200.0	202.0	201.0
	197.5	204.5	199.5	198.0	203.0	197.0	202.0	197.0	198.0	197.0
	198.0	202.5	198.0	197.0	203.5	203.0	200.5	202.5	196.5	197.5

Batch	C					D				
Furnace load	11	12	13	14	15	16	17	18	19	20
	198.0	199.5	200.0	199.0	201.0	204.5	199.0	203.0	199.0	205.0
	204.0	201.0	203.0	198.0	201.5	198.0	201.5	204.5	200.5	204.5
	199.0	203.5	197.5	201.5	198.0	199.5	205.0	198.0	198.0	198.5
	201.0	198.5	200.0	203.5	204.0	199.0	204.0	199.5	204.5	198.5

194

Specification limits are 200 ± 4 ohms.

(i)   Plot a multi-vari chart of these observations   *(11 marks)*
(ii) Use the chart to discuss what can be learned about the process.   *(7 marks)*

CHAPTER 14

PROCESS BASED QUALITY CONTROL CHARTS

A process based quality control chart controls a process to the tightest limits it is capable of achieving.

14.1   The need for process based charts

So far we have assumed that each variable has specification or drawing limits to which we must work. In some cases, however, we do not have such limits. For example:

1   Our process may be a new one, which we are still developing, and whose limits have yet to be decided. For the moment, we wish to control it to the closest limits it is capable of holding.

2   Many processes contain a series of operations, each depending on the others, and a check on the quality of the product itself is only possible at the end. Thus, consider the manufacture of castings in a foundry. The specification and drawings may set the quality of the final casting in terms of dimensional tolerances, hardness, porosity, etc., but they are unlikely to tell us how accurately we must control the moisture content of the moulding sand, or the pouring temperature of the metal. Therefore we shall wish to control these secondary qualities to the best they are reasonably capable of achieving.

3   Occasionally we may be obliged to produce with a process which is not capable of holding its drawing limits. We shall then need to control the process to the best it is capable of achieving, and since this will not be good enough, follow with 100 per cent inspection.

4   One school of thought argues that machines and processes should be controlled to the tightest limits they are capable of holding, *even when the specification limits are much wider*. We shall discuss this method further in Section 14.6.

14.2   The theory of a process based quality control chart

Suppose we have a process making components with a nominal weight of 175 g. To check its capability we weigh 50 successively made components, and plot our results as an ordinary frequency distribution curve for samples of 1 as shown in Figure 14.1a. Using the individual readings we estimate the process mean to be 175.8 g and its standard deviation to be 2.1 g. Hence assuming that our process mean stays constant, the inherent capability of the process is $175.8 \pm 3.09\sigma = 175.8 \pm 6.5 = 169.3$ and 182.3 g.

However in production we shall wish to take advantage of the increased sensitivity which we can achieve by averaging samples of say 5, and plotting against control limits, (see Sections 12.4 and 12.5). This will reduce the standard deviation by $\sqrt{5}$.

∴ Standard deviation of samples of 5 averaged =

$$\sigma_n = \frac{\sigma}{\sqrt{5}} = \frac{2.1}{\sqrt{5}} = 0.94 \text{ g}$$

Our frequency distribution curve now becomes as Figure 14.1b, and if we set capability control limits at $(175.8 \pm 3.09\sigma_n)$, we get:

$175.8 \pm (3.09 \times 0.94) = 172.9$ and 178.7 g as shown.

Where as in paragraphs 1, 2 or 3 of Section 14.1 we need a really tight control on the process, we also set 2 inner control limits at $175.8 \pm (1.96\sigma_n) = 175.8 \pm (1.96 \times 0.94) = 174.0$ and 177.6 g.

The inner control limits are set so that *each* cuts off 2.5% of the area under the curve as shown in Figure 14.1b.

If our process continued to perform exactly as it did when we took our sample of 50 pieces, almost every average of 5 should plot within the two outer control limits, and only 1 point in 40 (i.e. 2.5%) should be just (and only just) beyond each inner limit. Any of the following will warn us that the process average is changing.

a   One or more points beyond an outer limit.

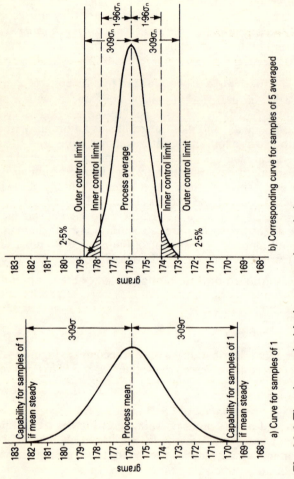

Fig 14·1 The theory behind process based charts

a) Curve for samples of 1

b) Corresponding curve for samples of 5 averaged

b   Two or more points close together beyond an inner limit, especially if they are some way beyond it.

It is often more meaningful on the shop floor to use the following terms. Inner control limits are called *warning limits*. Outer control limits are called *action limits*.

14.3   The range chart

The average chart described in Section 14.2 is usually used with a range chart which is basically identical to that in Figure 13.1a. It differs only if, as often happens, an inner limit is added to give greater sensitivity. We are free to choose whether or not to include inner limits, but as a rough guide if 1, 2 or 3 or Section 14.1 apply it should be used, but if 4 applies it is probably unnecessary. As with · the average chart, the inner control limit is set at a probability of 1 in 40, and acts as a warning if the process variability starts to increase.

14.4   A practical example of a process based quality control chart

In order to explain how a process based quality control chart is prepared on the shop floor, we will use the example which we introduced in Section 14.2. Notice as we proceed, how similar this chart is to the tolerance based chart in Figure 13.1. The completed chart is shown in Figure 14.2, and the steps for setting it up are as follows.

1   We draw the axes of both the average and range charts. At this stage the rest of the charts will be blank. If specification limits exist, they should be drawn in, but they will not play any direct part in the calculation.

2   Set up the process and start producing. Instruct the inspector to take samples periodically, (say 5 every hour), to measure them and plot sample average and range on the charts, as shown in Figure 14.2.

3   When we have at least 10 settled points, we are ready to set the control limits. As before we reject any unsettled or obviously spurious points, although this is not as easy as it sounds. Points may not be spurious merely because they are not where we expect them to be. If time permits it is best to repeat the observations from the start.

4   Since we are not using specification limits, we shall need to create a datum line, about which we can set the control limits. We do this by averaging all the averages of 5 together, to give the *process average* or as it is traditionally called, the *grand average*. In our example this is 175.78 g. We also average all the ranges together to get the mean range. In our example this is 4.6 g.

5   *Average chart*
   Outer control limits.   Multiply the mean range $\overline{w}$ by the constant $A'_{0.001}$. Add the result to the process average to get the upper outer control limit, and subtract it from the process average to get the lower outer control limit. Constant $A'_{0.001}$ varies with the sample size as follows:

No.in sample	2	3	4	5	6	7	8
$A'_{0.001}$	1.937	1.054	0.750	0.594	0.498	0.432	0.384

For our example we get:

$$
\begin{array}{ll}
\text{Outer Control} & \left[\begin{array}{l}\text{process}\\\text{average}\end{array}\right] \pm \quad (A'_{0.001} \times \text{mean range})\\
\text{limits} \quad = \\
\qquad = \quad 175.78 \quad \pm \qquad (0.594 \times 4.6)\\
\qquad = \quad 173.05 \quad \text{and} \qquad 178.51 \text{ g}
\end{array}
$$

   Inner control limits are calculated exactly as above, except that constant $A'_{0.025}$ is used instead of $A'_{0.001}$ It takes the following values.

No.in sample	2	3	4	5	6	7	8
$A'_{0.025}$	1.229	0.668	0.476	0.377	0.316	0.274	0.244

Hence for our example we get:

$$
\begin{array}{ll}
\text{Inner Control} & \left[\begin{array}{l}\text{process}\\\text{average}\end{array}\right] \pm \quad (A'_{0.025} \times \text{mean range})\\
\text{limits} \quad = \\
\qquad = \quad 175.78 \quad \pm \qquad (0.377 \times 4.6)\\
\qquad = \quad 174.05 \quad \text{and} \qquad 177.51 \text{ g}
\end{array}
$$

6   *Range chart*
   Outer control limit   Multiply the mean range by constant $D'_{0.001}$ and measure this amount up from zero range, to get the position of the control limit.
   Inner control limit   Repeat the above calculation using constant $D'_{0.025}$ The constants take the following values.

No.in sample	2	3	4	5	6	7	8
$D'_{0.025}$	2.81	2.17	1.93	1.81	1.72	1.66	1.62
$D'_{0.001}$	4.12	2.98	2.57	2.34	2.21	2.11	2.04

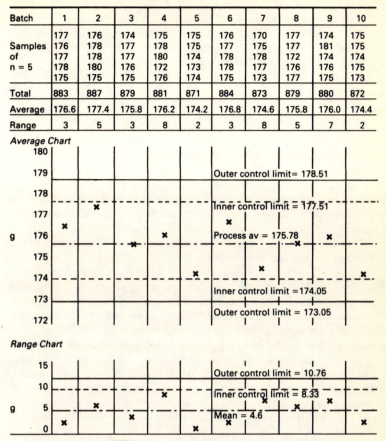

Batch	1	2	3	4	5	6	7	8	9	10
Samples of n = 5	177 176 177 178 175	176 178 177 180 175	174 177 177 176 175	175 178 180 172 176	175 175 174 173 174	176 177 178 178 175	170 175 178 177 173	177 177 172 176 177	174 181 174 176 175	175 175 174 175 173
Total	883	887	879	881	871	884	873	879	880	872
Average	176.6	177.4	175.8	176.2	174.2	176.8	174.6	175.8	176.0	174.4
Range	3	5	3	8	2	3	8	5	7	2

Average Chart

Outer control limit = 178.51

Inner control limit = 177.51

Process av = 175.78

Inner control limit = 174.05

Outer control limit = 173.05

Range Chart

Outer control limit = 10.76

Inner control limit = 8.33

Mean = 4.6

Process average = $\bar{x} = \dfrac{1757.8}{10} = 175.78$ g

Mean range = $\bar{w} = \dfrac{46}{10} = 4.6$ g

Average Chart
Outer control limits = $\bar{x} \pm (A'_{0.001} \times \bar{w}) = 175.78 \pm (0.594 \times 4.6)$
$= 173.05$ and 178.51 g
Inner control limits = $\bar{x} \pm (A'_{0.025} \times \bar{w}) = 175.78 \pm (0.377 \times 4.6)$
$= 174.05$ and 177.51 g

Range Chart
Outer control limit = $\bar{w} \times D'_{0.001} = 4.6 \times 2.34 = 10.76$ g
Inter control limit = $\bar{w} \times D'_{0.025} = 4.6 \times 1.81 = 8.33$ g

Figure 14.2 Example of a process based quality control chart

201

$$\therefore \text{ Outer control limit} = \overline{w} \times D'_{0.001} = 4.6 \times 2.34 = 10.76 \text{ g}$$
$$= \overline{w} \times D'_{0.025} = 4.6 \times 1.81 = 8.33 \text{ g}$$

Notice that throughout, we have resisted the temptation to round off the calculator figures unduly. This was done partly to enable readers to check the calculations, but also because if control limits are drawn at unrounded values, any plotted point will be quite clearly 'in' or 'out' of control limit. This avoids confusion on the shop floor.

7 We have now completed the charts shown in Figure 14.2.

14.5   American quality control charts

A number of companies in this country who have American principles, use charts which differ slightly from British Standards, although BS 5700 says that they are acceptable. In British charts the control limits are always set at exactly probabilities of 1 in 1000 for each outer limit, and 1 in 40 for each inner limit. This results in the number of standard deviations from process average being odd values i.e. $3.09 \, \sigma$ and $1.96 \, \sigma$, but since the control limits are set with constants, this is no disadvantage whatever. American companies set their control limits at exactly 3σ and 2σ, thereby losing the advantage of having exact probabilities. In practice either method is satisfactory, and the only effect of using American methods is that the chart constants change slightly. Notice too that a different set of symbols is used, and that inner control limits are omitted. Discarding the inner limits is satisfactory provided 4 of Section 14.1 applies, and the C_p value is around 1.5 or more. If it is less, or if 1, 2 or 3 of Section 14.1 apply, the reader is advised to include inner limits on the chart. Chart constant are as follows.

No. in sample	= 2	3	4	5	6	7	8
Average chart constant = A_2	= 1.880	1.023	0.729	0.577	0.483	0.419	0.373
Range chart constant = D_4	= 3.268	2.574	2.282	2.114	2.004	1.924	1.864

14.6   Use of process based charts, when specification limits exist

It is becoming increasingly common for companies to use process based charts, even though specification limits exist, and a tolerance based chart could be used. The object is to keep piece to piece variation to an absolute minimum and centred right on nominal. This reduces assembly and interchangeability problems, and increases performance and reliability of the final equipment. Initially of course, the increased number of process adjustments will increase quality costs and reduce output, but this is usually more than off-set by the reduced reject rate, fewer assembly problems and lower warranty costs.

Remember however that a chart based on process capability will control a process to the best of which it is capable, *even when that process is completely incapable of achieving its specification limits*! For this reason it is usual to start with a capability study as shown in Figure 11.21. The capability index C_p as explained in Section 11.8, must be computed and will hopefully be 1.33 or more. If C_p or either value of C_{pk} is less than 1.00 the process is not capable of achieving its specification limits, and if it is between 1.00 and 1.33 achievement will be difficult.

Alternatively the $\pm 3\sigma$ capability of the process can be estimated from a process based quality control chart. It is given by $(\sqrt{n}) \times$ (the difference between the upper and lower outer control limits on the average chart). Thus for our example:

$\pm 3\sigma$ process capability $= (\sqrt{5}) \times (178.51 - 173.05) = 12.21g$
$\therefore$ Process capability $= 175.78 \pm (\frac{1}{2} \times 12.21) = 175.8 \pm 6g$ say

If the process average can be reset to the specification nominal of 175.0 g, then the inherent capability becomes 175 ± 6 g approximately. (Readers who compare this estimate of the process capability with that in Section 14.2, will notice a slight discrepancy. This is almost inevitable when, as here, samples are used to estimate the standard deviation using two different methods.)

14.7 Taking samples, the sample size and frequency of sampling

When taking samples for process based charts, we usually select them from among the last pieces made, in order to get the 'latest news' about the state of the process. However the general considerations discussed in Section 13.7 still apply. Similarly the choice of sample size is exactly as set out in Section 13.8.

In principle the conditions upon which the frequency of taking samples should be based are the same as we discussed in Sections 13.9 to 13.13. However the process based chart explained in Section 14.4 assumes that the process average, (i.e. the central value to which the machine or process has been set), can be held absolutely constant. In practice many processes cannot be prevented from either drifting or jumping suddenly out of limit.

14.8 Processes which drift

Where a process average drifts steadily, we shall have to decide how far it can be allowed to go before it is reset. In effect we shall have to balance the increased variability of our product if we allow it to run too long, against the additional cost of resets if we keep the runs short. Where specification limits exist, or some practical limit can be assumed, a more precise calculation is possible as follows.

Suppose we wish to produce a diameter to 20.00 ± 0.05 mm. We take the usual 10 samples each of 5 pieces as in Section 14.4, and estimate that the mean range $\overline{w} = 0.015$ mm. We next set a value of C_{pk} to suit our requirements, as follows.

a   If it is important that no piece should be near either specification limit, set $C_{pk} = 1.5$ or even more.

b   If we wish to be reasonably sure that all pieces are within specification limit, set $C_{pk} = 1.33$.

c   If an occasional piece on or just beyond the specification limit is acceptable, set $C_{pk} = 1.00$. An easier alternative in this case is to use a tolerance based chart. Obviously the higher we set C_{pk} the shorter the run between resets. Suppose we want to be reasonably safe, without excessively short runs, so we set $C_{pk} = 1.33$.

From equation 11.8 we have:

$$C_{pk} = \left\lceil \frac{\bar{x}_L - L}{3\sigma} \right\rceil \qquad C_{pk} = \left\lceil \frac{U - \bar{x}_U}{3\sigma} \right\rceil$$

where $\bar{x}_L$ is the lowest value the process mean can be allowed to take, and $\bar{x}_U$ is the highest.
We solve these equations for $\bar{x}_L$ and $\bar{x}_U$.

$\therefore \bar{x}_L = (C_{pk} \times 3\sigma) + L$
$\quad \bar{x}_U = U - (C_{pk} \times 3\sigma)$

Now
$3\sigma = A'_{0.001} \times \bar{w} \times \sqrt{n} = 0.594 \times 0.015 \times \sqrt{5} = 0.0199$ mm
$\therefore \bar{x}_L = (1.33 \times 0.0199) + 19.95 = 19.976$ mm
$\quad \bar{x}_U = 20.05 - (1.33 \times 0.0199) = 20.024$ mm

Using $\bar{x}_L$ and $\bar{x}_U$ as the process average, we calculate the extreme upper and lower positions of the control limits in the usual way.

204

∴ Lower control limit =
$$\bar{x}_L - (A'_{0.001} \times \bar{w}) = 19.976 - (0.594 \times 0.015)$$
$$= 19.968 \text{ mm}$$
Upper control limit =
$$\bar{x}_U - (A'_{0.001} \times \bar{w}) = 20.024 - (0.594 \times 0.015)$$
$$= 20.032 \text{ mm}$$

The chart is now as shown in Figure 14.3. In practice the process average will be set as near as possible to 19.976 mm and allowed to drift until it reaches 20.024 mm. This will be achieved by ensuring that all averages of 5 plot within the control limits.

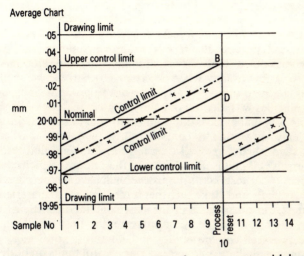

Fig 14·3 Process based chart for a process which drifts

If the process average has a consistent and predictable drift, then two sloping control limits AB and CD can be drawn as shown. The lower position of the upper control limit is then given by $19.967 + (0.594 \times 0.015) = 19.985$ mm, and the upper position of the lower control limit by $20.024 - (0.594 \times 0.015) = 20.015$ mm.

The range chart is not affected by a drift of the process average.

14.9 Processes which jump out of limit unpredictably

Where a process jumps out of specification limits at unpredictable moments, the method given in section 13.11 can be used to determine sample size and frequency. Where no specification limits

205

as such exist, we shall have to assume something suitable, so that this method can be used.

14.10 Interpretation of a process based quality control chart

The interpretation of a process based quality control chart is basically similar to the interpretation of a tolerance based chart, and therefore everything in section 13.14 applies.

14.11 Review of control limits

We shall hope to use our process capability chart as a means of improving the process itself. For example, suppose our chart suddenly goes out of limit. We shall immediately investigate and, because we know exactly when the change occurred, we shall be able to relate it to any known change in the process. Suppose it exactly coincides with the use of a new batch of materiel. We shall investigate why that batch is different from other batches. Chemical analysis may show that it contains much more of a particular impurity than usual. We shall then have to do controlled tests to satisfy ourselves that it is the addition of this impurity which caused the trouble. If our tests confirm this, we shall have learned that this impurity is deadly and make sure that future batches of materiel are free from it. As all batches in the past contained a little of this impurity, the result will be an improvement in the overall quality from the process. The variability and, therefore, the range will reduce, and we shall be able to reset our control limits on both the average and range charts. Thus, in quality control terminology, a variable which was unassignable has now become assignable.

Therefore, from time to time, we recalculate the control limits to see whether an overall improvement has taken place. If it has, we shall find that the control limits on the average chart have moved in towards the grand average line, and that the range control limits are lower. We must, however, beware of issuing vague instructions to the inspector, for example 'to recalculate the control limits every three months', because it can happen that a process has got worse during this period. Thus, suppose the level of our undesirable impurity had gradually risen, then when the control limits were recalculated the average chart control limits would widen, and the range limits would be higher! As we have a process capability chart it follows that, if the process becomes less capable, the recalculated limits will relax to match its reduced standards. Therefore, we must

206

tell our inspector that if, when he recalculates, the mean range proves to be greater than before, this must be reported for investigation. In general, we shall only accept wider limits if there is a compensating reason for them, for example if we are deliberately saving money by:

Buying cheaper, though lower quality materiel.

Employing a less skilled operator.

Using a less precise machine or other equipment.

14.12 Cusum charts

With a standard quality control chart, no action will normally be taken, so long as points plot within control limits. Thus a run of points, all above the grand average may not be noticed, because the position of each point is quite independent of those which preceded it. Sometimes this is unsatisfactory.

Suppose we are preparing a liquid chemical in which we wish the average content of a particular ingredient to be as near as possible to 10 g/litre. The liquid produced will be mixed in bulk before the next operation, so minor variations do not matter, so long as the *average* is kept at 10 g. For this we might decide to use a *cumulative sum chart*, or as it is usually called, a *cusum chart*. We start with a reference value, in this case the 10 g/litre, at which we wish to control the process, although in other applications it might be the average performance of the process established from past history. We sample test the process at intervals, and deduct the reference value from each observation. What is left, we then plot as a difference up or down from the last point. Thus suppose that our first 10 results are:

Observation = O	Reference value = RV	Difference = (O − RV)	Cumulative difference
10	10	0	0
11	10	+1	+1
9	10	−1	0
10	10	0	0
12	10	+2	+2
9	10	−1	+1
10	10	0	+1
8	10	−2	−1
10	10	0	−1
11	10	+1	0
Average 10			

These results are plotted in section AB of Figure 14.4.
Suppose our observations continue like this.

Observation value	Reference	Difference	Cumulative difference
11	10	+1	+1
10	10	0	+1
12	10	+2	+3
11	10	+1	+4
10	10	0	+4
11	10	+1	+5
13	10	+3	+8
12	10	+2	+10
9	10	−1	+9
11	10	+1	+10

Average   11

When we plot these results in section BC of Figure 14.11, we get a

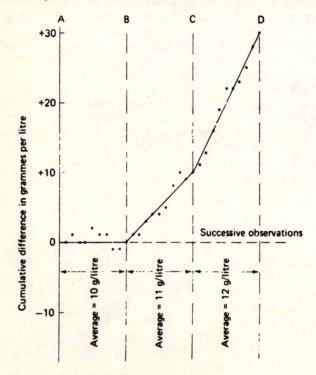

Figure 14.4   Example of a cusum chart

208

straight line going *upwards*, and this indicates that the process has changed to a *new average* level which is *higher* than the reference value. A check shows that it is averaging 11 g/litre instead of 10. In section CD of Figure 14.4, further observations are plotted, in which the average is 12 g/litre.

Interpretation of a cusum chart is therefore as follows:

1   A horizontal line of points means that the process is holding an average value equal to the reference value.

2   A *straight* line upwards means that the process has changed to a new *steady* average level, which is above the reference value. The steeper the line, the greater the difference between the new average and the reference value. (Conversely if the straight line is downwards, the new average is below the reference value.)

3   If the line is *curved* upwards, the new average is above the reference, and still increasing. Similarly if it is curved downwards, the average is below the reference and still reducing.

4   Notice that the position of a point on the chart represents the cumulative past history of the process, since observations were started. Thus there is no particular significance in whether the point is high up or low down on the paper. If points run out of the top of the chart, it is common practice to restart them again near the bottom. All that matters is the direction in which the points are heading. In our example, we must adjust the process so that they keep a horizontal course.

Use of a V mask

A number of methods are used to set limits to the permissible slope of the plotted points, the most popular of which is to use a V mask as shown in Figure 14.5. The mask is usually made of clear plastic so that points lying under it can still be seen. It is defined by the angle within the jaws of the V (usually denoted by 2θ) and a blanked off lead distance d. In use the mask is placed with its axis 0–0–0 horizontal, and with P over the last point plotted. If any of the plotted points is covered by the mask, the process average is deemed to have changed. If it is too high, then the plotted points will rise too steeply, and some of them will be hidden by the *lower* side of the mask BC. Conversely if the process average is too low, the plotted points will fall too steeply, so that some will be hidden by the *upper* limb AD. The two quantities, θ and *d*, are usually set using either a table or a nomogram, but in principle θ determines the maximum amount the process average can be above or below the reference value, and *d* sets the variability in successive samples about that average.

Advantages and disadvantages The chief advantage of a cusum chart is that it is very sensitive to small changes in the process average in the region of the reference value. It will also show large changes in average, but conventional charts will do this just as well.

It is not very sensitive to changes in variability, but where (as is often the case) each plotted point is an average of several observations, a cusum chart can be used in conjunction with an ordinary range chart. Another drawback of the cusum chart is that operators find them difficult to interpret. Hence they tend to be charts for quality engineers.

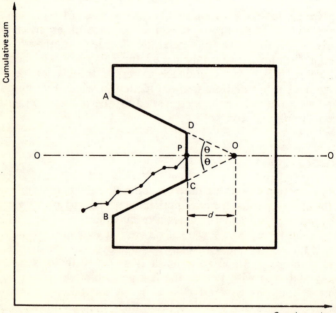

Figure 14.5 Use of a **V** mask

14.13 Questions

1 A machine is set to produce a diameter of 9 mm nominal, and a sample of five pieces is taken every hour from amongst the last made. Over the first 10 samples the following results were obtained:

Sample No. 1	2	3	4	5	6	7	8	9	10
9.05	9.05	9.04	9.04	9.06	9.06	9.04	9.06	9.05	9.03
9.03	9.04	9.05	9.04	9.04	9.04	9.07	9.03	9.05	9.06
9.03	9.06	9.04	9.04	9.05	9.05	9.06	9.03	9.05	9.04
9.04	9.04	9.06	9.05	9.05	9.04	9.06	9.04	9.06	9.05
9.06	9.05	9.04	9.04	9.06	9.04	9.05	9.05	9.05	9.03

1a Construct and plot appropriate average and range control charts, based on machine capability, and show clearly how the control limits were derived. *(15 marks)*

1b As an alternative to taking five pieces from amongst the last made, they could have been taken as a random sample from the whole of the last period's work. What considerations decide which should be used? *(5 marks)*

1c Under what circumstances is a chart controlling to process capability likely to be preferred to one controlling to drawing or specification limit, i.e. to a chart to modified limits?
(5 marks)

2 A capstan lathe was set to produce a diameter with a nominal value of 12.05 mm. Samples of four pieces were taken from amongst the last made, at intervals of 15 minutes, with the following results:

Sample No.

1	2	3	4	5	6	7	8	9	10
12.05	12.06	12.05	12.06	12.08	12.08	12.10	12.09	12.10	12.10
12.06	12.06	12.06	12.07	12.07	12.09	12.09	12.08	12.09	12.11
12.05	12.05	12.07	12.08	12.08	12.09	12.07	12.10	12.11	12.12
12.04	12.05	12.07	12.06	12.07	12.07	12.09	12.11	12.11	12.11

2a Plot the above data on average and range quality control charts. *(7 marks)*

2b Calculate and insert conventional control limits intended to control the machine to the best it is capable of achieving.
(7 marks)

2c Explain why conventional control limits will not be satisfactory in this case, and hence suggest suitable control limits, assuming that patrol inspection takes place every hour. *(6 marks)*

2d A customer has enquired the tightest limits which this machine can hold. What would be your reply assuming that inspection continues at hourly intervals? *(5 marks)*

CHAPTER 15

QUALITY CONTROL CHARTS
FOR
ATTRIBUTES

15.1   Use of attributes in quality control

As explained in Sections 3.3, 3.7 and 3.8, attributes are qualities
which are not measured in figures, either because they cannot be,
>   e.g. 'all threads to be clean',
or because it is not convenient to do so,
>   e.g. 'check with go/no go gauge'.
In quality control, attributes usually take a 'yes/no' form.
>   e.g. 'pass' or 'fail',
>   'works as intended' or 'does not work',
>   'has a minor blemish' or 'unblemished',
>   component is 'present' or 'absent'.
Wherever the choice between variables and attributes is roughly
equal, we should always choose variables. The considerations are
roughly as follows.

15.1.1   Advantages of using variables

1   Small samples, (e.g. 5 items), are sufficient to keep a check on
     both process average and variability.
2   Gradual changes such as drifts can be detected, and the

process reset *before* it goes out of specification limit. Changes in variability can be detected on the range chart.

3   Sudden changes in process average and variability can also be detected, but where this results in all work being out of specification limit, attributes will do this equally well.

15.1.2   Advantages etc. of using attributes

1   Many qualities cannot be measured conveniently as variables, e.g. appearance, taste, etc., although some tastes, for example sweetness, are often estimated on a scale of say 0 to 5.

2   Attributes are usually easier to check, and require a less skilled inspector.

3   Several types of defective can be observed and plotted together as total number rejected, but the chart should always include an analysis, so that types which often occur can be identified and investigated.

4   Sample sizes for attributes are much larger than for variables. For example, if the scrap from a process averages 1%, a sample of 100 is needed to have an average chance of finding one reject in it, and rather more to give a good chance of doing so. Samples can, and sometimes are, taken specifically to provide data for an attribute chart, but in the majority of cases we use data from 100% inspection which is being performed anyway.

15.2   Types of quality control chart for attributes

Quality control charts for attributes always control to process capability, since no one writes on a drawing, 'The scrap level shall be $2 \pm \frac{1}{2}\%$!'

Attributes divide into defectives and defects.

A *defective* is any item which does not comply with specification, and so includes scrap, rework, corrections, seconds etc.

A *defect* is any feature in an item which is undesirable, but which by itself does not render it unacceptable and therefore defective. Typically defects are small scratches, tiny blemishes etc. We may then stipulate that say 3 or more defects make the whole item defective, (i.e. any item with 3 or more defects will be rejected).

There are 4 basic types of quality control chart for attributes, and at the end of this chapter, we have summarised the considerations which decide which should be used in a particular case. The types are as follows.

214

p chart for percentage defective, where the sample size varies.

np chart for number defective, where the sample size is constant.

c chart for number of defects, where the sample size is constant.

u chart for number of defects per item, where the sample size varies.

These charts differ primarily in having different formulae for the process average and standard deviation. We will therefore explain the p chart in detail, and use it as a basic pattern for the other charts.

15.3   p chart for percentage defective

The p chart is used where we are dealing with defectives (e.g. scrap

| Dept. Electronic Assembly | Part. BMT 97 | Supervisor Val Jones | Inspector Tom Roy |

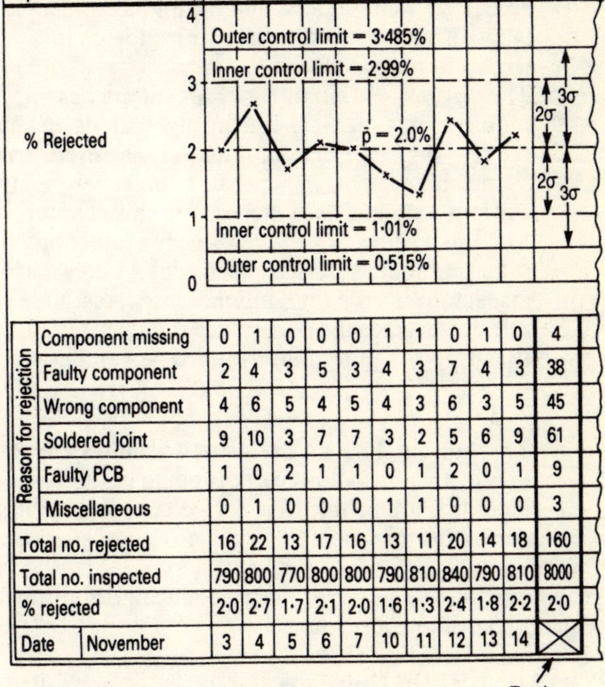

Reason for rejection											Totals
Component missing	0	1	0	0	0	1	1	0	1	0	4
Faulty component	2	4	3	5	3	4	3	7	4	3	38
Wrong component	4	6	5	4	5	4	3	6	3	5	45
Soldered joint	9	10	3	7	7	3	2	5	6	9	61
Faulty PCB	1	0	2	1	1	0	1	2	0	1	9
Miscellaneous	0	1	0	0	0	1	1	0	0	0	3
Total no. rejected	16	22	13	17	16	13	11	20	14	18	160
Total no. inspected	790	800	770	800	800	790	810	840	790	810	8000
% rejected	2·0	2·7	1·7	2·1	2·0	1·6	1·3	2·4	1·8	2·2	2·0
Date	November	3	4	5	6	7	10	11	12	13	14	

Totals

Fig 15·1 Example of a chart for % defective

215

or rejects), and the sample size varies. In almost any production shop, the number produced varies slightly from day to day, so if the results of 100% inspection of the product are used to provide data for the quality control chart, the 'sample' size varies correspondingly. The steps to set up this chart are in principle the same as we used for a process based chart for variables in Chapter 14. The example concerns a shop making electronic assemblies, and we proceed as follows.

1   We start with a blank chart, designed as Figure 15.1.
   a   At the top we put information which will enable us to identify the job. This will be especially useful later, if we should have trouble with this assembly, and need to investigate what went wrong.
   b   Below this we plot the percentage rejected. Make the scale long enough to include not only the upper control limits, but also any point which might have to be plotted above them. Out of limit points must be investigated and corrected immediately, and the impact on the shop floor is lost if they cannot be shown on the chart and boldly ringed in red.
   c   The bottom section of the chart can be designed to suit requirements, but it should *always* include an analysis of the reasons for rejection. It may also be useful to analyse by machine, process, operator, materiel or inspector. Various examples are included in this chapter.
   d   Vertical addition of the reasons for rejection, gives the total number rejected each day, below which the inspector puts the total number inspected. One over the other then gives the percentage rejected each day, which the inspector plots. Thus for 3rd November we have:

$$\% \text{ rejected} = \frac{16}{790} \times 100\% = 2.0\%$$

   e   The bottom line of the chart identifies the work. In Figure 15.1 each days work is being treated as a lot, but identification could be by batch, shift, individual assemblies etc.

2   We set up the process and start producing, and instruct the inspector to record his/her results.

3   When we have 10 or more typical settled points, we are ready to calculate the control limits. As before (Section 14.4 paragraph 3), if the process ran worse than usual during the observational run, the

points concerned should not be used, and must be eliminated. Since this is not always easy to do, it is best to repeat the whole run if time permits.

a   Estimate the process average, in order to provide a datum line for the control limits.

$$\therefore \text{Process average} = \bar{p}$$
$$= \frac{\text{Total no. rejected}}{\text{Total no. inspected}} = \frac{160}{8000} \times 100\% = 2.0\%$$

b   Estimate the standard deviation, using the formula given below.

$$\text{Average sample size} = \bar{n} = \frac{8000}{10} = 800$$

$$\text{Standard deviation} = \sigma = \sqrt{\frac{\bar{p}(100 - \bar{p})}{\bar{n}}} =$$

$$\sqrt{\frac{2.0(100 - 2.0)}{800}} = 0.495\%$$

c   Then outer control limits = process average $\pm 3\sigma$
and inner control limits = process average $\pm 2\sigma$

Strictly speaking we are now dealing with a binomial distribution, but it is convenient to treat it as though it was still Normally distributed. As this is an approximation however, there is no point in using 3.09σ and 1.96σ as we did in Chapters 12 to 14, so we settle for 3σ and 2σ.

$$\therefore \text{Outer control limits}$$
$$= \bar{p} \pm 3\sigma = 2.0 \pm 3(0.495) = 0.515\% \text{ and } 3.485\%$$
$$\text{Inner control limits}$$
$$= \bar{p} \pm 2\sigma = 2.0 \pm 2(0.495) = 1.010\% \text{ and } 2.990\%$$

These control limits are now drawn on the chart as shown. We should not be tempted to round off the calculations too quickly. It is useful in practice if control limits take odd positions which are not likely to be occupied by plotted points. Any point on the chart is then decisively in or out of control.

Notice that throughout quality control charts, n is always the number of items which contribute to one point on the chart, and *not* the total number reviewed when the limits were set.

15.4   The meaning of the control limits

Attribute charts are based on the capability of the process at the time the control limits were set. Thus in Figure 15.1 an average of

2.0% of work was being rejected at the time the process was observed. We are always dealing with samples. Even if, as in this case, we do 100% inspection, each days work is itself a sample of our long run production. Hence even if the process average really does stay at $\bar{p} = 2.0\%$ for evermore, the actual percentage of defectives observed each day will vary slightly. The control limits enable us to tell whether such variations are due to sampling differences, or whether the process average really has changed. It is usual to use probabilities from the Normal distribution as shown in Figure 11.16, even though it is not strictly correct to do so. Hence:

The *outer control limits* are regarded as being set at a probability of 1 in 1000 on each side. Since this is a very low probability, it means that in practice all plotted points should lie within the two outer control limits. Even one point outside means that the process average has changed, and we must investigate why.

The *inner control limits* are set at a probability of 1 in 40 on each side. Theoretically 1 point in 40 can be on or slightly beyond each inner limit, without indicating a change in the process average, but any of the following mean that the process average has changed.

a   Two points near together on or beyond an inner control limit.
b   One point so far beyond the inner control limit that it has nearly reached the outer limit.

15.5 Meaning of the lower control limits

It is at first surprising to find that we have lower control limits on charts for defectives or defects. Obviously if the process suddenly makes less defective work than usual this is all to the good. This is true, but we still need to be informed, and we then proceed as follows.

1   Check that inspection is still going as planned. The *apparent* number or percentage of defectives will drop if:

a   A new or inexperienced inspector misses some of the defective work.
b   Inspection gets behind production. If the inspectors for any reason, fail to keep up with production, there is a risk that at the end of the day they will work out their percentage as 'number of defectives found so far' divided by 'total made by production unit'. This will give a low point on the chart, followed tomorrow by an extra high point when they catch up. Notice that on the charts we have asked for the number *inspected* to be entered rather than the number *made*. Hopefully these two quantities are the same, but where this is not so, it is the number inspected which should be used.

218

2   If our inspection is all right, then it may be that our process really is better temporarily, in which case there must be some temporary change which caused it. If we can find what it is, maybe we can make that improvement permanent. To do this we need to be informed quickly when the improvement occurs, and for this we need the lower control limits on the chart. I had a case in which the percentage of defectives from a process suddenly dropped substantially below the lower control limits. Immediate investigation revealed that one of the raw materials being used was appreciably wet, and this was due to carelessness in bringing that batch from the stores on a wet day. Tests established that this particular operation was indeed improved if a certain amount of water was added to the ingredients. In future we stipulated that:

a   The ingredients must be dry.
b   A controlled amount of pure water would be added during the production operation.

15.6   Practical interpretation of a quality control chart for attributes

We instruct the inspector that every known change in processing conditions is to be entered on the chart, exactly where that change occurred. Deliberate changes will include the following.

1   The start of a new batch of materiel. Obviously if the product quality suddenly gets better or worse exactly where a new batch of materiel has been started, it is almost certain that the new batch is something to do with the change.
2   Different operator, especially if one is inexperienced.
3   Different inspector. Attributes are very subjective, and it is common to find that one inspector rejects something which his colleague will pass, and this will cause a sudden apparent change in quality. See Chapter 3 for help with this problem.
4   A different machine or process is used, or adjustments are made to the same machine.
5   A change in operating methods.

Make sure that unintentional changes are also entered, for example, 'batch dropped on floor', 'left in chemical bath too long' etc. If such mistakes are entered, we do not waste a lot of time looking for the cause of the resulting drop in quality.

In designing an attribute chart, we must ask ourselves, 'What information would be useful in reducing the number of defectives we make?'

1   The example in Figure 15.1 includes an analysis by type of fault. When we add up the total rejected and the total inspected over 10 days, we also total the 'reason for rejection' lines. This tells us at once that:

a   61 our of 160 = 38% of our rejections were due to dry joints. We should be able to find the cause, and reduce this considerably.

b   Similarly 45 out of 160 = 28% of our rejections were due to wrong components being used. We must have a close look at assembly, and maybe previous storage, to see what can be done to improve methods.

c   Some 38 out of 160 = 24% of our rejections were due to faulty components, and we shall have to look at vendor appraisal, goods inwards inspection and possibly handling within our own company.

Notice that this means that 38% + 28% + 24% = 90% of our rejections come from only 3 causes. This is a common pattern, which we shall discuss further in Chapter 16.

2   It is often useful on the chart to divide defectives into 'operator faults', 'machine or process faults' and 'materiel faults'. In this case make sure that what is recorded under operator faults, really is due to the operators. The same applies in principle to the other categories. We do not want to waste time investigating an apparently troublesome machine, if it is really the materiel which is causing the trouble.

3   The next step may be to show individual operators how they personally are doing. Sometimes however operators have a feeling that plotting the number or percentage defectives is 'putting all our sins on the wall for everyone to see'. I have found a simple solution to this. Plot the chart the other way up, and show the number or percentage good. The chart itself is exactly the same, and the control limits are unchanged. Thus from Figure 15.1 we have:

Process average good = $\bar{q}$ = (100 − 2) = 98%

Standard deviation   = σ = $\sqrt{\dfrac{\bar{q}(100 - \bar{q})}{\bar{n}}}$ =

$\sqrt{\dfrac{98 \times 2)}{800}}$ = 0.495% as before.

We set the control limits = $\bar{q} \pm 3\sigma$ and = $\bar{q} \pm 2\sigma$

Now the chart, as Figure 15.2 shows 'how good we are', and is often much more acceptable.

4   Be careful about using lower control limits on the shop floor. Thus apparently Figure 15.1 says to the operator, 'try to make at least 1% rejects, and on no account make less than ½%'! If the meaning of the lower control limits cannot be properly explained to operators, it may be best to omit them from shop floor charts, and only use them on charts which are kept in the quality engineer's office.

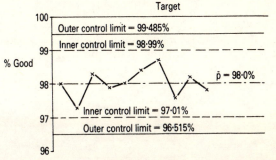

Fig 15·2 Part of fig 15·1, plotted to show % good

I have had considerable success with attribute charts which show only the upper inner control limit. I now call this a target, and draw it on the chart a little lower than its theoretical position. I then say to the operators, 'let's see if we can keep below the target'. If they succeed, and they often do, we have achieved a new and slightly improved process average. A new, but reasonable even lower target can then be set, and so on.

15.7   Making corrections when attribute charts reveal quality deficiencies

When an attribute chart shows a significant deterioration in quality, we must examine it carefully. If it is well designed, it will tell us almost exactly what is wrong. Notice in particular the pattern by which the process gets out of control, and which types of rejects account for the increase. The following are examples.

a   Sudden Change
If the reject rate suddenly jumps up, as shown in Figure 15.3a, there must be a corresponding sudden change in processing conditions. Hopefully the inspector has put a note on the chart at that point, e.g. new batch of materiel, different operator etc. Use the analysis by type of fault to pin point exactly what has gone wrong.

221

b Gradual Increase in Rejects

Try to determine exactly where the drift starts. Unfortunately, as Figure 15.3b shows, this is not always clear cut; there may be 2 or 3 points (A, B, C) at which it could have started. Any notes about process changes should help. Look for a corresponding gradual change in processing conditions, and again use the reject analysis to find out what has altered.

c Cyclic Patterns

Sometimes the pattern is cyclic. Thus in Figure 15.3c we have to find out what goes wrong first thing in the morning. Again the reject analysis should help.

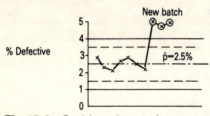

Fig 15·3a Sudden change in process average

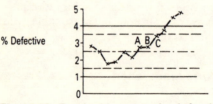

Fig 15·3b Gradual increase in defectives

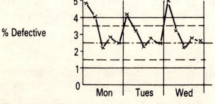

Fig 15·3c Example of a cyclic pattern

222

Some people do not use the inner control limits on attribute charts. This is a pity because the chart is then less sensitive, and the 'rule of 7' often has to be used to replace them. This rule says that the process average has changed if any of the following occur.

a   7 successive points all above the process average, or 7 successive points all below average.

b   7 successive points each rising above the previous point, or 7 successive points all falling.

The rule itself is sound, but it is inconvenient to apply to the shop floor. It is much easier to use the inner control limits. a and b above are unlikely to occur without crossing the inner limits. Indeed the inner control limits usually react quicker than the rule of 7.

15.8   Proportion defective chart

Sometimes charts for proportion defective are used. In this method our example in Figure 15.1 modifies as follows.

Process average =

$$\bar{p} = \frac{\text{Total number rejected}}{\text{Total number inspected}} = \frac{160}{8000} = 0.02$$

Standard deviation

$$= \sqrt{\frac{\bar{p}(1 - \bar{p})}{\bar{n}}} = \sqrt{\frac{0.02(1 - 0.02)}{800}} = 0.00495$$

NB Note that if this method is used the process average $\bar{p}$ must be expressed as a *proportion and not a percentage* defective.

This practice is statistically correct, but has no practical advantages. Indeed it has the disadvantage that shop floor workers will not understand proportion defective as easily as they will percentage.

15.9   Dealing with large variations in sample size

In Section 15.3 paragraph 3b, we calculated the standard deviation using the average sample size. This is satisfactory so long as the sample size does not vary by more than ± 25%. In the unlikely event that it does, the control limit for that point should be recalculated, using the $\bar{p}$ value already established for the process as a whole, and the actual number of items n on which that point is based. This means that each point concerned has its own individual control limits.

223

15.10 np chart for number defective

Where the sample size is constant, it is easier to plot the number defective rather than the percentage. The chart is still set up basically as Section 15.3, and we need only note the differences in calculating the process average and standard deviation. Our example in Figure 15.4 comes from a grey iron foundry making a small casting on a long run basis. The castings are batched into uniform lots of 500 and 100% inspected. Results shown are for 15 consecutive batches, when the process was in a stable condition. (In a foundry defective castings usually have to be scrapped and recast.)

1   Control limits
These are calculated as follows.

Total number of castings scrapped   = 185
No. of batches observed   15

$\therefore$ Process average $= \dfrac{\text{Total scrapped}}{\text{No. of batches}} = \bar{c}$

$$= \frac{185}{15} = 12.33 \text{ per batch}$$

Constant batch (i.e. sample) size   n = 500

Standard deviation for no. defective $= \sqrt{\bar{c}\left[1 - \dfrac{\bar{c}}{n}\right]}$

$$= \sqrt{12.33\left[1 - \frac{12.33}{500}\right]} = 3.47$$

$\therefore$ Inner control limits
$\qquad\qquad = \bar{c} \pm 2\sigma = 12.33 \pm 2(3.47) = 5.40 \text{ and } 19.27$
$\qquad$ Outer control limits
$\qquad\qquad = \bar{c} \pm 3\sigma = 12.33 \pm 3(3.47) = 1.93 \text{ and } 22.74$

2   Chart analysis
If we total the number scrapped for each reason we get:

	No scrapped	% of total scrap
sand inclusions	15	8.1%
broken/damaged	56	30.3
slag inclusions	31	16.7
misrun	76	41.1
blow	5	2.7
miscellaneous	2	1.1

Dept = Foundry	Section Grey Iron		Part No. XY640				Supervisor Vic Tucker							
Batch No.	1	2	3	4	5	6	7	8	9	10	11	12	13	14	15	

No scrap per batch of 500 (i.e. No defective)

26 24 22 20 18 16 14 12 10 8 6 4 2 0 — Outer control limit / Inner control limit / proc. av = $\bar{c}$ / Inner control limit / Outer control limit — Totals for 15 batches

Reason Scrapped		1	2	3	4	5	6	7	8	9	10	11	12	13	14	15	
	Sand inclusions	1	2	1	2	2	0	1	2	0	1	0	1	1	0	1	15
	Broken/damaged	4	2	5	3	4	3	6	6	2	4	3	5	4	2	3	56
	Slag inclusions	2	1	2	2	1	3	2	2	0	3	2	2	4	2	3	31
	Misrun	6	5	7	6	3	4	5	7	5	4	6	6	3	5	4	76
	Blow	0	0	1	0	1	0	1	0	0	0	0	1	1	0	0	5
	Misc	1	0	1	0	0	0	0	0	0	0	0	0	0	0	0	2
Total no. scrap.		14	10	17	13	11	10	15	17	7	12	11	15	13	9	11	185

Fig 15·4 np Chart for no. defective

We draw the following conclusions.

a   Misruns and slag inclusions together account for (41.1 + 16.7) = 57.8% of the total scrap. These must originate in either the cupola or metal pouring operations.

b   30.3% of scrap are broken or damaged. This must occur after pouring, probably during fettling.

With a bit of careful investigation, we should be able to reduce both of the above considerably.

(There are in fact over 80 reasons why a casting can be scrapped. For simplicity we have included only 5 in our example).

3 Traditional Formulae

Traditional text books usually quote the formulae for number defective charts as follows.

Process average $\qquad = \quad n\bar{p}$

Standard deviation $\quad = \sqrt{n\bar{p}\left[1 - \dfrac{n\bar{p}}{n}\right]}$

However no one would work out these quantities from n and $\bar{p}$, and those who use these formulae must mentally substitute $\bar{c}$ for $n\bar{p}$.

225

15.11 c chart for number of defects

The remaining two charts in this chapter concern defects. These are minor undesirable features such as small scratches, which individually do not render the item defective and therefore rejectable. Strictly speaking we are now dealing with a Poisson distribution, although this need not worry the reader.

The c chart is used where the sample size is constant. Basically it is set up as explained in Section 15.3, and we need only note the differences. The example in Figure 15.5 concerns the manufacture of glass sheets in batches of constant size, and results are given for 10 successive settled batches.

1   Control Limits
We calculate as follows.

Process average =

$$\bar{c} = \frac{\text{Total no. of defects}}{\text{No. of batches observed}} = \frac{117}{10} = 11.7 \text{ defects per batch}$$

Standard deviation = $\sigma = \sqrt{\bar{c}} = \sqrt{11.7} = 3.42$

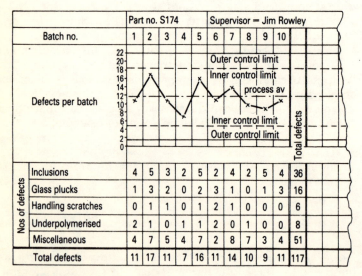

		Part no. S174					Supervisor = Jim Rowley							
Batch no.		1	2	3	4	5	6	7	8	9	10			
Defects per batch													Total defects	
Nos of defects	Inclusions	4	5	3	2	5	2	4	2	5	4	36		
	Glass plucks	1	3	2	0	2	3	1	0	1	3	16		
	Handling scratches	0	1	1	0	1	2	1	0	0	0	6		
	Underpolymerised	2	1	0	1	1	2	0	1	0	0	8		
	Miscellaneous	4	7	5	4	7	2	8	7	3	4	51		
Total defects		11	17	11	7	16	11	14	10	9	11	117		

Fig 15·5 Example of c chart

226

In the above we have used the term 'no. of batches' as being correct for that example. In the general sense it is the number of sub-groups into which the work has been divided, and hence quite simply the number of points on the chart during the observational period.

Inner control limits =
$$\bar{c} \pm 2\sigma = 11.7 \pm 2(3.42) = 4.86 \text{ and } 18.54$$
Outer control limits =
$$\bar{c} \pm 3\sigma = 11.7 \pm 3(3.42) = 1.44 \text{ and } 21.96$$

2   Chart analysis

a   Readers will notice that in carrying out the above calculations, we did not need to know the batch or sub-group size. Statistically this is true, but practically the batch size is a vital piece of information. Thus if in our example, the batch size was say 10,000 sheets, with an average of 11.7 defects per batch, the people concerned would be doing extremely well. On the other hand if the batch size had been only 5 sheets, with 11.7 defects per batch, their performance would be dreadful.

b   Analysis for type of defect gives.

Inclusions	36 defects	30.8% of total defects
Glass plucks	16 "	13.7% " "
Handling scratches	6 "	5.1% " "
Underpolymerised	8 "	6.8% " "
Miscellaneous	51 "	43.6% " "

Top of the list we find 'miscellaneous' at 43.6% of total defects. This is unsatisfactory because, as we do not know what types of defect they are, it will be difficult to take corrective action. It is often convenient to have a miscellaneous line on a quality control chart, because we cannot foresee every possible type of defect, but it should only contain the odd unclassified item. Where as in this case, miscellaneous dominates the analysis, we must find out what types of defect it contains, and add one or more named lines to the chart.

c   Inclusions at 30.8% head the classified list, and we must find out why they occur and act to reduce them.

15.12   u chart for number of defects per item

The u chart is used where we have defects from a variable sample size. The situation is similar to the p chart for defectives, which we solved by plotting the percentage or proportion defective. Similarly for the u chart, we plot the number of defects per item, or if more convenient per 100 or even 1000 items. Again the steps to set this chart up are similar to Section 15.3, and we have only to note the differences. Our example concerns a section of a paint shop who spray and stove a special panel. Results were recorded over a two week period, and the day and nightshift results were recorded separately. Provision on the chart has also been made for reviewing results at the end of each week. This is useful in many situations.

Preliminary inspection of the chart shows that we are averaging about 15 defects per shift, on an output of around 250 panels. If we do what is statistically correct, and plot defects per panel, we get:

$$\text{No. of defects per panel} = \frac{15}{250} = 0.06$$

This would not be very meaningful to the operators, so we have decided to plot the number of defects per 100 panels. Hence the first point on the chart is:

$$\therefore \text{No. of defects per 100 panels} =$$
$$\frac{\text{No. of defects}}{\text{No. of panels}} \times 100 = \frac{22}{250} \times 100 = 8.8$$

1 Control limits

Process average =
$$\bar{u} = \frac{\text{Total no. of defects}}{\text{Total no. inspected}} \times 100 = \frac{300}{4755} \times 100$$
$$= 6.31 \text{ defects/100 panels}$$

Average sample size $= \bar{n} = \dfrac{\text{Total no. of defects}}{\text{No. of shifts}}$
$$= \frac{4755}{20} = 237.75 \text{ panels} = 2.38 \text{ lots of 100 panels each}$$

Standard deviation $= \sqrt{\dfrac{\bar{u}}{\bar{n}}} = \sqrt{\dfrac{6.31}{2.38}} = 1.629$

$\therefore$ Inner control limits =
$$\bar{u} \pm 2\sigma = 6.31 \pm 2(1.629) = 3.05 \text{ and } 9.57$$
Outer control limits =
$$\bar{u} \pm 3\sigma = 6.31 \pm 3(1.629) = 1.42 \text{ and } 11.20$$

2 Chart analysis

a A quality control chart is a mine of information, and this one is richer than most. We can analyse it as follows.

Dirt or dust   =   15 defects = 5% of total defects
Dents or dings =   26   "   = 8.7%   "   "
Finger marks   = 129   "   = 43%   "   " ⎫
Damaged paint= 89   "   = 29.7% "   " ⎬ = 72.7% together
Uneven paint   =   26   "   = 8.7%   "   " ⎭

Notice that 43% of total defects are due to finger marks and another 29.7% are due to paint damage. This makes 72.7% of total defects caused either by careless handling, or because the handling methods, equipment etc. are unsatisfactory. We should be able to reduce this considerably, preferably by improving handling methods.

b Dayshift versus nightshift
If we analyse by shift, we get the following.

	Dayshift	Nightshift
Dirt and dust	6 defects	9 defects
Dents and dings	12 "	14 "
Finger marks	78 "	51 "
Damaged paint	56 "	33 "
Uneven paint	16 "	10 "
Miscellaneous	9 "	6 "
Total defects by shift	177	123
Total panels inspected	2495	2260
Defects per 100 panels	7.1	5.4

It appears that dayshift are appreciably worse than nightshift, and that the increase in defects is due to finger marks, damaged and uneven paint. We must consider this information in conjunction with our conclusions in *a* above.

c Mondays
There is some indication that Monday dayshift is bad. This may be due to a 'Monday morning feeling' amongst the operators, but it may also be because the plant has not stabilised after the week end shut down.

15.13   Choice of a quality control chart for attributes

The following is a guide to help decide which of the four standard attribute charts should be used in a particular case.

Dept Paint Shop **Section** C **Part** **Panel** **Part no.** B517 **Supervisor** Bob Clark **Plant no.** A6147

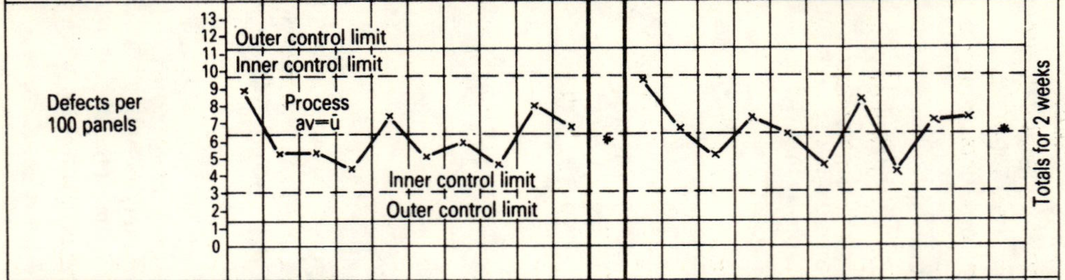

Date May
Shift (night/day)

Chart — **Defects per 100 panels** (scale 0–13), plotted as a u-chart with lines labelled:
- Outer control limit
- Inner control limit
- Process av = ū
- Inner control limit
- Outer control limit

Totals for 2 weeks (column at right)

Nos of defects	13 D	13 N	14 D	14 N	15 D	15 N	16 D	16 N	17 D	17 N	1-wk total	20 D	20 N	21 D	21 N	22 D	22 N	23 D	23 N	24 D	24 N	2-wk total	Totals for 2 weeks
Dirt/dust	1	0	1	1	0	2	0	1	0	1	7	1	0	0	2	0	0	1	1	1	2	8	15
Dents/dings	2	3	0	0	3	0	2	1	1	1	13	2	3	0	4	0	1	1	1	0	1	13	26
Finger marks	8	5	7	4	6	5	7	4	9	4	59	6	8	8	5	9	5	11	4	8	6	70	129
Damaged paint spot	6	3	5	3	7	3	5	2	8	4	46	6	2	4	6	4	5	7	2	7	0	43	89
Uneven paint spot	4	1	0	1	2	1	0	2	1	0	12	6	2	0	1	2	0	1	1	0	1	14	26
Misc.	1	0	1	2	0	1	1	2	0	0	8	1	1	1	0	1	0	1	1	0	1	7	15
Total no. defects	22	12	14	11	18	12	15	12	19	10	145	22	16	13	18	16	11	22	10	16	11	155	300
Total panels inspected	250	230	265	255	245	240	255	260	240	150	2390	235	240	255	245	255	245	265	245	230	150	2365	4755
Defects per 100 panels	8·8	5·2	5·3	4·3	7·3	5·0	5·9	4·6	7·9	6·7	6·1	9·4	6·7	5·1	7·3	6·3	4·5	8·3	4·1	7·0	7·3	6·6	6·3

Fig 15·6 Example of a u-chart

1   Distinguish between defectives and defects
a   Defective means the item is unacceptable because it does not
      comply with drawing or specification.
      e.g. broken, unusable, scrap, rejects etc.
b   Defect is applied to minor undesirable features which do not
      necessarily make the item unacceptable.
      e.g. tiny scratches, blemishes, dents, dings etc.

2   Charts for defectives
Decide whether the sample size (i.e. the number of items checked
for each point on the chart), is constant or varies.
a   Sample size varies – use a p-chart for percentage defective as
      Section 15.3.

Mean = $\bar{p}$ in %. Standard deviation = $\sigma = \sqrt{\dfrac{\bar{p}(100 - \bar{p})}{\bar{n}}}$

If a *proportion* defective chart is used as section 15.8

Mean = $\bar{p}$ as a proportion
Standard deviation = $\sigma = \sqrt{\dfrac{\bar{p}(1 - \bar{p})}{\bar{n}}}$

b   Sample size constant – use an np-chart for *number defective* as
      section 15.10

Mean = $\bar{c}$ (=$n\bar{p}$)
Standard deviation = $\sigma = \sqrt{\left[1 - \dfrac{\bar{c}}{n}\right]}$

3   Charts for defects
a   Sample size constant – use a c-chart for number of defects as
      section 15.11

Mean = $\bar{c}$ Standard deviation = $\sigma = \sqrt{\bar{c}}$

b   Sample size varies – use a u-chart for defects per item as
      section 15.12

Mean = $\bar{u}$ Standard deviation = $\sigma = \sqrt{\dfrac{\bar{u}}{\bar{n}}}$

15.14   Questions
1a   Outline the circumstances in which a control chart for
defectives would probably be preferred to one for variables.
(7 marks)

1b A department making 500 ties per day does 100 per cent visual inspection, and finds that over a typical period of 20 working days, the numbers of ties rejected are respectively as follows:

13 10 18 12 12 9 11 13 11 16 13 10 14 15 10 9 17 12 12 13

Without drawing the charts themselves, calculate the position of the inner and outer control limits for both the upper and lower positions for

(i)	a percentage defective chart	*(6 marks)*
(ii)	a number defective chart	*(6 marks)*

1c What are the merits of using each type of chart in *(i)* and *(ii)* above?   *(6 marks)*

Author's note.   The above question does not ask for the charts to be plotted, because it would then take more than the allowed time to complete. However the reader may like to plot it out for his own satisfaction.

A further question involving defective charts is given at the end of Chapter 16.

CHAPTER 16

CORRECTION OF QUALITY DEFICIENCIES

16.1 Sometimes the best-made plans go awry

If our quality planning and execution are perfect, then we shall have no scrap and no corrective operations. Since we shall not always achieve perfection, we must provide in our system for the correction of such quality deficiencies as may occur.

Thus, sometimes a batch gets right to the end of the production line and, just when it is due to go out, the final inspector finds a reason why it must be rejected. When this happens, the immediate panic is usually to correct that batch and dispatch it. After all, it is now overdue, and the customer is rapidly getting anxious because he has not received it. This is right and proper; such corrections must usually be done as a matter of urgency.

In our anxiety to get that batch out, however, we often forget that unless we correct the *cause* of that quality deficiency, the next time we make another batch of that type the chances are that the same thing will happen again and we shall have another batch of urgent corrections on our hands.

16.2 Sifting the evidence

Before we can come to any conclusions about what is wrong, we must carefully and systematically analyse and study the evidence. If we have a planned quality control system in operation, then we shall have quality control charts, etc., available to assist our investigation. However, even if we are just starting planned quality control, our investigations will still follow similar lines except that we shall not have so much information readily available to us. Although any investigation must be adapted to suit the type of production concerned and our experience with it, the following is fairly typical of the steps we shall expect to take.

16.3   Has the work been fairly rejected?

To answer this question we must begin by making sure that the quality standard demanded is clearly defined in practical terms. All variables must have tolerances, and attributes must have suitable comparative standards (Sections 3.3 to 3.8).

16.3.1   Rejection by our own inspectors

Where work has been rejected by our own inspectors, we can ask them to demonstrate its shortcomings. Inexperienced inspectors, faulty test equipment, etc., may cause satisfactory work to be rejected, and we must make sure that the fault is real, before we spend a lot of time tracing it. It it is, then we must be quite clear how the work or process falls short of the minimum standard required.

16.3.2   Rejection by our customers

Rejections by customers are liable to be more serious, because of their damaging effect on our company's reputation. An immediate apology and a promise of investigation is desirable in the interests of good relations, even if it subsequently transpires that our quality is all right, and that it is our customer who is wrong.

   If we are quite clear what our customer is complaining about, then we can proceed with the investigation. If not, we may have to pay him a visit and/or arrange for some of the rejected work to be returned to us. It is not uncommon for this first contact to reveal the basic cause of the trouble. For example:

1   Our customer's idea of the quality standard may be different from our own. Who is right is a matter for commercial negotiation. Remember, however, that our selling price will have been based on

our conception of the quality standard and that, if the standard is changed, our price may also require adjustment. Clearly from the factory point of view, if our production quality control system has produced the quality standard for which it was asked, it is no good blaming it if that standard proves to be incorrect. The fault may still, of course, lie in that part of our quality assurance which is within the orbit of our salesmen and designers.

2   Our customer's measuring equipment may be different from our own, and we shall have to co-operate in comparing the accuracy and precision of both sets of equipment. (See Section 3.5)

If it transpires that both the quality standard and its method of measurement are satisfactory, then we are left with two major questions to answer:

a   How did it happen that incorrect quality was produced in the first place, since our quality control system should have prevented this?

b   Given that the product quality was wrong, how was it possible for it to get through our quality control system undetected, with the result that it was sent out to the customer?

16.4   Assistance from the quality control charts

We must identify what went wrong and correct it. Almost any sort of record is useful at this stage, but it is an occasion when the quality control chart is particularly valuable. From the type of fault concerned, we shall be able to deduce which operators or areas of the production line must be responsible, and so we immediately call for the relevant quality control charts. Even if some months have elapsed since manufacture, and this is common with customer rejections, the charts will still yield the vital information. Thus, they will tell us:

1   Was the quality which was wrong included in the quality schedule or on the quality control chart, as suggested in Sections 8.10 and 8.11? If we did not schedule it for control then we cannot be surprised if it received no particular attention.

2   If control was scheduled, does the chart show that the operator, inspector, etc., claim to have carried out the specified checks? The chart will tell us which operator and inspector are concerned.

3   If the checks were carried out, were any quality difficulties

recorded, and if so what action was taken to overcome them? If no difficulties were recorded, then clearly either the control system was not being operated properly or the system itself is not foolproof.

16.5   Locating the cause of trouble

The source of our trouble must be somewhere in stages 2 and 3 of our quality control system, as given in Sections 1.3 to 1.6. Thus, if we are honest, we shall be obliged to answer 'No' to at least one of the following questions:

1   Was the method of manufacture satisfactory for the quality standard demanded? Did it comply with all the points we discussed in Sections 8.1 to 8.8?
2   Was the tooling and equipment adequate to achieve the quality standard? (Section 8.8.)
3   Was the materiel satisfactory? If not, then we have a triple question:
   a   Why was unsatisfactory materiel used for manufacture?
   b   If the raw materiel or components were bought, how did they get through our goods inwards inspection system as described in Chapters 6 and 7?
   c   If the materiel or components were made in our own factory, what went wrong with the quality control system etc.? How did it happen that they: *(i)* made them wrongly, *(ii)* released them to another department?
4   Were our operators sufficiently trained? Did they know the quality standard and the method by which they were to achieve it? It is unfortunately common to find that things went wrong because the operator was never clearly told what was required.
5   Was our shop floor quality control properly planned and executed?

16.6   Dealing with the 'culprits'

It is no use crying over spilt milk. Scrap which has been made cannot be unmade, and our actions must be directed towards seeing that we do not make another lot of scrap tomorrow. We must try to avoid dressing people down, and if we decide that this must be done, we must do it primarily with an eye to securing their co-operation in future. Unless we do this, we achieve nothing whatever.

16.7 Analysis of scrap and rework – the pareto curve

We can get further information by analysing the scrap and rework itself. A good quality control chart will have been designed to be largely self analysing. Thus in the examples in Figures 15.1, 15.4, 15.5 and 15.6, it is very easy to see the chief types of fault etc. being incurred. The relevant text in Sections 15.3, 15.10, 15.11 and 15.12 show how this information can be analysed. Where such information is not available, we can make a direct analysis. This is particularly useful where we are making a first survey of a department, which has as yet no planned quality control.

The principle is simple. We take a load of defective work and sort it in piles, with one pile for each type of fault. In practice we usually do the sorting on paper, using inspection reports etc. For the following example, we have reviewed all the defective work made by a diecast shop during one particular week. In Table 16.1 we have first listed all the reasons for defective work, *in strict descending order of quantity*. Thus there were more 'misruns' than 'not flat', and more 'not flat' than 'oxide inclusions', and so on. Next we have put the number defective for each reason. We have then converted the number defective into percentage of the total number defective. Adding up shows that there were 277 defective diecastings altogether, so for the first line we have:

$$\text{misrun} = \frac{80}{277} \times 100 = 29\% \text{ etc.}$$

In the last column we show the cumulative percentage defective. Thus we have:

misrun	= 29	= 29%
not flat	= 29 + 25 =	54%
oxide inclusions	= 54 + 16 =	70% and finally,
damaged	= 99 + 1 =	100%

Table 16.1 Data from which the Pareto Curve in Figure 16.1 was plotted

Reason defective	No. defective	% defective	Cumulative % defective
Misrun	80	29	29
Not flat	69	25	54
Oxide inclusions	44	16	70
Cropping burr	28	10	80
Cropping mislocation	25	9	89
Dirty	17	6	95
Incomplete	11	4	99
Damaged	3	1	100
Total	277		

We are now ready to plot the Pareto Curve shown in Figure 16.1. Vertically we put the cumulative percentage defective, using the right hand column of our table, and horizontally we put the reasons defective, in strict descending order of quantity, exactly as the left hand column. Inspection of the Pareto curve and table yields the following information.

Misrun was the worst single cause of defective work at 29% followed by not flat at 25% and oxide inclusions at 16%. We have now taken in a total of 70% of our defective work in only three categories. Clearly, if we wish to reduce the proportion of defective work we must have a drive against misrun, followed by not flat and oxide inclusions. It would be a waste of time to try to eliminate 'incomplete' and 'damaged', because these only account for 5% of the defective work between them. The practical reader will also notice that most of the defective work is coming from the diecasting operation itself, and comparatively little from the subsequent cropping operation.

The graph in Figure 16.1 is called a Pareto curve, after the Italian economist who used it for studying the wealth of Italy. It has a very general application. We almost always find that most of the defective work comes from a small fraction of the total possible causes, in the same way that most of the crimes in Britain are committed by a small fraction of the population. The Pareto curve is

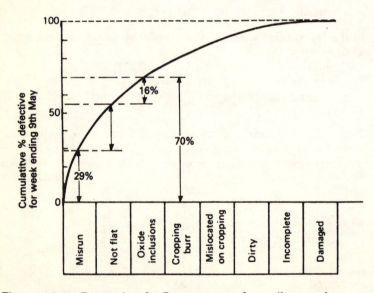

Figure 16.1   Example of a Pareto curve for a diecast shop

sometimes called an 80/20 curve, because we often find that some 80 per cent of the defective works comes from only 20 per cent of the causes.

The Pareto curve can be drawn in various ways to suit the problem. For example:

1 If all of the defective work is the same part number, it is usually convenient to plot in percentage of defective items as in Figure 16.1. If, however, a variety of products is included in the analysis, it is usually best to plot vertically the value in money that is lost due to the defective work. Otherwise, 50 small nuts at 3p each will count more than one complicated part worth several hundred pounds.

2 If we have a short-run shop, working on a variety of part numbers, then horizontally we can make an analysis by part number as well as an analysis by types of defective work. It is not unusual to find that one part number makes a large proportion of the total scrap value. Indeed, this will tend to occur if three conditions are fulfilled:

a The part concerned is made in largish quantities, compared with other production in the shop.
b It tends to run with a high scrap percentage.
c It is a valuable part, so that every time one is scrapped the money loss is large.

3 The following is a summary of some of the many ways in which defectives can be analysed on a Pareto curve.
Vertical Axis – we can plot:
e.g. Cumulative percentage or cumulative number defective
Cumulative cost of defectives, either in actual costs or in percentage of the total cost of defectives.
Cumulative weight, or cumulative numbers of batches (where appropriate). The vertical axis does not have to be plotted cumulatively, although it usually is. Some quality engineers prefer to plot number defective for each separate cause. This yields a diagram in bar chart form.
Horizontal Axis
The possibilities here are endless, and the following merely examples.
Types of scrap, rejects etc.
Part numbers rejected.
Plant, machine, tooling, method used etc. (Two nominally identical machines seldom produce exactly the same amount of defective work).

239

Materiel used. (A machine tool will make a much better job of working mild steel, than it will with say copper, even when the component made is identical).

Operator. (To detect differences between them, and pin point those who need help).

Inspector. (To detect differences between inspectors. On no account assume that these do not exist).

Departments or sections of a department.

Date of manufacture, etc.

16.8 The measles chart

The measles chart is a variation of the Pareto curve, and is useful if the location of the fault in the work is important. Figure 16.2 shows a sketch of a special sealed lamp in which trouble was experienced with leaks at the top, where it was sealed by an injection moulding operation. We, therefore, gave the inspector the factory drawing of the top together with a red pen, and instructed him that every time

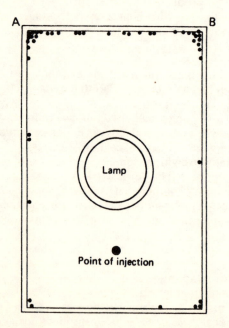

Figure 16.2 Example of a measles chart

he found a leak he was to put a red dot on the drawing, to show where it occurred.

His results are reproduced in Figure 16.2, and they show that most of the leaks occurred in the two corners A and B, which are farthest from the point of injection. We were, therefore, able to cure the trouble by altering the process conditions of injection, e.g. temperature.

Thus a measles chart can be used for any type of production which has a layout drawing, and particularly for electronic apparatus with a circuit diagram.

16.9 Analysis of manufacturing factors contributing to defective work

Sometimes we have no doubt which particular defect is causing most of the rejected work, but we still have to identify which section of the manufacturing process is at fault. For example, suppose we have a heat treatment process where a big proportion of the work finishes up either too hard (over top limit) or too soft (under bottom limit). With the help of the heat treatment engineer, we can set out the things which *might* contribute to our trouble. At this stage we try to include everything which *might* be concerned, and are very careful not to reject any possibility without a fair investigation.

This may be just a straight list, it may take the form of a family tree, or a popular method is to make a *fishbone* or *Ishikawa* diagram of it. An example of a fishbone diagram is shown in Figure 16.3, for the heat-treatment problem above. The central horizontal line sets out the overall objective of the process, in this case the satisfactory heat treatment of forgings. The main branches up and down from this centre line set out all the main sections of the operation within which the cause of the trouble could conceivably lie, e.g. materiel, equipment, operation, etc. Subsidiary branches then break each section down, and further even more subsidiary branches are inserted as required. Now we look at our evidence. The fact that work is sometimes too hard and sometimes too soft shows that, overall, we have a variability problem. Our investigation might proceed like this:

1   We satisfy ourselves that the hardness checks are being done properly. If there is more than one inspector we can compare results to see if they are much the same. Obviously, if heat treatment conditions are adjusted on the basis of inspection results, incompetent inspection could cause chaos.

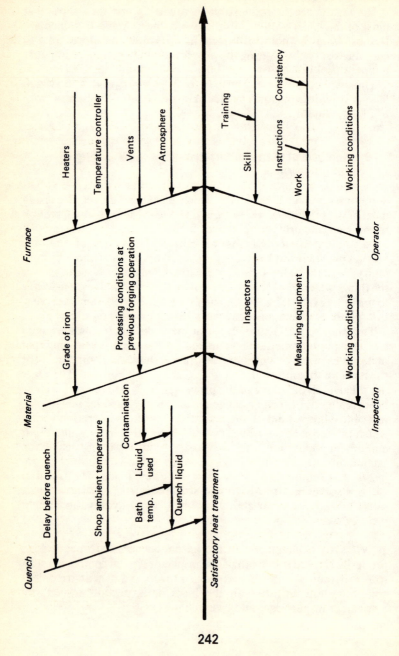

Figure 16.2 Example of a fishbone or Ishikawa diagram

2   We investigate whether the wide variability we are suffering is eliminated if we examine the results from:

a   One part number at a time. In this case, each part number probably requires its own heat treatment conditions, and a common treatment for all part numbers is unsatisfactory.

b   One furnace load at a time. If the variability within a furnace load is reasonably satisfactory, then our problem must be due to changes in *average* conditions from one load to another, for example:

    (i)   The furnace temperature controller allows the temperature to drift. If the controller has a recorder, this is easily checked, but otherwise we may have to make direct observations of it.

    (ii)   The time in the furnace or the quench routine is varying.

3   If variability is great even within one furnace load consisting of one part number only, then we shall suspect the temperature distribution within the furnace. Perhaps a bank of heaters has failed or a vent is blocked, etc.

4   Having analysed the variability into its obvious categories, it will be well worth our while to plot frequency distribution curves, and compare their shape with those given in Sections 11.3 and 11.4.

The approach to any particular problem must clearly depend upon the type of production concerned, but the above gives a fairly typical method.

16.10   Organising for corrections

We must provide a routine for the correction of quality deficiencies, otherwise no effective action is likely to be taken. Thus:

1   We must define what we mean by a quality deficiency which justifies corrective action. This will depend upon the type of work, etc., but the following are examples:

a   'Any part making more than 7% scrap.'

b   'Any machine which runs out of limit at a rate exceeding 15 times per 100 hours.'

2   The term 'quality deficiency' will sound pompous to the shop floor, so we shall need something more down-to-earth. The word

'Squawk' is useful. It creates the right mental image of someone calling urgently for the trouble to be put right.

3   We must arrange for squawks to be identified quickly. Where charts are used, we may ask the operators and inspectors to collect all charts which have been used into a single container, so that the quality engineer can analyse them for squawks.

4   Once identified, we must see that all available information about a squawk is immediately fed to the person detailed to take action. For example, it may be fed to the section supervisor or the planning engineer, etc. The person so detailed must be responsible for seeing that action is always taken, even if a minority of squawks is not within his sphere of responsibility. In such cases, he must coordinate effective action with the person who is responsible.

5   Unless the department concerned is small, we shall need an organised feedback showing what action has been taken, otherwise we shall soon find that those concerned 'just haven't had a chance to do anything about squawks' for a month or so!' Sometimes, an even more complicated system is required. For instance, where a method is unsatisfactory, the planning engineer may design or modify a jig, but this will achieve nothing unless we ensure that the jig is made and tested.

6   This brings us to the problem of setting the squawk value. For example, why did we say 7 per cent scrap in (1a) above, rather than any other value. Strictly speaking, a quality fault is worth correcting if what will be saved by doing so exceeds the cost of correction. In practice, we must also consider our corrective capacity. If the supervisors, engineers, etc., in a department can only deal effectively with two squawks per day, it is no good setting a squawk limit which throws up an average of four, because in attempting to deal with all four they are liable to effectively complete very few. Therefore, the squawk limit must be set so that the rate at which they are thrown up roughly equals the rate at which they can be corrected.

16.11   Questions

1   In a glass-making factory the numbers of defects per batch of 100 pieces of glass over a representative period were sub-divided as follows:

Batch No.	1	2	3	4	5	6	7	8	9	10	11	12	13	14	15	16	17	18	19	20
Glass plucks	1	0	2	1	3	0	1	1	2	0	0	1	2	1	1	0	0	1	2	1
Under-polymerised	0	0	1	0	1	0	0	1	1	0	0	1	0	1	0	2	0	1	0	1
Inclusions	3	3	2	3	3	4	2	3	4	3	2	3	3	5	2	4	3	1	3	4
Handling scratches	0	0	0	0	1	0	0	0	0	1	1	0	0	0	0	1	0	1	0	0
Miscellaneous	0	0	1	0	0	0	1	0	0	0	0	1	0	0	1	0	1	0	0	0

1a Draw a quality control chart for the total number of defects per batch, complete with inner and outer control limits, and plot the above data on it.
(17 marks)

1b Draw a Pareto curve for the whole of the data, analysing it by defect.
(8 marks)

2a Explain, in general terms, the principles involved in setting about locating and correcting the causes of quality deficiencies on a production line. *(12 marks)*

2b Describe how these principles have been or could be applied to a production line or service industry with which you are familiar *(13 marks)*

PART FOUR

THE DESIGN, ORGANISATION AND INTRODUCTION OF A QUALITY CONTROL SYSTEM

CHAPTER 17

LAUNCHING QUALITY CONTROL

17.1 Company organisation for quality

In Chapter 1, we agreed that everybody in a company has some contribution to make to quality and that, therefore, 'quality is everybody's business'. Unfortunately, if responsibility for quality is so wide, there is a real risk that in practice it will be nobody's business. To avoid this, overall responsibility for co-ordinating the company quality effort must be given to somebody, but the question is to whom.

As quality concerns everybody, the only person who is logically responsible for all quality is the very top man, for example the managing director, but he can seldom spare the necessary time. Therefore, responsibility for quality is usually delegated, and again we ask 'To whom should responsibility go?' There is no single answer to this and probably the perfect solution is yet to be found. In practice, the quality organisation of most companies is along the lines of one of the following.

17.1.1 Chief inspector type

Responsibility for quality co-ordination is delegated to a chief inspector, who controls the inspection organisation. His approval is necessary before anything is dispatched from the factory to the customer, and often he must also approve work before it can leave one department for another. His authority over the production departments is usually indirect. He cannot stop them from producing defective work, but he can stop them from dispatching it to another department or to the customer. Often, he will be called quality manager rather than chief inspector, and if he lives up to his name, he will do everything he can to assist the production departments to make right first time.

17.1.2 Advisory type

The quality manager may have a purely advisory role. He will help any department, including inspection, to solve its quality problems. He thus has what in management theory would be called a functional role, similar to that of production engineer, the safety officer, etc., and, like them, he usually needs some degree of authority to be successful. Thus, if a safety officer 'advises' the use of a particular guard, the department concerned is normally expected to act on this advice. Similarly, for this system to be successful, departments must be prepared to accept the advice of the quality manager.

17.1.3 Full authority for quality

In most companies, the quality manager is a very important person. He may be a director, and he has far-reaching powers to control quality. This type of quality organisation is discussed further in Chapter 30.

17.1 The quality role of top management

Whatever the quality organisation, it is essential that top management should back the quality effort, and that they should be seen to back it. There is always a risk that, having appointed a quality manager, top management will assume that quality is now taken care of and that they can forget all about it.

17.3 Putting management in the picture

The introduction of quality control is both hard work and very time consuming and, therefore, in general it can only be done one department at a time. Wherever we decide to start, we must first explain our objectives to the people concerned.

We begin with the managers or equivalent top line of supervision. It is best if the managing director or similar very senior man does this, so that the managers realise that quality control has his backing. Typical of what he may say will be that:

1   The board of directors has decided to introduce quality control, and they request the manager's help in doing this.
2   The quality manager will be responsible for co-ordinating the effort.
3   In each department a careful investigation will first be made, and proposals will then be fully discussed with the managers concerned and their approval obtained before anything in that department is changed.
4   The first department will be. . . .

As some of the managers may be very hazy about what quality control is, it may be useful to show them one of the videos obtainable from the Department of Trade and Industry. The managers will be expected through the normal channels of communication to inform the lower levels of supervision, etc. This will be supplemented by a works notice, etc., and where appropriate, use may be made of the company magazine.

17.4   The shop representatives

The shop representatives, e.g. the shop stewards, must also be told in much the same way as the managers were. Shop representatives will wish to be assured that quality control will not affect earnings. This assurance can be given with confidence, because a reduction in scrap, etc., if it has any effect at all on the earnings of pieceworkers, is likely to slightly increase them.

Detailed proposals are usually best discussed with the individual shop representatives concerned rather than with the general factory representatives, and they must be given every opportunity and encouragement to comment and make suggestions. They will not, of course, be formally asked to approve the proposals, but if it should happen that they obviously disapprove then we shall be well advised to try to understand why before going ahead.

17.5 Deciding where to start

The choice of the first department to receive quality control is often a difficult one, for clearly it is vital for the first project to be a success. Sometimes it seems as though every department has thought up reasons why it should not be first! In such cases, it may be best to start with incoming materiel since, usually, almost everyone will agree that they need improvement. Alternatively, there may be a department which is obviously in quality troubles, and knows it. Such a department may not yet be convinced that quality control will help but it may, nevertheless, be quite prepared to let the quality engineers 'have a go'. (A department which to the quality manager is obviously in trouble with its quality, but which has not itself realised this, may, however, be quite a different proposition to tackle.)

17.6 Starting quality control in a department

Having decided on the department, we first request an interview with the head of that department at a time which is convenient to him. At this, we shall:

1   Request his approval and co-operation. If for any reason this is not forthcoming, it will probably be better to start somewhere else. If we have top management's backing, it is unlikely that we shall encounter a direct refusal. However we might, for example, be told that in the next six weeks there will be panic to complete an urgent contract, and that it would be better to get this out of the way before starting quality control.

2   Assure him that at this stage we shall only observe and collect information. We promise to discuss proposals fully with him before attempting to alter or disturb anything.

3   Make a careful note of any suggestions he makes.

4   Ask him to tell all his supervisors and shop representatives what is afoot, requesting them to co-operate.

CHAPTER 18

COLLECTING AND ANALYSING QUALITY CONTROL INFORMATION

18.1 Collecting information

We now begin a careful collection and analysis of every bit of information which might help. As at this stage it will be difficult to foresee exactly what might be useful, we shall gratefully collect almost anything which is offered. Most information will come from one of the following sources:

1   From conversations with the staff concerned.
2   From departmental records.
3   By direct observation.
4   From quality control and allied literature.

In practice, we do not work down the above points stage by stage, in that order. Sources of information are interlocked, and the order in which it is collected tends to be partly a matter of convenience and partly decided by the apparent importance of the information.

1 Convenience Some operations may only be carried out at a specified time and so, if we wish to observe them, we must attend at that time. Again, a person we want to see may not always be available.

2 Importance Sometimes, quite early, it becomes apparent that certain information is going to be vital. For example, in a department where nearly all the production centres round one large piece of equipment it may be obvious, almost from the start, that a detailed determination of the capabilities of that machine will provide crucial information. As the necessary observational runs, etc., will take some time, the sooner they are put in hand the better.

For example, in the manufacture of some refractory materiel, the initial blending and mixing, etc., of the materiel is followed by a lengthy heat treatment in huge furnaces. Clearly, information about the temperature variation in different parts of the furnace is going to be important, and initial checks might be put in hand right away. These may be followed by more extensive checks, depending upon the results.

18.2   Conversations with the staff concerned

We must talk to each person concerned, at a time and place convenient to him or her. It is impossible to state in general terms exactly who these people will be, but they are likely to include:
1   All direct supervision staff.
2   Engineers and other technical people.
3   Inspection staff.
4   Possibly maintenance staff, and those who purchase and store materiel, etc.
It is important to:
1   See that no one is left out.
2   Talk to people in strict order of status in the company, for example the head of the department before the foreman, and the foreman before the assistant foreman, and so on.
As we must both find a convenient time and see people in the correct order, these conversations may spread over an appreciable period and we can collect other information in between them.

1   We shall take a notebook to write down any ideas and suggestions which are made. If we can possibly make use of them, we shall, because if we adopt suggestions from the staff members in the department, they will have an interest in making sure that their suggestions work, and therefore, a stake in ensuring that the whole quality control system works.

2   We shall try to make friends with each person, and try to convince him that quality control is there to help him or her.

3   We shall ask questions appropriate to the person concerned. Thus, we shall ask the supervisor about the sequence of operations

and the correct procedure at each stage. We shall ask the inspection foreman for details of checks carried out by his staff, numbers of each type of defective found, and so on. Do not be too narrow with these questions, however, or try to confine them too rigidly to that person's role. Because the members of a department must work together, they will overlap their knowledge. Make a point, where appropriate, of asking the same questions of several people to see whether we get identical answers. Often, although the questions are the same, the answers vary appreciably and then it is instructive to try to understand why there should be a difference. This may arise from differences in outlook.

For example, suppose that the department prepare a mix to which a percentage of water is added. We ask the production foreman what this percentage should be and he says 15%, while the engineer says 10% and the inspection foreman only 5%. We must clearly find out why these differences occur, and we must also take into account any information given in the specification and work instructions. Our investigations might reveal that:

a   15% water makes the mix easy to work, and the production foreman prefers it because it helps to keep up the rate of production.

b   5% gives a product with the best final quality, and hence the inspection foreman's preference. Unfortunately, during the various production operations, this yields components which are very brittle and, therefore, easily broken.

c   10% water gives a material which is easiest to handle on a subsequent operation in another department. The same engineer controls both operations but the foremen are different, and hence the difference in outlook.

Before we come to any startling conclusions about the above, we must go and see for ourselves what water the operators really put in. We may well find that in spite of the references to precise percentages the operators merely tip in about half a bucket, and then add a bit more if they think it needs it! Probably they will err on the generous side because, like the production foreman, they will know that more water makes the material easier to work.

We shall have to set a water content which is as near as possible to 5%, consistent with satisfactory working and subsequent processing properties. The way to set about this general type of problem is detailed in Section 21.2, sub-section (2).

4   Ask about the organisation of the department. Our new quality control system must not only be right technically, it must also be tailormade to fit the existing organisation and routines. It must

dovetail in with any projects done by the methods engineer, O & M staff, etc. Notice whether any difficulties in human relations are thrown up. Thus, a situation like the following is not uncommon:

a   The production foreman says, 'We do our best to produce good quality, and then the inspectors do their best to reject as much as possible. Half the time, I can't see anything wrong and we never get any information from the inspectors.'
b   The inspection foreman says, 'The general quality produced is well below what is required. We bend over backwards to pass as much as possible, so much so that one day the customer is going to complain and then I shall get the blame and have to tighten up. We used to send the production foreman detailed reports of all rejects, but he never looked at them. Three years ago, when the output increased, I found I couldn't spare an inspector any more to prepare reports that were never read.'

Clearly, we shall have to bring these two together again with our new quality control system. It will also be prudent to design a system which does not require more co-operation from them than is absolutely necessary.

5   Find out how the departmental cost system works, and what information is available.

18.3   The quality standard in practice

Very early, we must consider the impact of the first stage of quality control, as discussed in Section 1.4, and we must ask ourselves:
1   Do we know clearly what quality standard we have to make?
2   How do we check that we have in fact achieved the quality standard demanded?

In the example in paragraph 4 of Section 18.2, it is obvious that the production foreman and the inspection foreman have different ideas about the quality standard which is demanded. We shall have to consider:

1   What is the correct quality standard?
a   What do the relevant specifications and drawings say?
b   Where these do not make the quality standards clear, who is responsible for clarifying them? This may be a job for the quality control department liaising with the designer, or maybe either the production engineer or the inspection foreman can do it.

c   There may be relevant British Standard Specifications which would help.
d   Visual quality standards may be required (see Section 3.7).

2   Is the quality standard demanded higher than can be achieved with the operators, materiel and equipment available? If our capability runs as Sections 11.7 to 11.10, 12.1 and 18.6 show this to be the case, then we must face up to the situation, and either:
a   The department must be re-equipped with more accurate machines, tools, etc., operators retrained, better materiel bought, etc., to raise the quality standard to which it is capable of working; or
b   The designers must be told that they must not call for a higher quality than the department is capable of producing.
    The decision is often a difficult one, but no good can come of failing to be realistic and leaving the people concerned to get by as best they can.
    While clarifying the quality standard we must make sure that we have a satisfactory method of measurement, otherwise the department will never be sure whether they have got their quality right or not.

18.4   Departmental records

Every department has some records and, fairly early, it pays to investigate these to see what information is already available. Among them, we may find the following:
1   *Inspection records*   These usually show how much defective work has been found for each type of product, and often they also show what the fault was in each case. The defective work may be related to production batches, furnace loads, batches of materiel, machines, etc.
2   *Ordering particulars*   We shall need to know the quantities in which each type of product is made. Are we dealing with short or long runs? How is work loaded on to the department, and what warning does it get of what it has to make?
3   *Existing paperwork*   Collect together copies of every form used. Sometimes these can be adapted for quality control, and this saves introducing more paper.
4   *Cost records*   Cost information, if accurate, is most valuable since our quality control system must be designed with the object of saving as much money as possible.
5   *Personal records and sketches*   Often the staff in a depart-

257

ment have already thought about their quality problems, and may have sketched out something which they never completed.

6   *Work instructions* Where methods have been set down get hold of copies of them. Find out what the methods engineer believes to be the best approach.

18.5   Direct observation

There is no substitute for direct observation, and we must see for ourselves what the problems are. In every case, we must compare what is done with:

1   What the foreman says is done.
2   What the specification, drawing and work instructions etc., say.

Even then, we may not get the whole truth because the operator may change his pattern of work while we are watching. I remember a case in which castings had to be put into the bottom of a pit 2 m deep for special tests, and a hoist was provided for this purpose. When I went to see this job, however:

1   The operator laboriously carried each casting down the steps, one at a time, and then returned up the steps for the next.
2   The condition of the hoist, covered in dust, told me that it was never used and, when I asked the operator about it, he said that it was too slow to be convenient.

I accepted that the manually operated hoist would be slow, but I was still puzzled. Surely, I thought, it must be quicker and less tiring than carrying every casting down the steps. Later I found out the reason. The carrying of castings down the steps was only done because I was watching. When no one was looking, it was the practice to stand at the top of the pit and drop them in! As the castings were being checked for cracks, presumably any which cracked as a result of their fall were merely reported as defective!

In the course of our observations, we must get to know the operators and ask them for their suggestions. As we said in Section 9.5, most of them are very knowledgeable about their own operations.

18.6   Observational runs

Our direct observations are almost certain to include some formal observational runs with the object of establishing the capability and characteristics of a process or machine. In principle, these will be as discussed in Sections 11.7 to 11.10 and 12.1, but done on a broader basis such as the following:

1   Choose a typical machine doing a typical run.

2   Decide on the qualities to be checked, and these again should be typical of the production concerned. If possible they should be variables which can be checked quickly and easily.

3   Decide on the frequency of checks. Ideally, every piece made should be checked, but at the same time we should be able to keep up with the machine or process, as otherwise we may miss something important. Hence, it may be necessary to limit checks to one piece in two or three, etc.

4   Where a machine has several heads or channels of output, then the output of each must be kept separately and plotted separately, since the quality from one head may be quite different from that from the others.

5   Take care to see that the observational run in no way disturbs the output of the department. Thus, any existing patrol inspector should continue his normal checks, etc.

6   Start the observational run at the beginning of the shift, or perhaps at the beginning of a typical production run.

7   Try to measure and plot results as the run proceeds.

8   An observational run provides an opportunity to collect a lot of additional information. For example:
a   Notice whether the machine or process drifts as it warms up or as chemical baths become spent, etc.
b   Record the time and duration of every hold-up, why it was caused, and what was done to correct it.
c   Record all process changes, new batches of materiel, tool adjustments, etc.
d   Notice how often the inspector comes round, how many he checks, and what action he takes on his results.
e   Notice how often work is cleared from the machine or process.
f   We keep our eyes open. We shall be in the department for some hours, not specifically looking at the operators. They will, therefore, probably be more relaxed and behave more

nearly as they always do. Note anything which might help to design the new quality system.

9   An observational run should not, in general, last less than a whole morning and may be much longer. Often, it is best to start the run with no definite plans about its duration, and then to continue as long as useful information is being collected. Notice whether the quality changes when the process is shut down for the lunch break, etc.

10   Work out the machine or process capability, as described in Sections 11.7 to 11.10 and 12.1, but also list all the other information which comes to light. As a result of the observational run, it should be possible to decide which of the six patterns of variation given in Section 12.1 is appropriate.

11   Repeat the observational run, at least in part, for what the shop say is 'the worst machine in the shop' and also for 'the best machine'. We must know the worst, before we attempt to design the new quality control system.

18.7   Quality control and other literature

A lot of information can be obtained from quality control and other literature. We must, however, be careful not to be carried away by technically involved ideas. Remember that the foreman, etc., will not be familiar with complicated quality control theories, and sooner or later we shall have to explain our proposals to him.

If we are just starting quality control, this book will probably cover all our needs for some time and we should beware of launching into more elaborate techniques.

18.8   Analysis must be impartial

As we gather information, we shall begin to analyse it. This analysis must be systematically carried out, however, and we must resist the temptation to jump to conclusions. Thus, an inspector may show us a couple of dozen scrap pieces, with the remark, 'It's Frank Edwards; he's always making them like that.' Before we blacklist Frank Edwards, however, we must make quite sure that this really is the whole story. We may subsequently find out that:

1   The location stops on Frank Edwards's machine are so worn that they are useless; or that
2   This particular type of work is very difficult to do, and is always given to Frank because he is the best man in the shop, although even he makes an appreciable proportion of scrap.

18.9   Patterns of variation

The object of our analysis is to make the patterns of variation clear, and generally to understand the problem for which we must prescribe a remedy. We must progress from merely knowing how much of each type of scrap we make, to being able to compare the scrap rates from one machine to another, and from one operator to another, and so on.

Much of the work will probably prove to be straightforward and logical analysis of the information, and to help us we have:
1   The whole of Chapter 16 on quality deficiencies, and in particular:
     a   Pareto curves.
     b   Measles charts.
2   Frequency distribution curves as discussed in Chapter 11.

Analysis of information does not follow its collection in two clear steps. Analysis invariably reveals gaps in our knowledge and, therefore, the need for more information. This has to be collected and further analysed, and this process must be repeated until the problem is fully understood.

18.10   Need for action in other disciplines

Our analysis is primarily aimed at understanding the quality needs of the department. It is very common, however, to find that other needs come to light. For example:
1   The method may prove to be unsatisfactory, in which case method study must be systematically employed in order to effect an improvement, as discussed in Chapter 8.
2   Extensive operator training may be required, as considered in Chapter 9.
3   Plant maintenance may need improvement.
4   Production control may be the prime source of difficulty.
5   It is just possible that we may uncover the need for a more complicated technique like operational research.

Each of these needs must be negotiated with the specialists concerned, and an appropriate improvement made.

CHAPTER 19

THE FOUR FUNDAMENTAL TYPES OF QUALITY CONTROL SYSTEM

19.1   Starting to design the new quality control system

When our analysis is nearing completion it will be time to think about the design of our new quality control system, and we shall aim for a system which:

Will do exactly what is required.

Is so simple and practical, it looks as though it could only have taken five minutes to think up.

It will be based on the five stages of quality control which we set out in Section 1.10. Thus, whatever our type of production, we must make provision for:

1   Defining the quality standard in clear, practical terms.
2   Planning for satisfactory quality.
    a   The method of manufacture (Chapter 8).
    b   The equipment (Section 8.8).
    c   The materiel (Chapters 4 to 7).
    d   The selection and training of operators (Chapter 9).
    e   Inspection and shop floor quality control (Chapter 8).
3   Manufacturing right first time as far as is reasonably possible (Chapters 9 to 15).
4   Correction of quality deficiencies (Chapter 16).
5   Long-term quality control.

These reduce to four steps which we can check as we design our system:

1   *Start right*   Clearly, if production does not start right it is unlikely to be right at any stage. This is why we have put so much emphasis on:
     a   Defining the quality standard.
     b   Planning for satisfactory quality.
2   *Keep right*   Having started correctly, we must see that production keeps correct and that, if the quality shows signs of going outside specification or drawing limit, adjustments are immediately made to bring it back again. This is the role of shop floor quality control. It is necessary because, in general, we cannot ensure at the quality planning stage that the job cannot go wrong during production. The better we do our quality planning, the less shop floor quality control we shall need.
3   *Finish right*   If we really keep the quality right throughout the production run it is bound to finish right. Our concern here, therefore, will be primarily directed at the quality of the tooling, since this may require attention before the next run is commenced.
4   *Final inspection*   Final inspection is not so much part of the quality control system proper as a means by which we prove that our quality control system is working properly. If, on final inspection, everything is satisfactory it speaks well for our quality control.

19.2   The four basic types of quality control system

Quality control provides us with a large number of different techniques, the most useful of which have been described in Parts 2 and 3 of this book. In designing a quality control system, we must select those which are suitable for the production line in question and then blend them into a unified, practical whole. Few of these techniques are universally applicable. Each tends to have a certain range or class of work for which it is particularly suited. Developing this idea further, I have found that it is possible to classify almost any type of work as belonging to one of four basic groups. We shall define these as follows, and then discuss them in detail in the next four chapters.

Type A   Each small stage of production can be easily checked as soon as it is made. Most machine work comes into this class.

Type B   Interdependent production stages, where the product can only be checked at infrequent intervals. This class includes much of what we often loosely call the process industries.

Type C Assemblies.

Type D Service undertakings.

19.3 Effect of mechanisation and automation

There is no clear distinction between manual production, mechanisation and automation. At one end of the scale we have craft-type production, where only hand tools and a fair amount of labour are used, and at the other extreme we have completely automatic equipment, which works entirely unaided, with computers to monitor quality and correct processing conditions as required. Within these two extremes, many hybrid arrangements are both possible and entirely practical. Thus an assembly flow line may have some stages mechanised and others done by operators.

In each of the next four chapters, we shall consider first manual and single-machine production, where quality is controlled largely by the operator, and then mechanisation and automation, where quality is dictated and possibly controlled by the machine. Where work is done by craftsmen using hand tools, the rate of production is likely to be slow, and although the general quality standard may be high, it will suffer from unpredictable human variations. The watchful eye of the operator will however be ever-present. A piece of wood with a knot in it, or a screw without a thread, will be rejected, and no attempt made to use it.

Mechanisation means that we give the physical work to the machine. Because a machine does not suffer from human vagaries, the quality produced usually becomes much more consistent, but not necessarily consistently right; it may be consistently wrong! The following are examples:

1   If a cutting tool moves out of position, all subsequent production may be out of drawing limit.
2   A machine will attempt to use a screw without a thread, thereby damaging the assembly, and possibly itself as well. Hence it is most important that the materiels are of consistently satisfactory quality.

Automation implies that some degree of control is built into the machine. Ideally it has sensing devices which monitor all the process parameters, and then adjust them as necessary. Usually a computer of some sort is at the heart of the decision-making process. Often this is in the form of a large central multipurpose computer, and all equipment requiring control is 'on-line' to it. Indeed, the central computer does not need to be in the same factory, because telephone links can be used. However there is a distinct modern trend towards dedicated computers. These are smaller mini and micro computers designed specifically to do one job, or maybe a limited range of related jobs. We can see examples of this in some numerically controlled machines, and in specialised items of test equipment used in the electronics industry.

CHAPTER 20

DESIGNING A QUALITY CONTROL SYSTEM

TYPE A: WHERE EACH SMALL STAGE OF PRODUCTION CAN BE EASILY CHECKED AS SOON AS IT IS PERFORMED

20.1   The scope of Type A

Where we can easily check each small stage of production as soon as it is made, this is usually the most convenient basis for our quality control system. Thus, if we turn up a diameter we can immediately check it with a micrometer, and if we want to know whether medicinal pellets are the correct weight we can weigh them, etc. The following is typical of this class of work:

1   Most machine work, e.g. NC machines, lathes, milling machines, drills, etc.
2   Sheet metal work, and fabrication generally.
3   Diecasting.
4   Forging and hot pressing.
5   Manufacture of many plastics components.
6   Dressmaking, knitting, etc.
7   Any operation even in a process industry where the quality can be immediately checked, e.g. as a weight.

Consider Figure 20.1 where the row of symbols at the top represents the output of some machine or other operation in this class. Thus, it begins by making a run of pieces denoted by a circle. Then follows a 'one-off' denoted by a triangle, and this is clearly the shortest 'short run' which is possible. Next, we have a long run of the piece denoted by a square, and this could in principle be very long since only the limitations of the diagram make us stop after 22 pieces, and set up the piece indicated by a half moon. Consider the design of our quality control system, along the lines of the basic stages of quality control outlined in Section 19.1.

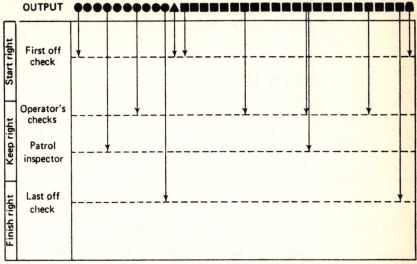

Type A easy to check each small stage of manufacture

Figure 20.1 Quality control of a Type A process

20.2 Start right

1 Define and clarify the quality standard
a All variables must have tolerances (Section 3.4).
b All attributes must have practical quality limits, such as visual quality standards (Sections 3.7 and 3.8).

2 Plan for satisfactory quality
a Make use of method study in order to ensure satisfactory methods, devised so that it is as easy as possible for the operator to carry them out correctly, and as difficult as possible for him to do them incorrectly (Chapter 8).
b Make sure that all tooling and equipment is adequate to achieve the quality standard demanded (Section 8.8).
c Ensure a supply of satisfactory materiel (Chapter 7).
d Select and train suitable operators and inspectors (Chapter 9).
e Prepare a quality schedule, in principle as described in Sections 8.10 and 8.11, and in detail in Section 20.3 below.

3   The first-off check   Insist on a correct 'first-off' check before the production run is allowed to proceed (Section 8.12). The 'first-off' inspector must remember that the object of this is not so much to check the first piece made, as to make sure that everything is satisfactory for the first period's run. In Figure 20.1 the arrows on the 'first-off' check line show which pieces will receive this check.

20.3   Keep right

In so far as the quality of our production can go wrong, we must provide checks to detect this quickly so that the machines, etc., can be reset before any, or hardly any, out-of-limit work has been made.

1   The quality schedule will state what checks must be applied during production and these may or may not be exactly the same as those for the 'first-off' checks. This will depend upon:
a   How likely each quality is to go wrong.
b   What it costs when it does go wrong.
We may be able to get some information about this from:
a   Our Pareto curves (Section 16.7) which will tell us which types of defective work are most commonly made.
b   Frequency distribution curves (Chapter 11) which will show which qualities are only just within the capability of the machine, and so are the most likely to get out of limit.
c   Our knowledge of the process. Thus, the diameter on an automatic lathe may change quite suddenly by quite a large amount, but the diameter of a punched hole is unlikely to change appreciably. If our method is such that the quality is unlikely to go wrong, then we do not need to check it so often.

2   Next we must decide how often checks must be made. This is basically a question of economics, and is fully discussed in Sections 13.9 to 13.13. In addition, it depends partly on the pattern of behaviour of our machine, and we shall know this from our observational runs (Sections 12.1 and 18.6).

3   The question of who is to do these checks is bound up with how difficult are they and how long they take. Consider first how much the operator can reasonably be expected to do.
a   If he can check each piece while the machine is working on the next, then it will probably be prudent to ask him to utilise his idle time in this way (Section 9.7). If his checks will hold up

production, then we must limit them severely. In Figure 20.1 the operator has been told to check every sixth piece, as shown on the line marked 'operator checks'.

b   Checks which the operator cannot conveniently do must be done by someone else. Often this person is called a patrol inspector, but in some cases it may be the setter or the supervisor. Consider the staff in the department concerned and ask, 'Who is the best man or woman to do it?' and not, 'What is he or she called?' In Figure 20.1, the inspector takes periodic samples. Notice that the piece checked may or may not be one which the operator has already checked. This is purely a matter of chance.

4   The choice of sample size is basically as discussed in Section 13.8. Thus, Figure 20.1 shows a sample of one, but clearly this will not always be the case. Operator checks will tend to be a sample of one because, in general, we shall do better to inspect more often (and so catch our machine quicker when it goes out of limit) rather than check more at each inspection. Furthermore, operators will be less likely to have time to average samples for control limits which is desirable if we are to make best use of a sample exceeding one. Where we use a patrol inspector, there will probably be a limit to the frequency with which he can conveniently visit the machine, but he is more likely to be able to undertake the averaging of his results, etc., at each visit. Hence, there is a stronger case for a sample exceeding one if the pattern of variation of the machine makes this desirable.

5   The routine of keeping each period's production separate, until the check at the end of that period has proved satisfactory, is most desirable (Section 8.14).

6   We must provide some method of ensuring that the operator actually does the checks he is paid to do. One simple way to do this is to ask the operator to mark the pieces which he checks. According to the type of work, this may be done with crayon, chalk or by inserting paper or plastics markers, etc. The routine then is that, when a patrol inspector finds something wrong with a piece which he checks, he checks the last piece which the operator claims to have checked and has declared all right. If this piece is found to be all right, then presumably the machine has only just gone wrong and the out-of-limit work in the last few pieces can easily be isolated. If the last piece checked by the operator is also wrong, then the operator is not doing his checks properly and must be corrected.

The patrol inspector must go backwards through the marked pieces, in order to locate where the change in quality occurred and so isolate all the out-of-limit work.

20.4   Finish right

It usually desirable for a production run to conclude with a patrol inspection, both to check that the run itself has finished satisfactorily and also to check the state of the tools. If these need resharpening, recutting, etc., then this should be done *before* they are returned to stores (Section 8.16).

20.5   Final 100 per cent inspection

Some contracts, particularly defence and similar government contracts, specify that 100 per cent final inspection must be applied. If we have a free choice, however, we shall try to make such final inspection unnecessary. It is nearly always possible to devise the production quality control routine so that nearly all the work which gets through the system as satisfactory is in fact all right. Unsatisfactory pieces, therefore, should only get through in any quantity when something happens which is not provided for in the routine, such as the occasional operator mistake. Act firmly where defective work gets through, because somebody has failed to work the quality control routine correctly.

Where components made in, say, a machine shop go next to an assembly shop within our own company, 100 per cent inspection is unlikely to be justified. Usually, it will be cheaper for the assemblers to throw out the occasional bad piece. There will be exceptions to this rule, for example in aircraft work, where safety is at stake. But, in general, if we think we need 100 per cent inspection it probably means that the quality control system itself is not sufficiently efficient, and we must have another look at it.

Where the output of a department is going directly to a customer, then customer reaction to any unsatisfactory work it contains must be considered. Remember, however, that the cost of any 100 per cent inspection must either come out of our profits, or from an increased price to the customer. Try, therefore, to achieve an acceptable quality level by improving the quality control system proper, and only resort to 100 per cent inspection when this proves to be impossible. Even when the customer specifies 100 per cent inspection, try to achieve an initial quality of production such that very little is rejected by this final inspection.

20.6 Mechanisation and automation

Where equipment is mechanised or automated, the same principles for designing a quality control system apply, but the emphasis changes.

Start Right   Correct initial set up is now of vital importance. Plugs, tapes, etc., used in NC or CNC machines must be right, or the whole run will be out of limit.

Keep Right   If manual patrol inspection is to be applied, then the sample size and frequency can in principle be determined from Sections 13.8 to 13.12. Typically the sample size will be $n = 1$ per outlet, but where a large volume of expensive production is concerned, the economic interval between inspections may be impossibly short, e.g. 5 sec. This indicates a mismatch between mechanised production and manual patrol inspection. When mechanisation of a production line is contemplated, it is important that we also consider quality control, which should be built into the machine. It should check its quality as it goes along, and if this is unsatisfactory, it should at least shut itself down, and give warning that it has done so. Ideally it should correct itself and continue production.

(Problems on the design of a quality control system are given at the end of Chapter 23.)

CHAPTER 21

DESIGNING A QUALITY CONTROL SYSTEM

TYPE B: INTERDEPENDENT PRODUCTION STAGES, WHERE THE PRODUCT CAN ONLY BE CHECKED AT INFREQUENT INTERVALS

21.1   The scope of Type B

There are many processes where the product can only be checked at infrequent intervals, so that a quality control system of the type discussed in the previous chapter becomes impracticable. Examples of this type are described below:

1   Many food processes   Thus, in making bread, we must obtain our materials, prepare and mix them, etc., and bake, before we can take a bite to find out whether our loaf is all right. Even then our check is destructive, so 100% inspection for taste is out of the question.

2   Many chemical and physical processes   In the manufacture of transistors, for example, it is not possible to check the functioning of the transistor as such until after it has been made. If it is then wrong, there is often little that can be done about it.

Similarly, in the manufacture of motor-car tyres, the raw rubber must be masticated, blended, calendered and then the tyre must be assembled and heat treated before the tyre itself can be checked.

3   Some engineering processes   Examples of this type are:
a   Foundry work.
b   Plating, painting and other forms of metal finishing.

c   Processes with a lengthy time cycle, as sometimes occurs in heat treatment, the manufacture of refractories, etc.

Take foundry work as being typical of the family of processes which comprise this group. When we make a casting, there are roughly nine operations which must be completed before we can check whether the casting itself is good. They are:

1   Make the pattern.
2   Prepare the sand.
3   Prepare and melt the metal.
4   Make the mould.
5   Close the mould.
6   Pour the metal.
7   Cool.
8   Knock out.
9   Clean up and fettle.

Only when all of these have been completed can we check whether our casting is good or not, and as this sequence may take two or three days, if checks then show that our castings are bad we may have a great deal of unsatisfactory work already in our long pipeline, i.e. possibly 2 or 3 days' production. Checks at the end of the production line are, therefore, of little use as the basis of our quality control system.

With this type of production, it is usually best to argue that, if everything is correctly made with satisfactory materiel and equipment, then all production must be good. This argument is somewhat idealistic, of course, but it forms the basis of our quality control system, which again goes in four steps.

21.2   Start right

1   Define and clarify the quality standard
a   All variables must have tolerances (Section 3.4).
b   All attributes must have practical limits, such as visual, audible or taste quality standards, etc. (Sections 3.7 and 3.8).

2   Define and plan the method of manufacture   Since we propose to base our control system on method, it follows that our method must be defined with considerable care. At every stage of the process, we must set down precisely what is to be done, expressing as many parameters as possible in figures complete with tolerances. For example:
a   Distribute 48 ± 1 g of powder A evenly on a nickel plate 300 mm square.

b   Cure at $240 \pm 3°C$ for 180 ± 5 seconds.

Some processes may appear to contain an element of 'black art' or 'mystery'. The supervisor, operators and even perhaps the engineer will tell us that the process cannot be controlled by ordinary scientific means, because the quality varies all the time, and only experience with the process can help in deciding what to do, and even that is not always satisfactory.

Now it is a well-established scientific fact that, if we repeat the same operations, on exactly the same quality and quantity of materiel, we shall get exactly the same result every time. How then does it happen that these 'black art processes' are relatively common? The reason must be that in these departments they *do not* always carry out exactly the same operations on exactly the same quality and quantity of materiel, and hence they do not always get the same result. Additional variations may then be caused by arbitrary adjustments made by the 'experts' in order to regain control.

We must not be demoralised by assertions that formal quality control has no chance. We must diligently set out every detail of the method, and the probablity is that this will be most revealing. We ask as many people in the department as possible to tell us what the method is, and compare their answers. We shall almost certainly find that they differ, because each person will have his own opinion based on his own particular experience. For example:

Joe White says, 'I put on 50 g to make quite sure that there are no thin patches, but the temperature must be 250°C.'
Fred Black says, '45 g is enough, otherwise it cracks, and a temperature of 230° is plenty.'

As quality engineers, unless we happen to know which of these opinions is right, we shall have to fix the two parameters arbitrarily to start with, and then make sure that everyone observes them. Thus, we might set the weight of powder at 48 ± 1 g, and the press temperature at $240 \pm 3°C$. We shall go right through the whole process setting every parameter, and giving it a tolerance based on our knowledge of the process capability. This may not immediately yield the best method, but at least we know what the method is, and we can control it. Thus, if 48 g then proves to be too high, we can reduce it to say 46 g. Previously, when everyone put on different weights, we had no effective control at all and no possibility of finding out what the best weight was.

We must not be put off because we are told that something is not critical. For example, 'We just throw in a handful; it's not critical.'

Provide a measure for everyone to use, so that we know what volume is put in. No parameter should be left uncontrolled, however loudly the department protest that it is not important.

3   Provide satisfactory equipment   Again we must make sure that the equipment provided is adequate to achieve the quality standard required (Section 8.8). With processes, we often have a chance to provide automatic controls. Thus a temperature of $240° \pm 3°C$ will require control equipment, and if it is not economic to buy it, then it is no use pretending that we are controlling to that accuracy.

4   Materiel   Materiel for a process often presents its own peculiar problems. Where relevant, we shall apply the routines described in Chapters 4 to 7 but, in addition, we may have uniformity problems especially if we are dealing with natural materiel. Thus, if we buy flour, its quality may vary according to where the wheat was grown, natural rubber may vary from plantation to plantation, perhaps even from tree to tree, if we are able to investigate that closely. Even inorganic materiel is not free from this problem. The impurities in copper, selenium, tellurium, etc., even after they have been purified, still vary according to the location of the mine from which the ore was obtained.

In such cases, we may decide to homogenise, that is to mix several batches thoroughly together to obtain a large batch of uniform quality. Sometimes a degree of blending may be included. We decide that we will keep a particular impurity constant at a certain level, e.g. $0.1 \pm 0.02\%$, and so we check the impurity content of all incoming batches, and then blend them together in the right proportions to achieve our agreed level of impurity.

In a foundry, the quality of the sand used for moulds depends in part on its spectrum, that is on the proportions of large and small particles which it contains. Now sand from different quarries will tend to have different spectra. Therefore, it is common practice to check the spectrum of each load of sand when it arrives, and then to blend it with other sands in just the right proportions to achieve a constant spectrum over a reasonably long period.

5   Operators   We must obtain and train suitable operators, as discussed in Chapter 9.

6   First-off checks on the method   First-off checks will still be necessary every time a machine is prepared or an operator gets ready for a fresh run. We may not be able to check the product, but we can still check the method, equipment and set-up, etc. For example:

275

a   Has the correct equipment been correctly set up?
b   Are temperatures, weights, concentrations, speeds and feeds, etc., all correct?
c   Is the correct materiel being used?
d   Is the operator carrying out the correct method, in the correct sequence?

To ensure that the operator knows what the correct method is, we must break down the standard method which we prepared in (2) above, into job instructions with key points as Section 9.3.

21.3 Keep right

Now we must ensure that our method is observed right to the end of each production run. One way to do this is to use the equivalent of a patrol inspector, except that we shall probably call him a quality control assistant. He will make periodic visits to the operators and machines to check that the process parameters and operations are correct, for example:

1   That the curing temperature is still $240 \pm 3°C$.
2   That the operator spreads the correct weight of powder evenly over the plate, etc.

We can still give each operator a quality control chart, but this time it will list the key points of the method, and the quality control assistant will enter on each visit whether or not they are being observed, by a tick or a cross. Parameters which are in figures, such as temperature, can be plotted as a variables chart with specification limits, even though it is not always possible to use control limits.

Even on a process, there are usually some points where a quality control chart can be based on a direct check of the quality of the product. Thus, in the foundry, when the sand has been prepared, a sample can be checked for moisture and clay content, etc., and used as a basis for controlling sand quality.

21.4 Finish right

A last-off check on the method used for the run usually has little value, unless it is possible to check the condition of the equipment in preparation for the next run.

21.5 Final inspection

As before, we try to make final 100 per cent inspection unnecessary.

If we decide to do it, its purpose will probably be one of the following:

1 To prevent defective production from reaching the next operation, or maybe the customer, and in some cases because the customer has insisted that it shall be done.
2 To confirm that the quality control system proper is working satisfactorily and to give the alarm if it is not. We shall be very careful, however, that we do not attempt to use final inspection as the quality control system in its own right.

21.6 Mechanisation and automation

Much of Section 20.6 applies. If the process has been mechanised to increase throughput, without regard to quality control, an inbalance between the two is likely, and the patrol inspector may be unable to keep up. Mechanisation must include corresponding improvements to the quality control system.

Some processes have a number of interrelated parameters which must be controlled. Continuous optimisation between them is needed, and this calls for a computer. Sometimes this is done by putting the plant on-line to a mainframe computer: more likely it has its own dedicated computer. The computer may also control complicated tests on the final product. As mechanisation and automation increase, the operator has an ever-decreasing effect on quality. Ultimately, an operator in the true sense is almost eliminated. His or her job becomes that of plant minder, with little or nothing to do until the control equipment indicates unsatisfactory processing conditions. The operator must then locate the fault and correct it.

(Problems on the design of a quality control system are given at the end of Chapter 23.)

CHAPTER 22

DESIGNING A QUALITY CONTROL SYSTEM

TYPE C: ASSEMBLIES

22.1 The scope of Type C

Under assemblies we include every case where components, large or small, are fitted or fixed together. Thus, in principle, we range from, say, the assembly of a nut to a bolt at one extreme to the assembly of, say, a diesel locomotive or an aircraft at the other. The principles of our quality control system will be the same even though its intensity and complexity may vary considerably.

22.2 Analysis of incorrect assemblies

At the start of a quality control project on an assembly line, a Pareto curve of rejected assemblies is often most revealing (Section 16.7). Assembly takes place after various components have been made and, in some cases, the components themselves are fairly complex. Thus, it is not uncommon for a Pareto curve to reveal that most of the causes of rejection originate *outside* the assembly department. The following example of a light electrical assembly line illustrates this point:

Reason for rejection	Percentage of all rejections	Cumulative total (%)
Faulty transformer	35	35
Faulty choke	24	59
Component not available	20	79
Wiring faults	12	91
Soldering faults	6	97
Miscellaneous	3	100

On this line, a high percentage of assemblies were being rejected on final test so that, at first sight, it looked as though the assembly operators were very unsatisfactory. However, the above Pareto curve paints a very different picture. Notice that 35% of the rejections were due to faulty transformers, and a further 24% to faulty chokes. Neither of these is anything to do with the assemblers. Furthermore, both transformers and chokes were made in the same component supply department, hence underlining the need for better quality control there. Next, we have 20% rejections because a component is not available and, therefore, the assembler cannot put it in. These were faults in the production control department, and it illustrates how quality control will often draw attention to problems originating outside its popularly recognised sphere (although there is no reason why we should not do quality control of production control or, indeed, any office work).

Thus, in this example, 79% of the faults originated outside the assembly department, and the quality engineers concluded that they must tackle these first, before dealing with the 21% which originated from within it.

22.3 Design of assemblies

In Section 3.1 we discussed the designer's general contribution to quality control. In assembly work, however, the designer has additional scope because he can design so that as far as possible the components will only go together the correct way. For example:
1   Components which must go a particular way round should not be designed so that they will go equally well either way.
2   Small differences should be introduced so that similar components cannot be interchanged.

279

22.4 Start right

1 Define and clarify the quality standard All variables must have tolerances (Section 3.4), and all attributes must have practical limits, such as visual or audible quality standards (Sections 3.7 and 3.8). Thus, we may have to define what we mean by a 'satisfactory soldered joint' or a 'moderately tight nut'. The latter we may be able to define by means of a torque spanner.

2 Plan a satisfactory method Assembly work is a particularly happy hunting ground for the methods engineer, for there are considerable savings to be made. There are also opportunities to work with the designer, to ensure that assemblies will only go together the correct way. Jigs, etc., can often be designed so that they will only accept components if they are inserted into it in the correct way (Sections 8.3, 8.4 and 8.5).

3 Plan the equipment Some assembly lines use relatively little equipment, and therefore, it is very easy to forget that satisfactory equipment is an essential part of our quality control system (Section 8.8).

4 Plan materiel As our example in Section 22.2 showed, the materiel used may prove to be the vital key to trouble-free assembly.

1   *Materiel purchased* from outside suppliers will need to be controlled as Chapters 4 to 7.
2   *Where materiel is manufactured* within our own company, it may be wise to improve quality control in the supply departments, before tackling the assembly.

5 Select and train operators In most assembly work, there is considerable scope for the operators to go wrong. In particular, we must see that they are trained in any basic skills required, such as soldering, stripping wires, the principles of fitting, etc. Next, we must provide each of them with a job instruction card showing the steps and key points of each type of assembly to be made (Chapter 9).

6 First-off checks On assembly work, as much as on machine work, there is scope for a 'first-off' check. If the first assembly of a particular batch or run is incorrect, it is very likely that the rest will also be wrong.

22.5 Keep right

In so far as we have been *unable* to ensure that our assemblies cannot go wrong, so we shall have to do assembly shop floor quality control. Therefore, periodic checks will be required by the operator, inspector, supervisor, etc. Our position is probably a little like that discussed in Chapter 21 for processes in that, although we can check that each component is correctly assembled, we cannot usually check until an assembly is completed whether or not it actually functions as intended. Thus, we have to argue that, if every assembly is correctly made, with correct components, to a correct design, then every assembly must work when completed, and so we need a control system as outlined in Section 21.2.

A quality control chart, either per operator or per production section or department, may be useful so that both operators and supervisors know how well or otherwise they are doing. Much, but by no means all, assembly work is concerned with attributes, and Figure 15.1 shows a typical chart for such a section.

The sequence in which assembly operations are done often affects the probability of mistakes, as the example in Section 8.5 illustrates.

22.6 Final inspection

In many cases, assembly is the final manufacturing operation before dispatch to the customer and, therefore, 100% test and inspection is commonly applied. Its object may be to:
1   Comply with a customer's contract (this is often the case with government defence contracts, etc.).
2   Prevent a faulty assembly from reaching the customer. (A customer buying, say, a record player will not have stipulated by contract that 100% final inspection and test must be applied, but he/she will nevertheless expect it to work satisfactorily, and it will reflect on the manufacturer if it fails to do so.)
3   Adjust transformer taps, resistors, carburetter settings, etc., to obtain best performance.

As always, we should regard this final test and inspection as *proof* of our quality control system, rather than as the system itself. Anything which has gone wrong anywhere during manufacture will, we hope, be discovered on final test. The information which we get will, therefore, be most valuable. A Pareto analysis, probably grouped initially in the departments in which the faults originated, will show us where further quality control effort is required. Our aim must always be to have a minimum of rejections on final inspection.

22.7   Mechanised and automated assembly

Sometimes only one or two stages of an assembly flow line are mechanised; the rest is done by operators. At the other extreme, the whole assembly can be made and checked by the machine. It is particularly important to ensure that all components are satisfactory, unless the machine will check what it uses. Ideally it should also check every stage of assembly as it goes along and correct itself, or at least give warning, if anything goes wrong. Either a central or a dedicated computer can be useful in carrying out a complicated sequence of tests. It can supply a printout of every parameter, although it is more likely that it will be programmed to print out only parameters that are out of limit.

(Problems on the design of a quality control system are given at the end of Chapter 23.)

CHAPTER 23

DESIGNING A QUALITY CONTROL SYSTEM

TYPE D: SERVICE UNDERTAKING

23.1 Examples of a service undertaking

In this chapter we are concerned with organisations which provide a service, rather than manufacture a product, and the following are examples:

Wholesale and retail distributors.

The Post Office.

Transport undertakings such as British Rail, bus companies and airlines.

Educational establishments.

Medical services.

The armed forces.

Government Departments.

Maintenance organisations, both those which exist solely for this purpose, such as car repair garages, and those which are part of a factory organisation.

Clerical work.

When manufacturing, we carry out a prescribed performance in order to obtain a satisfactory end product. We can regard a service as one where the prescribed performance is an end in itself, and there may be no end product. Then we can apply the quality control principles we have already discussed.

23.2 Define the service required

A manufacturing organisation must begin by surveying the market to find out what its customers require, and its designers must then reduce this to a fully defined quality standard, in the form of a manufacturing specification. In the same way, a service undertaking must start with a survey of the needs of their market. From all the information which is available, they must produce a clear specification of operational requirements. For example:

1   A retail organisation needs to decide where shops will be established, what range of goods they will sell, and in what quantity.
2   A bus company needs to know what routes will be covered, and what passenger density is anticipated.
3   The armed forces must work from an overall statement of defence needs, to a detailed specification of what, where, when and how much.
4   A college must define as precisely as possible what it means by a student who is adequately educated and trained to be, say, a quality engineer.

23.3 Plan to provide the required service

This will broadly follow the five basic sub-stages which we discussed in Chapter 1.

1   Plan the method   We must decide as precisely as possible how our organisation will work. For example:
a   A retail organisation must decide how it will organise and lay out a shop, what storerooms it wants, and with what conditions, etc.
b   A bus company must consider how routes can be economically dovetailed together, so that buses and their crews are not idle, yet there is always a bus at the time and place required.

2   Obtain equipment   Next we must obtain the equipment which we require, for example:
a   A retail organisation must obtain suitable counters, shelving, scales, refrigeration equipment, delivery vans, etc.
b   A bus company must obtain buses, and ensure that they are reliable. No doubt they will need a maintenance organisation, which will require a service quality control system in its own right.

c   A water company must decide on pumping equipment, and an electricity board on alternators, etc.

3   Obtain materiel   We must obtain an adequate supply of satisfactory materiel, but the magnitude of the task will vary enormously with the type of undertaking. Thus:

a   To a wholesale or retail organisation, the purchase of saleable goods with the required quality, quantity, price and delivery, is so important that it may well be the most important single task they have to perform.

b   To a bus company, the purchase of diesel fuel is a relatively small problem, which can be calculated fairly precisely.

c   The purchase of, say, shells for the army presents a problem which is peculiar to the armed forces. Apart from practice and trial firings, the army probably hope that they will never need to use them, yet in an emergency, adequate supplies must be available, and the soldiers must be able to rely on them to function correctly.

d   Electricity and gas boards must ensure that they have adequate supplies of the correct grades of fuel. Notice that part of their materiel is the final output of another service undertaking, British Coal.

4   Select and train personnel   Service undertakings have in principle the same problems as do manufacturing organisations, in selecting and training suitable staff. Indeed many people work for both at different times in their lives.

5   Plan the operational quality control   Throughout we shall plan so that, as far as possible, the service must be performed as intended. Where we cannot be certain that this will happen, we shall have to provide additional safeguards, probably in the form of spot checks, equivalent to the patrol checks of industry.

23.4   Perform the service correctly to plan

At last we are ready to perform our service to the specified quality standard. The better our planning has been done, the less the trouble we shall have in carrying it out. Our problems may however be aggravated by having our staff scattered, as is the case with maintenance men and vehicle drivers. Again we consider the three phases.

1   Start right for example
a   A shop window display can be checked to see that it is correctly priced and described. Under the Trade Descriptions Act, incorrect descriptions may result in legal action.
b   A bus inspector can ensure that buses leave the garage on time, displaying correct destination boards.
c   The output of an alternator can be checked when it is started up.

2   Keep right   We must now ensure that our service keeps to its plan, e.g.:
a   A bus inspector can board buses at random times, to check that they are running to timetable, and that tickets have been correctly issued.
b   College students are set tests from time to time, to check that their education is proceeding as planned.
c   Shop supervisors can make snap observations on the way their staff serve customers.
Sometimes other checks can be included, for example:
a   The output of an alternator can be continuously recorded and controlled.
b   The time a bus passes a point can be recorded by instructing the conductor to insert a card in an automatic clock recorder.

3   Finish right   In many cases a customer receives a service in person, so that it is not possible to do a 'final inspection before despatch'. If a haircut has been incompetently done, probably nothing can be done until the hair has grown again. We can still however use information from a final check to plan for better quality in future, even if alas we have a dissatisfied customer now. For example:
a   We can check the time a train arrives at its destination.
b   We can check a repair job on, say, a car, before handing it back to the customer.

23.5   Correct the cause of any quality shortcomings in our service

In addition to all the information we have already discussed, we are sure to have a feedback from our customers in the form of complaints, comments, etc. It is clearly important to see that these are dealt with quickly and courteously, but in addition it is most important to learn from our mistakes. We must do our best to improve the basic planning and execution of our service, so that shortcomings in our service do not recur.

23.5 Questions

1 Discuss practical ways of tackling quality control for *two* of the following:

- *a* A food processing line.
- *b* An electronic assembly shop.
- *c* Clerical work.
- *d* A foundry.
- *e* A transport undertaking. *(25 marks)*

2 Describe a suitable quality control system for *two* of the following:

- *a* A plastics workshop making small components: most of the machines have operators working on short to medium runs, but some are mechanised, and only require the operator to load them occasionally with raw powder, and remove finished work; the latter are on long runs.
- *b* A workshop making wooden 'adventure' toys for schools, e.g. climbing frames.
- *c* A small workshop cutting and sewing ladies' dresses.
- *d* A department heat treating small components.

(25 marks)

3 Select any *two* of the following, and outline a suitable quality control system for *each*. (Candidates should state any further assumptions they make to define practical operating conditions.)

- *a* A section of a machine shop containing 24 automatic lathes, in which runs are fairly long.
- *b* A small company which contracts to clean the windows of other industrial concerns.
- *c* The manufacture of printed circuit boards on to which components are assembled and wired, but which are not incorporated into equipment at that stage.
- *d* A small foundry making non-ferrous castings up to about 4 kg. *(25 marks)*

Author's note: Each of the above questions asks for only two systems to be designed because more could not be completed in 30 minutes. The reader however might care to attempt them all.

CHAPTER 24

QUALITY CONTROL OF SHORT RUNS

24.1 The approach to short runs

If the reader has to deal with short runs, then he should read this chapter in conjunction with Chapter 20, 21, 22 or 23 as appropriate. Basically, there are two main ways in which we can deal with short-run production:

1   We can control the features which are common to every run.
2   Where each type of product repeats from time to time, we may be able to plan its quality control system once and for all, and then use it every time a batch of that product is made.

24.2 Controlling on the features that are common to every run

Quality control is not as difficult as it may appear to apply to short-run production. The important thing to realise is that any one department only does one class of work. This is bound to be so, because machines and equipment are always built to do a given limited range of work, and operators only have a limited range of skills. Thus, when the foreman tells us that, 'All our runs are different; we never get two things alike,' we need not take him too literally. Consider, for instance, the following examples which are deliberately exaggerated in order to make the point:

1   In a short-run sheet metal shop, every job has roughly the
     same operations, for example to:
     a   Cut sheet to size.
     b   Punch holes and slots, etc.
     c   Bend to shape.
     d   Weld, etc.
2   In many electronic circuit assembly departments, the
     sequence of operations is roughly to:
     a   Insert components in printed circuit board.
     b   Solder.
     c   Test.
If we give some thought to the particular short-run shop for which
we wish to design a quality control system, we shall soon discover
the features which are common to every production run, and we can
then use them as the basis of our new system. Broadly, there are two
ways in which we can do this.

1   We can use a chart for defectives or defects   The first possibility,
which is almost always applicable, is to use a number or a
percentage defective chart, plotting one point for a day's work, a
morning's work or per batch etc., depending on the rate of
production. Thus, a chart of the type shown in Figures 15.1, 15.4,
15.5, or 15.6 are independent of run length. Where the average
number or percentage of defectives is roughly constant, regardless
of the actual part number being made, it is even possible to use
control limits.

2   We can control on the method   A defectives chart has of course
the objection that it waits for faulty work to be made before calling
attention to it. We may be able to overcome this by basing our
control system on the method, as we did in Section 21.2. This again
is not dependent on run length.

24.3   Having an individual quality plan for each product

Where each individual type of product repeats from time to time, it
is possible to have an individual quality plan for each. For example,
in most machine shops, each part number has a method card or
maybe a planning route card showing the method which is to be
followed each time that part number is made. In the same way, we
can provide an individual quality control chart and quality schedule,
etc., for each part number.
   Thus, the short-run department is given a complete set of quality

control charts, one for each part number. The routine is that whenever a part number is set up, the inspector gets the chart for that part number out of the file and puts it in the holder on the machine. This tells the setter what checks will be applied, which are specially important, and shows him what troubles were incurred the last time that part number was made. When the run is finished, the chart goes back into the file and another is put up in the holder. Even a one-off gives no trouble; the chart can always be got out quicker than the machine or process can be set up.

With this system, we can control on variables as well as on attributes. In a few cases, we may even be able to use control limits for variables. We set the control limits on the first run, and then use them for subsequent runs. Some care is necessary, however, because if in the meantime the machine wears appreciably, the control limits will no longer be appropriate for the next run.

In general, control limits for variables are difficult to apply to short runs because the run tends to be finished before we can complete the routine, given in Sections 13.3 and 14.4, for setting the control limits. We can, however, use pre-control charts as discussed in Section 13.17.

24.4 Question

Discuss the difficulties involved in controlling the quality of short run or batch production, and hence suggest how a satisfactory quality control system can be devised. (Your answer may be related to a production line with which you are familiar.)

CHAPTER 25

THE DESIGN OF A
QUALITY CONTROL CHART

25.1   Chart sizes

Whatever our type of production it will not be long before we need a quality control chart of some sort and, although there is nothing difficult about its preparation, it does need to be approached in the right way.

We shall not want our charts to be all shapes and sizes, so we must start by choosing one of maybe two sizes which we shall use as standards. As charts spend more of their time in the file than they do out on the job, they must fit economically into our storage arrangements. Therefore, find out the largest size which will just fit into the files which you will be using. Other considerations permitting, there is a lot to be said for making the charts to one of the international paper sizes. Thus A4 is a convenient size for charts which are to take one or two variables, along with some attributes. If a lot of data must be entered, and we wish to interest a group of operators, then we may prefer A3. For small individual charts A5 may be large enough.

25.2   The chart holder

When the chart is in use, it must be readily visible to all who should use its information. As the operator often has the greatest need, such charts must be strategically placed on the machine or process where the operator cannot help seeing them. Therefore, for protection, the chart will need a simple holder with the following features:

1   A solid back to provide a rest for on-the-spot entries.
2   Provision for hooking the chart on to the machine or process once entries are complete.
3   It should be painted in a distinctive bright colour so that it is easy to see. If that colour is uniform throughout the factory, it soon becomes associated with quality control.
4   Each holder should bear the words, 'Quality Control Chart', as a form of publicity.
5   Where the work is dirty, or machines are likely to spray oil about, the holder will need a piece of clear plastic in front to keep the chart clean. If this is designed to slide to the right, then a right-handed person can use it as a hand rest while making entries, so keeping dirty marks off the chart.
6   Sometimes it is possible to put slots in the plastic so that entries can be made without removing it.

If charts are out in the thick of production, it is inevitable that occasionally one will come to grief. This need cause us no undue concern. It is better for them to die usefully on 'active service' than to idle their days away in an inspector's drawer.

25.3   Standard chart layouts

Although we can use any design of quality control chart we choose, the chances are that many and possibly all our needs will be met by one of the three designs illustrated in Figures 25.1–25.3 which we can regard as standard.

In Figure 25.1, the basic chart consists almost entirely of graph paper, and this is intended to be used where the qualities concerned are all to be plotted as variables. Notice that every alternative vertical line is printed a little heavier, and extended upwards to make 'boxes' at the top, for further information. The × of each point is plotted on the light vertical lines in between.

Where the qualities to be checked are a mixture of variables and attributes, then the paper shown in Figure 25.2 is useful.

The design shown in Figure 25.3 is for use where only attributes have to be recorded. Notice that where not too many qualities are to be plotted it is possible to divide the chart horizontally across the middle, and so get two complete lines of information on one side. The charts from which these illustrations were made were about A4 in size.

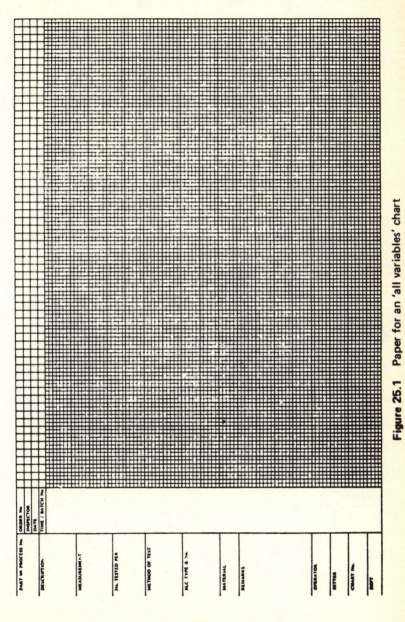

Figure 25.1 Paper for an 'all variables' chart

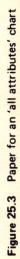

PART NO. | ORDER NO.
DESCRIPTION | INSPECTOR
| DATE
| TIME

ISSUE NO. | I | INSPECTORS CHECKS
OPERATION | R | RE-SETS
SECTION | PREVIOUS M/C ERROR
M/C TYPE | MTLS & CASTING FAULTS

PLANT NO.
MTL.
SETTER
OPERATOR(S)

INSPECTOR CHECKS PER HRS
CODE
A = ACCEPTED
C = CORRECTED
R = RETURNED
S = SCRAP

REMARKS MAKE ANY COMMENTS

OVERALL APP'Y

100% INSPECTION RESULTS | TOTAL QTY. | TOTAL REJECTS

OPERATORS CHECKS *
OPERATOR CHECKS PER HRS | TIME
COMPILED BY | 1st. OFF INSPECTION STAMP

Figure 25.3 Paper for an 'all attributes' chart

25.4 Information on a quality control chart

Although we can and indeed should put any information on the chart which might be useful, the following is typical.

25.4.1 On the left-hand side of the chart

1   The part number or process number, and its name or description for example:
      ABQ 314 Pump Body
2   The name of the operator, setter, supervisor, etc., and the name of the department or section.
This helps to make these people feel part of the system, as well as permitting later analysis of each individual operator's performance. Use the operator's complete name, e.g. 'Mary Hicks', not just 'Hicks'.
3   The number to be inspected, and the frequency of inspection.
4   Leave space so that the method of inspection can be recorded where necessary.
5   Provide for any other information. Written notes from the operator, inspector, setter, etc., are often most valuable. Sometimes, instead of putting this information down the left-hand side, it is more convenient to put it along the top.

25.4.2 At the top of the chart

Here we put information which may change in the course of a production run, for instance:
      The order number.
      The inspector's initials.
      The date.
      The time of inspection or, alternatively, the batch number.
Where the operator's name may change, as when there is both a day and a night shift, then the operator's name should also appear at the top.

25.5 Special quality control charts

From time to time, jobs will come along with special requirements and we shall find it desirable to design a special chart for them. In general, it is as well to keep to the same size of paper, otherwise we shall upset our filing arrangements. However, we can include additional information. For example:

1 We can include the results of any final inspection.
2 Where there are subsidiary operations, successful completion of these can be recorded. For example, after forging it, it may be useful to record the completion of grinding, heat treatment, etc.

25.6 The preparation and duplication of quality control charts

In preparing quality control charts, we must use paper sparingly. We do not want to be accused of littering the factory with tons of paper. Charts of the type illustrated in Figures 25.1–25.3 will take 50 to 60 entries, in one row, on one side of the paper. If we can get two rows of information per side, this makes 100 to 120 entries. By using sufficiently thick paper or thin card both sides of the chart can be used, and we have a possible maximum of 200 to 240 entries per piece of chart paper. Thus, if checks are made once per hour, one piece of chart paper lasts about six weeks on day shift, or three weeks if there is also a night shift.

The information to go on to each chart comes from the quality schedule, as discussed in Sections 8.10 and 8.11, and the labour of transferring this information on to each new sheet is not very great in most cases. However, it is better to avoid even this by getting a supply of standard charts as shown in Figures 25.1–25.3 and using them as originals. The checks relevant to a specific process, operation or part number, etc., are then entered on this original, and photocopies are made from it as required for use on the shop floor. This method has several advantages:

1 It eliminates the work of drawing duplicates.
2 It avoids mistakes. If the original is correct, all the prints are bound to be correct.
3 The original can frequently be used as the quality schedule, so eliminating that as well.

25.7 Charts for new quality control systems

When we devise a new quality control system, we may not be able to hit upon the best chart design immediately. Furthermore, operators, inspectors, supervisors, etc., may, on seeing our proposals, make suggestions which should be included. Again, jobs which at first sight require a special chart often settle eventually to a standard pattern. Hence, we should not rush into print with our first proposals.

An easy way to overcome this is to have a supply of completely blank paper, the size of the standard chart. When we require a new chart, we draw our proposals as an original and run off a few copies at a time, as required. If we wish to modify the design, we merely redraw the original. Only when we are sure of our design do we go into print.

25.8 Points concerning the operating routine

Try to establish a standard operating routine which as far as is applicable can be used throughout the factory. Inevitably, supervisors, operators and inspectors sometimes get moved from one department to another, and it helps if they still recognise the quality control system as a familiar and useful friend. For example:

1   The limit at which a machine or process is to be stopped and reset could always be drawn with a solid red line. (Where duplicated charts are used, as discussed in Section 25.6, then this will have to be a solid black line.)
2   Out-of-limit points should always be ringed in red.
3   The action taken when points are out-of-limit and all machine resets, process adjustments, new batches of materiel, etc., are always recorded. This information often proves to be the most valuable part of the chart.

CHAPTER 26

INSTALLING THE NEW QUALITY CONTROL SYSTEM

26.1   Preparing to sell the new system

We have now investigated the quality problems of our department, analysed the information we collected and designed our new quality control system. Next, we have to sell our ideas to the personnel concerned, and install the new system. It sounds simple, and yet it is no exaggeration to say that this will probably take us as long as all the rest put together.

We begin by preparing examples of any charts or forms we propose to use, and then fill them in with typical information preferably drawn from existing records. We shall need to do this in any case, to satisfy ourselves that the design is convenient. We also collect together anything else which will help us sell our system.

26.2   Explaining our proposals

We have not said anything about being in the department concerned since Chapter 18, and this may seen rather a long time. It is in fact bad for the department to be left too long, because interest wanes and the cynical conclude that the problem has beaten us! It seldom happens, however, because from time to time we almost always have to return to gather more information. If not, we should deliberately show ourselves, to keep the interest alive.

Now that we are ready to proceed, however, we return and request an interview with the head of department, at a time convenient to him. At this we shall:

1   Explain our proposals carefully, emphasising the ways in which they will help.
2   Ask for his criticisms and suggestions.
3   Seek his approval to try the proposals out on a small scale, for example on one machine or one section, etc. The agreement is that we will show by demonstration that the new system works and, if for any reason it does not, we shall take it out again. This is a fair agreement. If the new system does not work, it would be stupid to retain it. Needless to say, however, we shall take very good care to see that it does work!

Our request for criticisms and suggestions need some comment. Having spent some hours designing our new system, our natural reaction will be to feel reluctant to alter it, unless the suggestions made are obviously better. Yet, in fact, we must go along with the express object of incorporating every suggestion we possibly can, in order to make as many people as possible feel that they have a stake in making the new quality control system succeed. Only if a suggestion is obviously inferior shall we reject it, and even then we shall carefully explain why. It we are doubtful about a suggestion, then we make a note of it and promise to consider it carefully, and return with our opinion.

When we have convinced the head of department, we must do the same with each grade of supervision, in strict order of seniority, not forgetting production engineers, inspection foremen, etc. We shall talk to exactly the same people mentioned in Section 18.2, in exactly the same order. This time it will take a little longer, for proposals must be discussed in detail and charts, etc., redrawn as required. Sometimes, we may even have to go back up the line to the more senior people again, to get approval for a major change which has been suggested.

In due course, we shall reach the shop steward or other shop representatives. Our approach to them is much the same as that adopted for top supervision. The only difference is that we do not have to ask formally for their approval to go ahead. In theory, we inform them. However, we must still listen to their criticisms and adopt their suggestions with exactly the same care. If they are worried about our proposals, we must try to understand why and attempt to allay their fears. It is difficult to get a quality control system to function well if either the supervision, shop stewards or the man on the shop floor is against it.

Next, we explain it to the operators who will be concerned with the first pilot run. Selection of those to be 'first' requires careful consideration but usually, by the time we have done observational runs, we have a pretty good idea who is likely to be co-operative and enjoy trying out something new. If anybody says of our proposals, 'It won't jolly well work', we must resist the temptation to reply that 'it jolly well will', because this creates an impasse! The correct reply is, 'Why, Fred, what's the snag?' and then, 'Would you explain it to me?' and perhaps 'Would you show me?' Finally, if we still have doubts we ask, 'Can I try it for myself?' People seldom protest about proposals just to cause trouble, but often the snag they have foreseen is a minor one and we shall have no difficulty in overcoming it. Large or small, however, it is our job to find a satisfactory solution.

Avoid technical terms when talking to the shop floor, but on no account talk down to them. Do not present the proposals in too serious a vein. A few quips help, but not at their expense. Do not hide any snags in the proposals. On the contrary ask for help; someone familiar with the work can often think of a way to get over them.

26.3   The pilot quality control system

When at last the selling is complete we fix a day, the sooner the better now, to launch the pilot scheme. This is the most critical moment of all, particularly if it is the first scheme in our company. Everyone will be watching to see if our quality control really does work. If it had to be taken out again and modified, the loss of prestige would be considerable and selling it a second time doubly difficult. If preparations have been carefully made, however, there is no need to fear this but we must be on our guard to see that all goes smoothly.

Everything must be ready and we must be there, whatever the hour in the morning. If possible, start the new scheme off without disturbing the old, because this gives the shop confidence. Equally, if practicable, we do every job in the new system ourself and then show and teach the operators. There is nothing like trying proposals out on ourself, to see if they work, and if they do we are then in a strong position to discuss snags with other people.

Keep everybody, but particularly the operators, well in the picture. Discuss progress with them, and praise their efforts. Show particular eagerness to solve any snags which may arise, whether they are caused by our oversight or not. Always refer to it as 'your quality control system' and never as 'ours'. After it has been installed, it will be theirs permanently.

If the operators are interested, they will work with us often solving snags for themselves. If not, they may delight in thinking up snags for us to solve. It is quite usual for the original proposals to suffer some modification during the pilot stage, and to be all the better for it.

26.4 Enlargement and consolidation

We shall visit the new quality control system at least twice a day during the early stages, and be prepared to stay for longer periods whenever necessary. Soon we hope that the pilot scheme will have settled in well enough for us to request the head of department to withdraw the old quality control system in favour of the new, and to allow us to spread the innovation.

If the department is large this will take some time. On each occasion that a few more operators are added, the new system must be carefully explained to them, and the addition to the system must be carefully watched over, much as the pilot scheme was.

Meanwhile, the original pilot scheme will still require attention. For years perhaps, the department have operated their old system of quality control. Now, to begin with, they will regard the new system as a 'try out'. Even after they are satisfied that it works, it may be some weeks or months before they regard the new system as the accepted one, in the sense that they would not go back to the old even if they had a chance. Throughout the whole of this period, the new system needs very careful, fatherly care. It can easily falter and die.

Therefore, we must visit each part of the new system regularly. When a group of operators is first put on to the system, they must be visited twice a day with continuous attention where necessary. In a day or so, this will become once per day and after two or three weeks, twice a week. This reduction in the frequency of visits goes on until eventually the system is inspected once per month. I would suggest that you continue to visit every system once per month, permanently.

Once the system has settled in, make sure that its equipment is of a permanent nature. Thus, as a try out, we may have used:

Makeshift forms and charts.

Odd bits of wire to put up chart holders.

Gauges, etc., borrowed from another department.

All such points must receive attention.

26.5 Calculate the savings

When the quality control system is complete it is important to calculate the savings made. Top management should want to know what these savings are, and we must in any case tell them. This is part of the task of selling quality control to management.

The calculation is not always easy. We always know the cost of defective work, etc., after quality control has been put in, but often little information exists about what it was before. Many accounting systems do not easily separate quality costs from other costs. Thus, any accurate calculation may be difficult. Fortunately, however, the savings from quality control are nearly always large compared with the cost of putting it in and operating it, and there is, therefore, usually no difficulty in showing that a very satisfactory saving has been made, even if its exact magnitude is in doubt.

26.6 Question

1 It has been decided to install a formal quality control system in a production department which has previously relied on a few inspectors working on an accept or reject basis.

1a Explain briefly what information should be collected, and how this information should be analysed, in order to decide on the appropriate quality control techniques to be used.

(12 marks)

1b Suggest how a suitable quality control system could be designed, and the points to be watched in getting it successfully installed. *(13 marks)*

CHAPTER 27

THE DESIGN OF EXPERIMENTS

Note. This chapter is retained for its usefulness to the quality engineer, but it is no longer required for City and Guilds Certificate No 743.

27.1 Introduction

At any time during the planning, installation or day-to-day maintenance of a quality control system, a quality engineer may wish to carry out experiments, in order to improve his understanding of the processes concerned. Sometimes these can be done under laboratory conditions, but many must be done on the production plant itself.

27.2 Significance tests

Suppose we have a production process which produces an average of 70 kg of satisfactory output, from each batch of materiel fed into it. One day one of our assistants says that by making certain alterations to the processing conditions, he has been able to produce a satisfactory yield of 80 kg. Should we congratulate him, or tell him kindly that his discovery is of little value? Our answer will depend upon how that process normally behaves.

1   If the process is very consistent at 70 kg, seldom varying by

more than 1 or 2 kg up or down, then a single batch of 80 kg is quite remarkable, because it has never happened before.

On the other hand, if the process varies considerably about its average of 70, so that outputs of both 60 and 80 are quite common, then there is nothing unusual about one batch of 80 kg. If of course the new process *averages* 80 kg over a lot of batches, that would certainly be noteworthy, but this will require more results to establish. At the moment the new process is not proven.

We can now restate our problem in more scientific terms. If we have sufficient past records, we can plot the output of our usual process as a frequency distribution curve, along the lines explained in Section 11.6, and the result might be as shown in Figure 27.1. Curve (2) corresponds to (2) in our discussion above. Although the mean is 70 kg, the standard deviation about that mean is large at 10 kg. If the curve is approximately Normal, we can apply the percentages given in Figure 11.16. Notice that the output of 80 kg which has been claimed is exactly 1 standard deviation above the mean, and Figure 11.16 shows that the chances of being 1 standard deviation or more above the mean are $(13 \cdot 59 + 2 \cdot 14 + 0 \cdot 132 + 0 \cdot 003) = 15 \cdot 865\%$. Now $15 \cdot 865\%$ is roughly 1 in 6, meaning that the old process achieves 80 kg on 1 batch in 6. Hence there is nothing very significant about it happening once on the new process.

With curve (1) in Figure 27.1 the position is quite different,

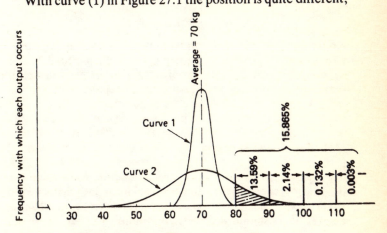

Figure 27.1 Assessing the improvement offered by a new process

305

because the standard deviation is only 3 kg, so that there is only a chance of about 1 in 1,000 of getting an output of even 79 kg from the old process. Therefore if our new process has achieved 80 even once, this is no accident. The new process must really be better than the old.

We can now set out our argument in general terms, so that we can apply it to any similar case.

1   We begin by assuming that the new process is no better than the old. This is called a *null hypothesis*. We then consider whether there is sufficient evidence to show that this hypothesis must be wrong.

2   We estimate the probability that the new result is due to chance variations, in a process that is really no better. If we say that it is quite likely that the new results are due to chance, then we say that the result is *not significant*, i.e. it is unproven. It is consistent with our null hypothesis. If the result is very unlikely to be due to chance, we say it is highly significant, because the new process is almost certainly better than the old. The descriptions usually assigned to probability values are as follows:

Probability = α = 0.10 or more, not significant without more evidence

α = 0.05 probably significant

α = 0.01 significant

α = 0.001 highly significant

Notice that whereas a low probability means that the new process is almost certainly better than the old, a high probability does not necessarily mean that the new process is no better. It merely means that there is not yet enough evidence to decide.

We can of course collect further information by doing additional tests with the new process. Thus suppose we make n batches to the new process, and they *average* 80 kg. This is mathematically analogous to the situation shown in Figure 12.8 for the heights of men, and to be fair to our new process, we must compare this average with the frequency distribution curve, which we should get by plotting averages of samples of n from the old process. This would have a shorter base and steeper sides, and in accordance with Eq. (12.1) its standard deviation would be given by:

$$\sigma_n = \sigma / \sqrt{n}$$

If we now let $\bar{X}$ be the mean value of the old process and $\bar{x}$ the observed mean value of the new process, then the number of standard deviations, z, by which $\bar{X}$ is displaced from $\bar{x}$ is given by

$$z = |\bar{X} - \bar{x}|/\sigma_n$$
$$\quad = \sqrt{n}|\bar{X} - \bar{x}|/\sigma \qquad (27.1)$$

(The vertical lines in $|\bar{X} - \bar{x}|$ mean 'take the smaller from the larger'.)

If the standard deviation of our old process is well established from a lot of observations, we can use Eq. (27.1) directly:

Thus for our example
$\bar{x} = 80$, $\bar{X} = 70$ and $\sigma = 10$
and if $n = 5$ observations averaged together, we get
$z = \sqrt{5}(80 - 70)/10 = 2.24$

We now consult tables, such as *Statistical Tables for Science, Engineering Management and Business Studies*, by J. Murdoch and J. A. Barnes, in which we shall find the areas in the tail of a Normal distribution. These are of course the figures in Figure 11.16 in more detail. This gives us that:

$\alpha = 0.0125$

Comparing this with our standards of significance, we conclude that our result is almost low enough to be called significant (0.01) and is certainly much better than probably significant (0.05). Thus there is a good chance that our new process really is better than the old one.

27.3   Student's t

The foregoing assumed that we knew the standard deviation of our old process fairly accurately. Where this is not so, we have to estimate it from the observations we make. To do this we use Eq. (11.1):

$$\hat{\sigma} = \sqrt{\frac{\sum_1^n (x_i - \bar{x})^2}{(n - 1)}}$$

We rewrite Eq. (27.1) as follows:

$$t = \sqrt{\bar{n}}|\bar{X} - \bar{x}|/\hat{\sigma} \qquad (27.2)$$

This is known as Student's t test, Student being the pen name of its originator. Because we have only an estimate of the standard deviation, we must now use a table giving the percentage points of the t distribution. (Murdoch and Barnes' tables contain this.) This table requires the number of degrees of freedom, which as far as we are concerned is $v = (n - 1)$. Thus if in our example, our value of 10 for the standard deviation is only an estimate from our sample of 5, we have:

$$\bar{x} = 80$$
$$\bar{X} = 70$$
$$\hat{\sigma} = 10 \qquad \text{whence from Student } t \text{ tables we get:}$$
$$t = 2.24 \qquad \alpha = \text{a little less than } 0.05$$
$$\gamma = (5 - 1) = 4$$

Hence our observations show that the new process is probably significant, but we cannot be as certain as we were when we knew precisely what the standard deviation was.

Students t is called a *significance test*, and we can use it whenever we want to find out whether a sample whose mean is $\bar{x}$, could have come from a frequency distribution whose mean is $\bar{X}$, and whose standard deviation is estimated to be $\hat{\sigma}$.

27.4 Correlation

Suppose we suspect that the percentage of a particular materiel which we add to a product affects its final electrical resistance. This has not mattered in the past, but now a customer requires consignments in which this resistance has been controlled to defined specification limits. We therefore need to determine corresponding limits for the percentage of added materiel.

We decide to do an experiment in which we deliberately treat batches with different percentages of the additive, and measure the resulting electrical resistance. We have thus got two variables, the percentage of the additive and the resistance, and to check the relation between them, we shall probably plot a graph of our results. This might look like any of the plots shown in Figure 27.2. If our graph is similar to *(a)*, we shall conclude that there is good *correlation* between the additive and the resistance. It is a linear relation, which we can estimate roughly by drawing a ruler line as shown. Ideally all experimental points should lie exactly on the line, but in practice this seldom happens.

Indeed we should be lucky to get a result as good as *(a)*. More likely we would get result *(b)* where the correlation is not nearly so good, and it is difficult to decide which position of the line fits best.

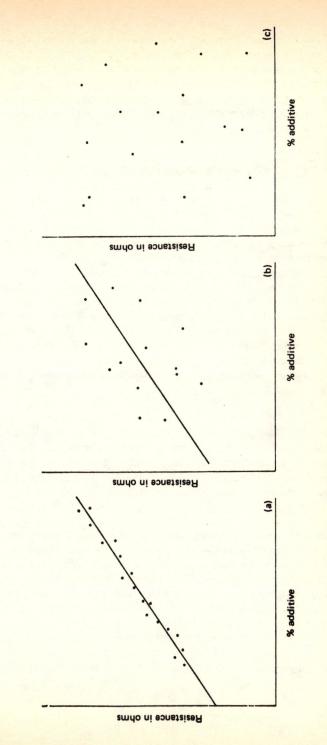

Figure 27.2 Examples of: (a) good correlation; (b) partial correlation; (c) no correlation

If we were very unlucky, we might get *(c)* which shows no correlation at all. This does not necessarily mean that the additive and resistance are completely unrelated. It may be that un-controlled variables in the process swamp any relationship. It would however, mean that we could not use the percentage additive in order to control the resistance, until we had got the stray variables under better control.

27.5 The principle of least squares

In many cases a line fitted by eye is adequate for practical purposes, but it is possible to calculate a 'best fit' line, based on what is known as the *principle of least squares*.

When we worked out a standard deviation in Section 11.5, we subtracted the mean value from each observation in turn. Now it would obviously be possible to do this calculation with any other number, instead of the mean. However by its nature, the mean is always in the middle of the observations, and this would not be quite true of any other number, especially if it was nowhere near the mean. As a consequence the differences $(x - \text{chosen number})^2$ would tend to be larger, and so therefore would the final answer.

We now apply this principle to the problem of choosing the best fit line. Suppose that we have tested five different percentages of the additive, and obtained the following results.

% additive	0.1	0.2	0.3	0.4	0.5
Resistance in ohms	7.3	10.5	12.2	15.3	18.5

We can plot this data on a graph as shown in Figure 27.3. The points do not form a perfect straight line, but they leave us in no doubt that they have a linear relationship. Now any straight line can be represented by an equation of the form:

$$y = mx + c \tag{27.3}$$

In our problem x is the percentage of additive and y is the resistance, whilst m and c are constants.

If we put $x = 0$ we get $y = c$ and therefore c is the value of y for which x is zero. If in Figure 27.3 we fit a line by eye, we can see that c must be roughly 4.5. Now m represents the slope of the line, and the figure shows us that:

$$m = \frac{18 - 4.5}{0.5} = 27 \text{ approximately}$$

Therefore our rough estimate for the equation for this relation is:

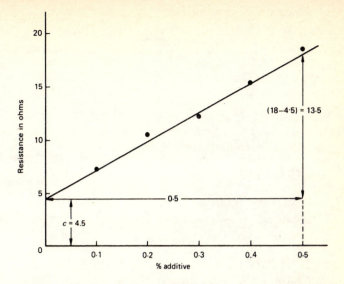

Figure 27.3 Fitting a straight line to experimental data

$$y = 27x + 4.5 \tag{27.4}$$

Of the five sets of observations which we have, only the 0.4 per cent addition giving 15.3 ohms happens to lie exactly on this line. If we insert any other pair of observations into the equation, it will not balance exactly. Thus for the first pair, we have:

Observed resistance   **7.3**
Calculated resistance = $27x + 4.5 = (27)(0.1) + 4.5$ **= 7.2**
Discrepancy   **= 0.1**

If we work out the discrepancies for each pair in turn, we get:

     0.1, 0.6, 0.4, 0, 0.5

Now the principle of least squares says that the best fit line is the one for which the sum of the squares of these discrepancies is a minimum. For our example, this gives:

     0.01 + 0.36 + 0.16 + 0 + 0.25 = 0.78

However these discrepancies relate to a line which we fitted by eye, and there is almost certainly another line which will give a better fit, and therefore a lower total of these squares. There are a number of ways of finding the best fit line, but the following is the most straightforward.

1   Prepare a table as follows:

x	y	xy	x^2
(% additive)	(Resistance)		
0.1	7.3	0.73	0.01
0.2	10.5	2.10	0.04
0.3	12.2	3.66	0.09
0.4	15.3	6.12	0.16
0.5	18.5	9.25	0.25

Totals $\Sigma(x) = 1.5$ $\Sigma(y) = 63.8$ $\Sigma(xy) = 21.86$ $\Sigma(x^2) = 0.55$

Σ means 'summation of' and in this case merely implies that we must total each column.

2   Insert these totals in the following simultaneous equations:

$$(\Sigma x^2)m + (\Sigma x)c - (\Sigma xy) = 0$$
$$(\Sigma x)m + nc \quad - (\Sigma y) = 0$$

Therefore,

$$0.55m + 1.5c - 21.86 = 0$$
$$1.5m + 5c - 63.8 = 0$$

Solving these equations for m and c gives:

$$m = 27.2 \qquad c = 4.6$$

3   Hence our best fit line is:

$$y = 27.2x + 4.6$$

It requires a knowledge of calculus to prove that the equation deduced by the above method does in fact give the lowest possible total to the sum of the discrepancies squared. The reader not so equipped may however like to check that the total for the best fit line is lower than for our line fitted by eye. (It is in fact 0.648 against 0.78.)

Notice that the least squares calculation can easily be carried out on any set of pairs of observations, regardless of whether or not they form anything approaching a straight line. It will still give a best fit line for a case like that shown in line (c) of Figure 27.2, even though there is no useful relationship at all. Hence we should only use this method where it is reasonably evident that a straight line relation exists. (There are methods of checking the degree of correlation, and readers who are interested should consult a standard book on statistics.)

27.6 Sources of experimental error

When we carried out the experiment in the last section, we hoped that all the variations which we observed in the electrical resistance were caused by deliberate changes which we had made to the quantity of additive. In practice this is never strictly true. However careful we are there will always be uncontrolled sources of variation, and we can easily guess what some of these might be. For example:

1   Variations in the quality of consignments of the materiel.
2   Variations in the way batches were processed. These will be partly due to the plant, and partly due to the operators.
3   Errors in estimating the resistance produced, and in weighing the additive.

We can get some idea of the magnitude of these variations by treating a succession of batches with the same quantity of additive, and observing how the resistance varies. If the variation is very little, we conclude that there are no large uncontrolled variables. If however the variations in resistance are comparable with those which we observed when we were deliberately varying the additive, then we can only proceed if we can separate the uncontrolled variables from those which we deliberately caused. Where uncontrolled variables occur completely at random, we can reduce their effect by *replication*. This means that at each percentage of additive, we make a number of tests, and average the results together. We are in fact eliminating errors of precision as we discussed in Section 3.5, but we shall not be able to eliminate inaccuracies in this way. Thus suppose that the consignments on which we carried out our experiment already contained 0.1 per cent of the additive, instead of being free of it as we assumed. Then all our results would tend to be the equivalent of 0.1 per cent too high, and no amount of replication would eliminate this error.

Suppose now that a consignment of materiel as received from the supplier is just sufficient to make five batches for our process. We decide to allocate a single consignment for our tests, using the top 1/5th for the batch at 0.1 per cent, the next 1/5th for that at 0.2 per cent, and so on. This however would leave us wide open to errors. Perhaps the top has been contaminated in transit, and the materiel gets progressively purer towards the bottom. If the contamination affects the reaction, it could be that the differences in resistance which we observed were not due to changes in the additive at all, but to changes in the contamination.

Errors of this type are called *systematic errors*, and we shall try to eliminate them by:

1   Eliminating all extraneous sources of variation.
2   Randomising those which remain.

By *randomisation* we mean that we shall try to ensure that all remaining sources of variation have an equal chance of affecting all of our observations in the same random way, so that they can be reduced to an acceptable magnitude by replication. In our example, we might begin by homogenising, that is thoroughly mixing, the consignments immediately before test. We shall then carry out our tests in random order. This can easily be done with playing cards. If we allocate say the ace, 2, 3, 4 and 5 of diamonds to denote the five percentages of additive, and the same of spades to denote the part of the consignment, then we can thoroughly mix each group of cards, and draw them in random order. The diamonds will tell us the order in which the different percentages are to be applied, and the spades the part of the consignment to use. We could equally use random number tables, and in more complicated tests, this is the easiest way.

27.7   Factorial design

As we originally did it, our test involved only one observation at each percentage of additive, but in practice we would probably make several. If we decide on five tests at each percentage, we should need five consignments of materiel. If we can we shall mix all five thoroughly together, and then use random numbers to decide the order of the tests. If this is not practicable, then we shall make sure that each of the five batches treated at one percentage have come from different parts of a different consignment, and that they are treated in random order. This is called a *factorial design*, and when done as described, it is said to be *balanced*. The following is an example. (We have used letters so that the design is quite general for any similar experiment.)

	Batch Number				
Part of consignment to be used	1	2	3	4	5
Section 1	A	E	D	C	B
Section 2	E	C	A	B	D
Section 3	C	A	B	D	E
Section 4	B	D	E	A	C
Section 5	D	B	C	E	A

27.8 Questions

1a Explain the statistical basis of Student's t test. *(10 marks)*

1b A press makes plastic components which are known to have a mean weight of 121.1 g. A test is run using a new materiel and 10 components are weighed as follows:

120, 121, 119, 120, 120, 122, 121, 118, 120, 119g.

(i) Estimate the standard deviation of the process when working with the new materiel, showing every step of the working. *(7 marks)*

(ii) Assuming that variability has not been changed by the use of the new materiel, and that the frequency distribution is approximately Normal, use a suitable significance test to determine whether the new process uses less materiel per component than the standard process. (All steps in the calculation must be shown.) *(8 marks)*

2a Explain the principle of 'least squares'. *(12 marks)*

2b Using this principle to deduce the best straight line equation relating the following two variables x and y:

x	−4	−3	−2	−1	0	1	2	3	4	5	6
y	−31	−29	−27	−24	−19	−17	−13	−12	−7	−6	−3

(13 marks)

3a What is meant by 'randomisation of the variables' in an experiment? Explain in general terms how this is done. *(12 marks)*

3b A manufacturer has a new type of car in production and now wishes to determine how many kilometres it will do to a litre of petrol, in order to compare this with predictions.

(i) Outline how such an experiment might be devised and executed.

(ii) How might the results be presented?

CHAPTER 28

AN OUTLINE OF RELIABILITY

28.1 Definition of reliability

Our products must not only work correctly when first manufactured, they must continue to do so for as long as our customers reasonably expect. Hence we must see that they are reliable. Suppose we have a new television set, and we want to know whether it will work reliably for say five years, under normal domestic conditions. There is only one certain way to find out, and that is to work it for five years under these conditions. If at the end of this time it is still working satisfactorily, then it was a reliable set. The trouble is that we have had to wait five years for the result, and the set is now largely worn out.

Hence in practice we cannot be certain in advance about the reliability of any particular item, and we have to use probabilities. If for example experience shows that 95% of our television sets are reliable under the conditions stated, then we say that they have a reliability of 95% or 0.95. As explained in Section 5.2, probabilities are usually expressed by the numbers from 0 to 1.0, so that a reliability of 1.0 means certain to work as intended, and reliability 0 means absolutely certain not to work as intended. We can now define reliability as follows.

Reliability is the probability that an item will perform as required, under stated conditions, for a stated period of time.

Notice that the reliability quoted applies to 'stated conditions'. If our television set was to be used in a club instead of a home, then it would probably receive rougher treatment, and we could not expect it to last so long. We must also state what maintenance will be required, to achieve the reliability we quote.

If we put a large number of similar items on life test, and observe when each fails, we can write:

$$\text{Reliability at any time t} = R(t) = \frac{\text{No. surviving at instant } t}{\text{No. at start when } t = 0}$$

(28.1)

28.2 Failure rate

When an item is no longer capable of performing its required function, we say that it has failed. We must however be clear what its required function is. Thus a racing car intended to reach 300 km/hr will be considered to have failed if it only reaches 250, whereas a family car might be considered very satisfactory if it would do 150 km/hr.

Suppose we are able to put 10,000 of a particular part on life test. We note when each part fails, and replace it on test with a good one. After the test has run for many hours, we analyse the results, and find that on average seven parts have failed for each 100 hours, and that this figure appears to be quite constant. This however related to 10,000 parts, and so in order to express a meaningful failure rate, we relate it to one part and one hour:

$$\text{Average failure rate} = \frac{7}{100 \times 10,000} = 0.000007 \text{ per hour}$$

Because failure rates are often very small, it is common, especially in the electronics industry, to express them as probability of failure per million hours:

Average failure rate = 7 per million hours

Failure rates are often constant, but they can vary and in theory have a different value for each instant of time. Hence we can write, for a very large number on test:

$$\text{Instantaneous failure rate} = z(t) = \frac{\text{No. failing per hour at instant } t}{\text{No. still surviving at instant } t}$$

Where the instantaneous failure rate is either constant or is averaged over a convenient period of time, the symbol λ is usually used instead of $z(t)$. Notice that we still refer to the number failing

317

per hour, even when dealing with an instant in time, in the same way as we might refer to a car reaching 150 km/hr, 'just for an instant'.

28.3 The failure probability density function

In our example, we decided to replace any part which failed, so that there were always 10,000 on test. If we had not done this, the number on test would have gradually reduced, and hence the number of failures per hour would have reduced, even though the failure rate remained constant. Hence we can write:

$$
\begin{bmatrix} \text{Observed number of} \\ \text{failures per hour,} \\ \text{at instant } t \\ \text{(out of 10,000)} \end{bmatrix} = \begin{bmatrix} \text{Number} \\ \text{surviving} \\ \text{at instant } t \end{bmatrix} \times \begin{bmatrix} \text{Instantaneous} \\ \text{failure rate} \end{bmatrix}
$$

Again expressing this in terms of one part on test, we have:

$$
\begin{bmatrix} \text{Observed number} \\ \text{of failures per} \\ \text{hour, at instant } t \\ \text{per part on test} \end{bmatrix} = \begin{bmatrix} \dfrac{\text{Number} \\ \text{surviving at} \\ \text{instant } t}{\text{Number at start} \\ \text{when } t = 0} \end{bmatrix} \times \begin{bmatrix} \text{Instanteous} \\ \text{failure test} \end{bmatrix}
$$

$$
= \quad R(t) \quad \times \quad z(t) \qquad (28.2)
$$

The expression in Eq. (28.2) is called the failure probability density function, and given the symbol $f(t)$. Therefore

$$
\begin{array}{l}\text{Failure probability} \\ \text{density function}\end{array} = f(t) = R(t) \times z(t) \qquad (28.3)
$$

28.4 The mean time between failures

If an item has a constant failure rate of 0.001 per hour, we shall expect it to fail and have to be replaced on average every 1000 hours. This would therefore be called the *mean time between failures* or MTBF, and given the symbol θ. Notice that the MTBF is the reciprocal of the failure rate. Thus in our example:

$$
\text{MTBF} = \theta = \frac{1}{\lambda} = \frac{1}{0.001} = 1000 \text{ hours} \qquad (28.4)
$$

Where it is not practical to replace an item which has failed, we refer to the *mean time to failure* or MTTF.

28.5 The bath-tub curve

Suppose we have a large number of parts, which we are able to put on a life test together. We observe, but do not replace failures, and plot a graph of failure rate against time, as shown in Figure 28.1. Because of its shape, this is called the *bath-tub curve*, and it divides into three sections:

1 The early failure period In the first few hundred or so hours of test, the failure rate may be relatively high. Possible causes are:

a Manufacturing faults which were not detected in the factory. This may indicate deficiencies in our factory quality control system.

b The design may be deficient. This is most likely when a new and relatively untried design is concerned.

c Where we are concerned with failures in the customers' hands, they may be due to misuse or inexperience.

2 The constant failure rate period Once parts with inherent weaknesses have failed and been replaced, it is common, especially for electronic parts, to find that the failure rate settles down to a constant and quite a low value for a considerable time. This is therefore called the constant failure rate period.

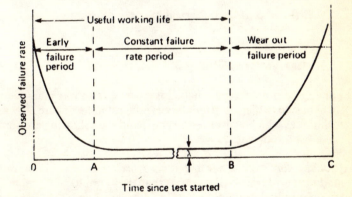

Figure 28.1 The bath-tub curve

3 The wear out failure period Since nothing lasts for ever, there will come a time when the bath-tub curve begins to rise again, probably at an ever-increasing rate. This is therefore called the wear out failure period. If our products are to be reliable for the whole of their planned working life, wear out must not begin until after it has finished. Sometimes when technical improvements are likely in the near future, it is economic to plan for a short working life, at a correspondingly reduced manufacturing cost, so that the equipment can then be replaced by a more up-to-date one. This is called *planned obsolescence*. It may also be used in the fashion trade, to encourage customers to buy new designs, rather than make do with old ones.

28.6 Calculation of reliability when the failure rate is constant

Where the failure rate is constant, we can calculate the reliability after any time t from

$$\text{Reliability} = R(t) = e^{(-\lambda t)} \tag{28.5}$$

Thus suppose that the failure rate is 0.00002 per hour, and we wish to know the reliability after 10,000 hours of operation. Then

$$R(t) = e^{[-(0.00002) \times (10,000)]} = e^{[-0.2]}$$

Now 'e' stands for exponential, which we look up in tables such *Statistical Tables for Science, Engineering Management and Business Studies* by J. Murdoch and J. A. Barnes, and find that

$$R(t) = 0.8187 = 0.82 \text{ or } 82\% \text{ approximately}$$

28.7 Design for reliability

For an equipment to be reliable, it must be faithfully manufactured to a design which is itself inherently reliable. There are many techniques which assist the designer, and the following are some of the most important.

1 Use reliable parts, derated as necessary Since any equipment is made up of parts, it is essential that they should be reliable. The techniques which we discussed in Chapters 6 and 7 for controlling the quality of purchased materiel are most useful for ensuring that only reliable parts are accepted.

The reliability of individual parts can often be improved by *derating* them. Thus we may decide that resistors with a nominal rating of 1 watt shall be used in our equipment at 0.5 watt, in order to lengthen their life.

2 Use as few parts as possible   An equipment will only function as intended if all its vital parts work properly. The more parts there are, the greater the risk that there will be one which fails, so causing the whole equipment to fail. We can illustrate this quite simply.

Suppose we have an equipment in which all the parts have a reliability of 0.90 or 90 per cent, and that every part is vital, in the sense that if one fails, the whole equipment fails. If our equipment only contained one vital part, then:

Reliability of equipment = 0.90

If there are 2 vital parts, then since both must work, we use the multiplication rule, explained in Section 5.3. From this

Reliability of equipment = (0.90 × 0.90) = 0.81

Continuing this argument, we get:

For   3 parts, reliability = $(0.90)^3$ = 0.73
For   4 parts, reliability = $(0.90)^4$ = 0.66
For   5 parts, reliability = $(0.90)^5$ = 0.59
For 10 parts, reliability = $(0.90)^{10}$ = 0.35

Our equipment reliability is now dropping rapidly. Fortunately however parts are usually much more reliable than 0.90, but as none of them are perfect, the fewer we use, the better. When parts or other items in an equipment are such that if one fails, the whole fails, they are said to be *in series*.

3 Redundancy   Even though we use the most reliable parts available, and keep their numbers to a minimum, we may still find that the reliability of one unit in the equipment is insufficient to achieve the overall reliability demanded. Where cost and weight considerations permit, we may decide to include two or more of that particular·unit, arranged so that the whole equipment will continue to work, so long as at least one of these units survives. This technique is called *redundancy*, and the units are said to be *in parallel*.

The reliability of a block of units in parallel can most easily be deduced by considering the probability of overall failure. Suppose that one unit of an equipment has a reliability of only 0.88, and that this cannot be economically improved in time to meet delivery requirements. The designers decide therefore to insert a block of three parallel units into the equipment. We can calculate the overall reliability of this block as follows:

Probability 1 unit fails = (1.00 − 0.88) = 0.12

Since the block will function if any one or more units is working, complete block failure will only occur if all 3 units fail. This requires the multiplication rule discussed in Section 5.3.

Probability all 3 identical units fail
$$= 0.12 \times 0.12 \times 0.12 = 0.001728$$

Therefore,

Reliability of block $\quad = (1.00 - 0.001728) = 0.998272$
$$= 0.998 \text{ say}$$

In the above example, all three units were energised for the whole time the equipment was working. This is called *active redundancy*. Sometimes it is convenient to keep a unit in reserve, and only start it up when the first unit fails. This is called *standby redundancy*. An example of this is the standby generator which a hospital keeps, so that it can light the operating theatre if the mains supply should fail during an operation.

Sometimes, although some failures are permissible, more than one unit must function to keep the equipment working. This is called *partial redundancy*. A simple example of active partial redundancy is the spokes of a bicycle wheel. One or two spokes can fail, but so long as the broken ends are removed, the cycle is still rideable, but clearly we cannot ride it with only one spoke! As an example of standby partial redundancy we can take a car, where we have a spare wheel which we can bring into service if one of the four road wheels fails. However for the car to function, at least four of the five wheels must be in working order.

28.8   Reliability prediction

Suppose a customer asks us to design and make a special piece of equipment, with a guaranteed reliability. It would obviously be foolish to push ahead with design and manufacture, trusting to luck that when the equipment was finally installed, it would have the reliabilty demanded. Months later we should find out that we had failed.

It is essential therefore to predict the final reliability right from the first conception of the design, and then at every stage we:
1   Recalculate the prediction, using additional information as it becomes available.
2   Modify the design as necessary.
The first prediction, before the design proper has started, is likely to be the most inaccurate, and then at every stage our accuracy

improves, until when the equipment finally goes into service, we discover its true reliability. At the start we shall be relying mostly on past experience, but it is unusual for a company to undertake to make a complex piece of equipment of a type which is very different from anything it has previously made. Nearly always there is a background of experience on which we can draw.

We divide the equipment into identifiable sections. Thus suppose we have to produce a special tunnel oven for a new type of cereal. We break this down into:

1   The oven itself with reliability = R_o.
2   The conveyor mechanism with reliability = R_c.
3   The temperature control equipment with reliability = R_t.

The overall equipment reliability might be specified directly in reliability, or as a failure rate or an MTBF. Suppose that a reliability of not less than 0.85 is demanded. Now the sections of the equipment are effectively in series, because if one of them fails, the whole equipment will fail. We can therefore write:

$$R_o \times R_c \times R_t = \text{not less than } 0.85 \qquad (28.6)$$

Suppose we made an oven like this last year, and its reliability was at least 0.99. We also made a conveyor mechanism which was similar, except for being a bit longer. Its reliability was about 0.97. It is the control equipment that worries us, because it contains 6 identical instruments each controlling the temperature of one section of the oven, and all the cereals will be scrap, if any one of them fails. We can now allocate a target reliability to the control equipment, using Eq. (28.6):

$$0.99 \times 0.97 \times R_t = \text{not less than } 0.85$$
$$\therefore \qquad R_t = \text{not less than } 0.885$$

But the six instruments of the temperature controllers are also in series, so if r is the reliability of one section, we have:

$$R_t = r \times r \times r \times r \times r \times r = \text{not less than } 0.885$$
$$\therefore \qquad r = \text{not less then } 0.98$$

Our development engineers must now devise an instrument for one control section of the oven, with a reliability of at least 0.98, or alternatively we may call in one of the firms who specialise in this sort of work. If we should find that 0.98 is not easily obtainable, it is still open to us to improve the reliability of either the oven itself or the conveyor.

Where the reliability is quoted as a failure rate, this is divided directly between the sections. Thus if we are permitted five failures per million hours we could provisionally allocate say one to the oven, one to the conveyor and three to the control equipment.

28.9   Reliability life tests

Much of the reliability information which we require for prediction must come from specially designed tests.

1   Life tests   Most reliability tests are basically life tests, in which the items concerned are operated as nearly as possible as the customer will use them. Tests are usually continued until some or all of the items have failed, and their times to failure recorded.

2   Accelerated life tests   Many parts have a very long life, e.g. an MTBF exceeding 10 years is not uncommon, and hence an ordinary life test would take an unacceptably long time. Accelerated life tests are therefore often used, and these take two main forms:

a   When operation in practice is intermittent, it may be possible to make it continuous for the purposes of the test. A home film projector, for example, will only be used occasionally by its owner, but in the factory it could be run continuously thereby compressing many years of use into an acceptable number of hours.

b   Electronic parts in particular are often continuously loaded in normal use, and so in order to accelerate the test, we have to increase this load, and probably the ambient temperature as well. Thus what is normally a 1 watt resistor might be operated at 2 or 3 watts, at an elevated temperature. The chief difficulty with this type of test is to correlate results with practical use. Thus a statement that a component has a mean life of 200 hours under some specified accelerated test, tells us little unless we know the equivalent number of hours of normal use.

3   Environmental tests   Often our real interest is not to see whether the items concerned will work in a clean temperature-controlled laboratory, but whether they will be satisfactory in the conditions under which our customers will operate them. Hence we may do environmental tests, in which we simulate conditions of temperature, humidity, vibration, shock, mud, dirt, sand, sea water and so on.

28.10   Reliability acceptance tests

There are two main types of reliability test:
1   Reliability acceptance tests, which we shall discuss here.
2   Reliability measurements, which we shall consider in the next section.
   In theory, reliability acceptance tests are analogous to sampling inspection of incoming batches of materiel.

1   We take a random sample of the items to be tested.
a   They may be actually drawn from a batch, but often they are advance samples, before bulk supplies are ordered.
b   Cost usually prohibits tests on large equipments, and so we are mostly concerned with parts and small assemblies.

2   The items are usually tested for a preset time, but the test may be stopped if the allowed number of failures is exceeded (this is c in quality control terms).

3   Acceptance tests are based on an operating characteristic, and the theory in Chapter 5 applies to them. A reliability engineer will talk about 'demonstrating a certain reliability (say 0.95) at a certain level of confidence (say 90%)'. The reliability to be demonstrated is related to the lot tolerance percentage defective of Section 5·9·1. Thus if a fraction 0.95 are reliable, then $(1.0 - 0.95) = 0.05$ must be unreliable, and this corresponds exactly to an LTPD of 5%. The confidence level is effectively $(1.0 - consumer's\ risk)$, so that in our example the consumer's risk is to be $(1.0 - 0.9) = 0.10$ or 10%.

4   The batch or supply of items will be accepted if at the end of the preset time the number of failures observed does not exceed the number allowed by the sampling plan.

28.11   Reliability measurements

Acceptance tests are concerned with demonstrating that the reliability of the items is satisfactory for some purpose. In general they do not provide enough information to give any adequate estimate of the actual reliability or MTBF. For this we must use a reliability measurements test. This is similar in principle, but normally lasts longer. It is, for example, essential to continue until some failures have occurred. When the test is stopped, we estimate the MTBF from:

$$\text{Estimated MTBF} = \frac{\text{Total time all items survived on test, regardless of whether they failed}}{\text{Total number of failures}}$$

Thus if 10 items were put on test for 1000 hours, and 3 failed at 300, 672 and 806 hours whilst the remaining 7 were still working at the end, we should calculate:

$$\text{Estimated MTBF} = \frac{300 + 672 + 806 + (7 \times 1000)}{3}$$

$$= 2926 \text{ hours}$$

Because our sample size is small, the above might not be a very accurate estimate of the MTBF. If the reliability is required, we convert the MTBF to failure rate and insert it in Eq. (28.5).

28.12 Questions

1a Draw a typical bath-tub curve and name both its axes and its *three* main sections. *(6 marks)*

1b Fifteen similar components are put on life test and failures observed to occur at the following times, measured in hours from the start of the test:

20, 100, 130, 220, 270, 330, 470, 670, 870, 980

The test finished after 1000 hours with 5 components still surviving. Assuming that the failure rate is constant, estimate for the components

(i) the mean time to failure (MTTF). (Treat as MTBF). *(5 marks)*

(ii) the failure rate. *(4 marks)*

(iii) their reliability after 100 hours in operation. *(5 marks)*

1c A small assembly contains 6 of the above components connected in series. Estimate its reliability for an operating life of 50 hours. *(5 marks)*

2a Define the term 'reliability'. *(3 marks)*

2b A system consists of three units whose reliabilities are, respectively, 0.95, 0.90 and 0.80. What is the reliability of the system if these units are connected in series? *(3 marks)*

2c Explain briefly the basis of reliability prediction. *(19 marks)*

CHAPTER 29

THE USE OF COMPUTERS IN QUALITY CONTROL

29.1 Introduction

A computer is able to do simple calculations extremely quickly. To enable it to perform a complex calculation, it must be provided with detailed step by step instructions, called the *program*. If there is the slightest mistake in the program, the computer will either say it does not understand, or will give a wrong answer. It usually has no ability to deduce what the correct instruction should be. Computer manufacturers provide many ready made programs for commonly required calculations. Where no program exists, it is only likely to be economic to prepare one for a calculation which is going to be required many times, working on different numerical data.

Programs collectively are called *software*, and the computer itself is the *hardware*.

29.2 Developments in computer use

The modern trend is towards *dedicated* computers, which are intended for one application only. Thus a process may have its own *minicomputer* to monitor and adjust continuously the settings of its various process parameters, in order to ensure a consistently good quality product. Where the computer is so small that it contains only one integrated circuit, it is called a *microcomputer*. The central

327

mainframe computer still exists in some companies, and it is then often possible to link a minicomputer *on-line* to it, so that the minicomputer can make use of data etc., stored in the main computer.

Many pocket and desk calculators have in-built programs, called functions, so that frequently required calculations can be done at the touch of a button. Those most useful to the quality engineer include mean, standard deviation, natural logarithms and exponentials, powers of numbers (especially squares and square roots) and factorials. Even shop floor inspectors can be provided with simple calculators for working out averages and ranges for quality control charts, or for acceptance sampling by variables.

Small table top type computers can now be obtained, which are designed to be linked to a test jig. When manufactured components are placed in the jig, the computer records their measurements, and from the data it collects, it plots out average and range charts, histograms and other frequency curves, process capability data, etc. as required. Computers of this type can be obtained from Mitutoyo (UK) Ltd., Kingsway, Walworth Industrial Estate, Andover, Hampshire SP10 5LQ.

29.3 Analysis of data

A computer is useful for analysing large quantities of data, as the following examples show.

1 Scrap and other defective work

This can be analysed, Pareto-style, into type of fault, cause, part number, machine used, batch number, operator, inspector, department responsible, etc. Provided data are available, the analysis can be in terms of money rather than numbers defective.

2 Customer returns

Failures in the customers' hands can equally be analysed into type of equipment, the type of part which has failed, the cause of failure, the age of the equipment, how much it had been used, and the type of work on which it had been engaged, etc. If code numbers permit the manufacturing conditions to be identified, then analysis can proceed as in (1) above into department responsible, machine,

328

materiel, batch, operator, etc. It may also be possible to analyse customer use into faulty operation, faulty storage, faulty installation, bad maintenance, etc. Better training and instruction manuals will help customers to avoid these failures.

29.4   In-process uses of computers

These have already been explained in Sections 19.3, 20.6, 21.6 and 22.7.

29.5   Computer control of complex tasks

Many equipments, especially those which are fundamentally electronic, need a complex succession of tests to ensure that they function correctly and are properly adjusted for optimum performance. If this is done manually it is time-consuming, and any test which is not essential is likely to be omitted. Suitably programmed, the computer can carry out these tests as quickly as the equipment can take them. It can then print out a complete set of results, or merely report those parameters which are out of limit.

29.6   Design and analysis of experiments

The computer can easily generate random rumbers for the design of an experiment, for the taking of truly random samples from a batch, etc. It can also be used for analysing experimental results. Thus it can find the line of best fit, not only for the linear case discussed in Section 27.5, but also where a higher-order curve must be fitted.

29.7   Control of purchased supplies

Again we can use the computer to generate random numbers for batch sampling, where this is worthwhile. It can analyse information from incoming inspection, suppliers' test reports, laboratory analyses, etc. It can also work out vendor ratings, and keep them up-to-date on an ongoing basis.

29.8   Reliability testing

As we saw in Sections 28.10 and 28.11, reliability tests tend to be complicated, and there is often a lot of data best analysed by computer. For economic reasons, tests are usually made on parts and units, rather than on complete equipments, and the computer can then be used to work out the overall reliability of the assemblies and equipments built from them. This technique is known as *testing by parts*.

At the design stage, reliability predictions are often made from published data, such as that given in the American MIL-STD-HBK-217. Amongst other things, this gives failure rates for many types of component, mostly electronic, together with allowances to be made when they are working under arduous conditions, such as exposed on the deck of a ship. The equipment reliability can then be predicted if the arrangement of these parts in series or parallel (Section 28.7) is known. A computer can store all these data, so that if it is given a list of parts to be used, their arrangement and the working environment it can not only predict the overall failure rate, but it can draw attention to the sections of the equipment where failure is most likely to occur.

29.9   Computer aided design (CAD)

As designs become more complex, so it becomes almost essential to use a computer for the necessary calculations. This is particularly so where the problem is primarily one of optimisation. Out of perhaps thousands of combinations of the relevant parameters, the best combination must be chosen. The designer might hit upon a reasonable set of conditions, but in many cases only the computer can find the best with certainty.

29.10   Computer aided manufacture (CAM), and similar applications in defence

Many modern equipments used either in industry or in defence, are computer controlled. Quality control of the design, manufacture and testing of the required software, follows the same basic steps as that for hardware, but great care is required. Once a mistake has been made in a program, it is often extremely difficult to find and correct.

Defence requirements for software are set out in AQAP-13, whilst AQAP-14 is the guide to it.

29.11 Questions

1 Explain the quality uses which can be made of dedicated computers, (i.e. computers which are specifically designed for one task, or a range of related tasks). *(25 marks)*

2 Explain the uses and limitations of a computer, when assisting the control of quality. *(25 marks)*

CHAPTER 30

QUALITY ASSURANCE

30.1 The changing quality scene

In recent years customers have become much more critical about
the quality and reliability of products supplied. Thus the Ministry of
Defence will only purchase from companies approved to an
appropriate AQAP standard, (see Sections 30.2 onwards). Many
industrial concerns will only purchase from companies approved to
BS 5750, as sections 30.3 onwards, or who have been appraised and
approved by their own quality engineers as explained in Chapter 4.
In addition there is a tendency for industrial purchasers to demand
that their suppliers use statistical methods as described in Chapters
11 to 14. Purchasers of domestic equipment have too often found
that quality and reliability have not come up to their expectations,
and regrettably they have increasingly bought imports from the far
east.

All of the above has spurred British manufacturers to make
major improvements in quality, but much time has been lost, and
the need for a substantial improvement in product quality and
reliability is now urgent. Increasingly what was once the inspection
department is being developed into the quality assurance department, with a quality manager or quality director in charge. *Quality
assurance* is responsible for overall surveillance of everything to do
with quality throughout the company. Thus it is concerned with the
quality aspects of sales, research, design, development, pre-

production, materiel, plant, tooling, operators, inspectors, manufacture, storage, packaging, transit, installation, commissioning, customer comments and complaints.

30.2 Allied quality assurance publications (AQAP's)

In the mid 1960's, NATO adopted what at that time was an advanced set of quality assurance systems, which it issued as a series of Allied Quality Assurance Publications, (AQAP's). Our own Ministry of Defence decided to make use of these standards, and initially issued them as a series of Defence Standards numbered 05-21 upwards. Recently they have reverted to the now updated AQAP's, of which the most important are AQAP-1, AQAP-4, AQAP-6, AQAP-9 and AQAP-13.

30.3 British standard 5750

Over the years many large industrial concerns devised their own quality assurance requirements, which they then imposed on their suppliers. These were mostly somewhat similar, but differed considerably in detail. The problem was that a manufacturer who supplied several of these large concerns, found it very difficult to satisfy all their differing requirements economically. Small companies seldom had sufficient commercial strength to impose requirements, and too often had to put up with whatever the supplier sent.

Various attempts were made by a number of organisations to establish some sort of national quality standard, and this was finally achieved by the British Standards Institution, in the form of BS 5750. Since then many medium and small companies have achieved the standard required and been approved to BS 5750. Unfortunately many of the large companies who already had systems of their own have refused to change, and so remain outside the national system.

30.4 International standards ISO 9000 to 9004

A number of countries have adopted similar quality assurance system requirements, but again differing in detail. Hence for some time, work has proceeded to try to produce an international standard, which most countries would accept. Finally this has been achieved and published by the International Organisation for Standardisation (ISO) as a series of standards numbered ISO 9000 to ISO 9004. These in turn have been published by British Standards as an updated version of BS 5750:1987 in 4 parts numbered 0, 1, 2 and 3. Part 0 incorporates both ISO 9000 and ISO 9004, and parts 1, 2 and 3 correspond exactly to ISO 9001, 9002 and 9003 respectively.

30.5 Summary and comparison of current standards

We now have two sets of current quality assurance standards, namely the AQAP system of the Ministry of Defence, and BS 5750 which incorporates ISO 9000. These two systems are not identical, but have a considerable similarity. Each system has 3 key standards, which correspond with each other as follows.

AQAP-1 and BS 5750 part 1

These standards are used where a contract requires design work, and/or where manufacture requires close quality control throughout.

AQAP-4 and BS 5750 part 2

These standards are used where an approved design already exists, but close inspection and test will be required throughout manufacture.

AQAP-9 and BS 5750 part 3

These are used where an approved design already exists, and the product is sufficiently simple that a competent person can ensure complete conformance to requirements by inspection and test after manufacture. Note however that it would be unwise to have no in-process quality control at all, because the reject rate on final test would probably be unacceptably high.

Guides to the standard

AQAP-2 is a guide to AQAP-1, and AQAP-5 is a guide to AQAP-4.

The corresponding British Standard guides are incorporated in BS 5750 part 0.

Calibration

In order to obtain approval under the AQAP system, all measuring devices must be calibrated in accordance with AQAP-6 and its guide AQAP-7. In the British Standard system, calibration requirements have now been incorporated in the main BS 5750 specifications, and BS 5781 which was originally used for this purpose is no longer required.

30.6   Obtaining approval

A company wishing to obtain approval under either an AQAP or BS 5750, must apply to either the Ministry of Defence or BSI stating:

1   For which of the standards in 30.5 approval is requested.
2   The precise range of product or service it is offering.

Companies who supply defence equipment will need an AQAP, those serving industry an appropriate part of BS 5750. Companies working in both fields will probably need approval under each. As the corresponding standards are similar, this is not as bad as it sounds, but watch carefully for the differences between them.

MOD or BSI as appropriate will then send a small team of assessors, hopefully knowledgeable in the type of work involved. They will check the applicant's quality assurance system fairly thoroughly, to satisfy themselves that it complies with the standard for which approval is sought. At the end the company concerned will be placed in one of 3 categories.

1   Significant non-compliance   This means that the company concerned has failed to get approval.

2   Significant number of minor non-compliances   The assessors have found a scatter of things which need correction, but when this has been done, approval will be given.

3   Minor problem areas   Approval has been granted, subject to a few minor comments.

Contracts offered by the Ministry of Defence have an appropriate

AQAP level attached to them. Thus a contract requiring AQAP-1 will only be awarded to a company approved to AQAP-1 for the type of work concerned. In principle the same applies to BS 5750, but individual customers do not always apply their rights rigorously. If a manufacturer accepts a contract to one of these standards, (e.g. AQAP-1) then the standard agreed becomes a term of contract, and a company which failed to comply could be sued for breach of contract. The guides however are purely advisory and do not comprise part of the contract.

30.7 Contents of the standards

Each pair of standards set out in section 30.5, (e.e. AQAP-1 and BS 5750 part 1), are very similar, but not identical. It is therefore essential for anyone wishing to obtain approval, to obtain a copy of the latest edition of the relevant standard, and comply with it to the letter. Nevertheless a company approved to say AQAP-1, would have no difficulty in making the necessary additions, (e.g. training), in order to comply with BS 5750 part 1 for the same range of products or services.

The standards offer a very good set of quality assurance systems, which any company could use to advantage, regardless of whether approval is sought. However approval is an excellent commercial accolade, and there are few companies who would not benefit from having it. It is not possible in this book to give complete details of all of these standards, but the following is a brief summary of the contents of AQAP-1, so that the reader may have some idea what is involved.

The principle throughout is that the customer, in this case the Ministry of Defence, states exactly what is required, and the contractor, (i.e. manufacturer), is responsible for meeting those requirements, and for keeping adequate records to show that he has done so. For AQAP-1 where design is involved, the Ministry will probably state the functional properties of say a new weapon, leaving the manufacturer to design the hardware to achieve this. MOD will appoint a Quality Assurance Representative (QAR), to keep in touch with each contractor, with authority to inspect work in that contractor's premises as required. (Under BS 5750 the QAR is called a Purchaser's Representative (PR) but has exactly the same role.)

The following is a summary of AQAP-1's stipulations.

1 A quality manager or equivalent must be appointed with

authority to ensure that all quality and reliability requirements are met.

2   Prescribed procedures, usually in the form of a *quality manual*, must be prepared, giving details of the whole of the company's quality organisation and arrangements. These must be reviewed periodically, and corrected and updated as necessary. These reviews are called *quality audits*.

3   Designer's responsibilities must be clearly defined. Manufacturing drawings and specifications must satisfy requirements completely. Tolerances must be rational and allow for interchangeability. The issue and recall of drawings etc. must be properly controlled.

4   The contractor is responsible for the quality and reliability of all materiel he obtains, and each materiel must have a precise written purchasing specification. Vendor appraisal is encouraged, and goods inwards inspection or its equivalent must monitor all incoming consignments, and ensure that they are satisfactory.

5   Written work instructions must be provided throughout, not only for manufacture and test, but for every other operation, for example, packaging.

6   In-process checks must verify everything which cannot be checked later, and final test and inspection must complete the evidence of full conformance.
a   All test and inspection equipment must be calibrated to AQAP-6.
b   Records of all checks must be kept.
c   At each stage work must be segregated by *materiel status* into
       (i)   awaiting inspection,
       (ii)   checked and found satisfactory,
       (iii) checked and found unsatisfactory.

7   Effective corrective action must be taken immediately unsatisfactory work occurs, or in a situation where it could occur.

8   A complete set of records must be kept of all of the above, and these must be kept until disposal is authorised by the Ministry. This is typically 5 years, but may be longer if the product concerned has a long working life.

9   Handling, storage, packaging, installation etc. must all be closely controlled.

10   Each contract must have its own *quality plan* or equivalent. When the contract is in prospect, the contractor must review all its requirements, and confirm that he understands them fully. He must then draw up a quality plan, showing which of his quality facilities, (as shown in the quality manual), will be required, and how he is going to satisfy any demands of the contract which are not already available. The Ministry must approve the plan.

30.8   BS 9000

All British Standards numbered from BS 9000 up to 9999 deal with electronic components of assessed quality. Again although far from identical, the 9000 system follows the same general lines as are set out for AQAP-1 in section 30.7.

30.9   The role of the quality manager

The role of the quality manager is roughly as follows.
1   He/she has direct line control of the quality assurance department. Sometimes, particularly in small companies he controls other associated functions, such as the works test laboratory, purchase department and stores, plant mainten- ance etc. In the food industry the quality manager is usually responsible for hygiene.
2   He is responsible for surveillance of all quality matters throughout the rest of the company. Obviously he must not usurp the authority of the other departmental heads, but if for example, there is a problem with the quality of a particular design, he must have the authority and ability to resolve it with the chief designer. The same applies to a quality problem anywhere in the company.
3   The quality manager must act as the customer's represent- ative. If any customer has a quality problem, complaint etc., they will usually contact the quality manager, and expect him to get things put right, *regardless of where in the organisation* the trouble originates.
4   The quality manager has in effect the job of introducing, organising and controlling all that we have discussed in this book. He will utilise all the information which the quality

assurance system collects, and he will be striving always to achieve a satisfactory quality and reliability as cheaply as possible.

30.10 Questions

1 Outline the quality assurance system in a company with which you are familiar. What improvements to the system would you suggest, and why?

2 What is the purpose of the Ministry of Defence's standard AQAP-1. Explain briefly what is involved in complying with it. (An answer related to BS 5750 part 1 would be equally acceptable.)

TABLE 1 AQL sampling inspection table

A.Q.L. Batch size	0·065%			0·10%			0·15%			0·25%			0·40%			0·65%			1·0%			1·5%			2·5%			4·0%			6·5%		
	n	P	F	n	P	F	n	P	F	n	P	F	n	P	F	n	P	F	n	P	F	n	P	F	n	P	F	n	P	F	n	P	F
2–50	All			All			All			All			32	0	1	20	0	1	13	0	1	8	0	1	5	0	1	3	0	1	8	1	2
51–90	All			All			80	0	1	50	0	1	32	0	1	20	0	1	13	0	1	8	0	1	5	0	1	3	0	1	8	1	2
91–150	All			125	0	1	80	0	1	50	0	1	32	0	1	20	0	1	13	0	1	32	1	2	20	1	2	13	1	2	8	1	2
151–280	200	0	1	125	0	1	80	0	1	50	0	1	32	0	1	20	0	1	50	1	2	32	1	2	20	1	2	13	1	2	13	2	3
281–500	200	0	1	125	0	1	80	0	1	50	0	1	32	0	1	80	1	2	50	1	2	50	2	3	20	1	2	20	2	3	20	3	4
501–1,200	200	0	1	125	0	1	80	0	1	50	0	1	125	1	2	80	1	2	80	2	3	80	3	4	32	2	3	32	3	4	32	5	6
1,201–3,200	200	0	1	125	0	1	80	0	1	200	1	2	125	1	2	125	2	3	125	3	4	125	5	6	50	3	4	50	5	6	50	7	8
3,201–10,000	200	0	1	125	0	1	80	0	1	200	1	2	200	2	3	200	3	4	200	5	6	200	7	8	80	5	6	80	7	8	80	10	11
10,001–35,000	800	1	2	500	1	2	315	1	2	315	2	3	315	3	4	315	5	6	315	7	8	315	10	11	125	7	8	125	10	11	125	14	15
35,001–150,000	800	1	2	500	1	2	500	2	3	500	3	4	500	5	6	500	7	8	500	10	11	500	14	15	200	10	11	200	14	15	200	21	22
150,001–500,000	1,250	2	3	800	2	3	800	3	4	800	5	6	800	7	8	800	10	11	800	14	15	800	21	22	315	14	15	315	21	22	200	21	22
Over 500,000	2,000	3	4	1,250	3	4	1,250	5	6	1,250	7	8	1,250	10	11	1,250	14	15	1,250	21	22	800	21	22	500	21	22	315	21	22	200	21	22

The above is an example of how suitable sampling plans can be selected from BSS' 6001. The method of use is as follows. Suppose the batch size is 500 and the A.Q.L. is to be 1·0 per cent. Take the sample of 50 (Column n) and check it. If the number of defectives does not exceed 1 (column P) the batch is passed; if it is 2 or more (column F) it is failed. n is sample size, P is max. defectives for batch to pass, F is number of defectives (or more) for batch to fail. For further details see section (5.7).

This table has been taken from DEF-131A, by kind permission of the Controller of Her Majesty's Stationery Office.

TABLE 2 Choosing the most economical AQL. (For details about the use of this table, see Section 6.8)

RATIO = $(a + r) \div (i)$

Batch size	0.1	0.2	0.3	0.4	0.5	0.6	0.7	0.8	0.9	1.0	2	3	4	5	6	7	8	9	10	20	30	40	50	60	70	80	90	100	150	200	250	300	400	500	600	700	800	900	1000	1500	1600
2–50	2.5	2.5	2.5	2.5	2.5	2.5	2.5	2.5	2.5	2.5	2.5	2.5	2.5	2.5	2.5	2.5	2.5	2.5	1.5	1.5	1.5	1.0	1.0	1.0	1.0	0.65	0.65	0.65	0.40	0.40	All	All	All	All	All	All	All	All	All	All	All
51–90	2.5	2.5	2.5	2.5	2.5	2.5	2.5	2.5	2.5	2.5	2.5	2.5	2.5	1.5	1.5	1.5	1.5	1.5	1.5	1.0	0.65	0.65	0.65	0.65	0.40	0.40	0.40	0.40	0.25	0.25	0.25	0.25	All	All	All	All	All	All	All	All	All
91–150	2.5	2.5	2.5	2.5	2.5	2.5	2.5	2.5	2.5	2.5	1.0	1.0	1.0	1.0	1.0	1.0	1.0	1.0	1.0	0.65	0.65	0.4	0.4	0.4	0.4	0.4	0.4	0.25	0.25	0.25	0.15	0.15	0.15	0.15	0.15	All	All	All	All	All	All
151–280	2.5	2.5	2.5	2.5	2.5	2.5	2.5	2.5	2.5	2.5	0.65	0.65	0.65	0.65	0.65	0.65	0.65	0.65	0.65	0.65	0.4	0.4	0.4	0.25	0.25	0.25	0.4	0.25	0.15	0.15	0.15	0.10	0.10	0.10	0.10	0.10	0.10	0.10	0.10	All	All
281–500	2.5	2.5	2.5	2.5	2.5	2.5	2.5	2.5	2.5	2.5	0.4	0.4	0.4	0.4	0.4	0.4	0.4	0.4	0.4	0.25	0.25	0.15	0.15	0.15	0.15	0.15	0.15	0.15	0.15	0.15	0.10	0.10	0.10	0.10	0.065	0.065	0.065	0.065	0.065	All	All
501–1,200	2.5	2.5	2.5	2.5	2.5	2.5	2.5	2.5	0.25	0.25	0.25	0.25	0.25	0.25	0.25	0.25	0.25	0.25	0.25	0.25	0.25	0.15	0.15	0.15	0.15	0.10	0.10	0.065	0.065	0.065	0.065	0.065	0.065	0.065	0.065	0.065	0.065	0.065	0.065	All	All
1,201–3,200	2.5	2.5	2.5	2.5	0.15	0.15	0.15	0.15	0.15	0.15	0.15	0.15	0.15	0.15	0.15	0.15	0.15	0.15	0.15	0.15	0.15	0.10	0.10	0.10	0.065	0.065	0.065	0.065	0.065	0.065	0.065	0.050	0.050	0.050	0.050	0.050	0.050	0.050	0.065	All	All
3,201–10,000	2.5	2.5	0.15	0.15	0.15	0.15	0.15	0.15	0.15	0.15	0.10	0.10	0.10	0.065	0.065	0.065	0.065	0.065	0.15	0.10	0.10	0.065	0.065	0.065	0.065	0.065	0.065	0.065	0.065	0.065	0.065	0.050	0.050	0.050	0.050	0.050	0.050	0.050	0.050	All	All
10,001–35,000	2.5	2.5	0.15	0.10	0.10	0.10	0.10	0.10	0.10	0.10	0.10	0.10	0.10	0.10	0.10	0.10	0.10	0.15	0.15	0.10	0.10	0.065	0.065	0.065	0.065	0.065	0.065	0.065	0.065	0.050	0.050	0.050	0.050	0.065	0.050	0.050	0.065	0.050	0.065	All	All
35,001–150,000	2.5	0.10	0.10	0.10	0.10	0.10	0.10	0.10	0.10	0.065	0.10	0.10	0.065	0.065	0.065	0.065	0.065	0.065	0.065	0.065	0.065	0.065	0.065	0.065	0.065	0.065	0.065	0.065	0.065	0.050	0.050	0.050	0.050	0.050	0.050	0.050	0.050	0.050	0.065	All	All
150,001–500,000	0.10	0.10	0.10	0.10	0.10	0.10	0.10	0.10	0.10	0.10	0.10	0.10	0.065	0.065	0.065	0.065	0.065	0.065	0.065	0.065	0.065	0.065	0.065	0.065	0.065	0.065	0.065	0.065	0.065	0.050	0.050	0.050	0.050	0.065	0.050	0.050	0.065	0.050	0.065	All	All
Over 500,001	0.10	0.10	0.10	0.10	0.10	0.10	0.10	0.10	0.10	0.10	0.10	0.10	0.065	0.065	0.065	0.065	0.065	0.065	0.065	0.065	0.065	0.065	0.065	0.065	0.065	0.065	0.065	0.065	0.065	0.065	0.065	0.050	0.050	0.050	0.050	0.050	0.050	0.050	0.065	All	All

a is cost of one item in batch; *r* is cost of repairs, etc. if one defective item gets into production lines; and *i* is cost of inspecting one item. All indicates 100 per cent inspection.

TABLE 3 Constants for the use of control limits on quality control charts.

13.2 Tolerance based quality control charts

Average chart

Draw each control limit a distance equal to ($A''_{0.025} \times$ mean range), *inside* each specification or drawing limit.

Range chart

Draw one control limit, a distance equal to ($D'_{0.001} \times$ mean range), starting from zero range, and measuring upwards.

Values of constants

Sample size	2	3	4	5	6	7	8
$A''_{0.025}$	1.51	1.16	1.02	0.95	0.90	0.87	0.84
$D'_{0.001}$	4.12	2.98	2.57	2.34	2.21	2.11	2.04

For information on the use of these constants, see section 13.2.

14.4 Process based quality control charts

Average chart

Inner control limits Draw each control limit a distance equal to ($A'_{0.025} \times$ the mean range), *out* from the process average.

Outer control limits Draw each control limit a distance equal to ($A'_{0.001} \times$ the mean range), *out* from the process average.

Range chart

Inner control limit Draw one control limit a distance equal to ($D'_{0.025} \times$ mean range), upwards from zero range.

Outer control limit Draw one control limit a distance equal to ($D'_{0.001} \times$ mean range), upwards from zero range.

Values of constants

Sample size	2	3	4	5	6	7	8
$A'_{0.025}$	1.229	0.668	0.476	0.377	0.316	0.274	0.244
$A'_{0.001}$	1.937	1.054	0.750	0.594	0.498	0.432	0.384
$D'_{0.025}$	2.81	2.17	1.93	1.81	1.72	1.66	1.62
$D'_{0.001}$	4.12	2.98	2.57	2.34	2.21	2.11	2.04

American constants (14.5)

Sample size	2	3	4	5	6	7	8
A_2	1.880	1.023	0.729	0.577	0.483	0.419	0.373
D_4	3.268	2.574	2.282	2.114	2.004	1.924	1.864

Quality control charts for attributes

Book section	Chart type	Application	Process average	Standard deviation
15.3	p	% defective	$\bar{p}$	$\sqrt{\dfrac{\bar{p}(100 - \bar{p})}{\bar{n}}}$
15.8	p	Proportion defective	$\bar{p}$	$\sqrt{\dfrac{\bar{p}(1 - \bar{p})}{\bar{n}}}$
15.10	np	Number defective	$\bar{c} = n\bar{p}$	$\sqrt{\bar{c}\left[1 - \dfrac{\bar{c}}{n}\right]}$
15.11	c	Number of defects	$\bar{c}$	$\sqrt{\bar{c}}$
15.12	u	Defects per item	$\bar{u}$	$\sqrt{\dfrac{\bar{u}}{\bar{n}}}$

ANSWERS TO NUMERICAL QUESTIONS
(Provided by author)

Chapter 2

2b *(ii)* 2% at which the total cost is £1400.
3a *(iv)* 3.54%, £2,828.

Chapter 5

1b *(i)* 0.1829; *(ii)* 0.1667; *(iii)* 195.
2a *(i)* 0.0544; *(ii)* 0.1333; *(iii)* 0.4544; *(iv)* 0.5878.
3b *(i)* 0.0474, 0.0537; *(ii)* 0.2381, 0.0818; *(iii)* either; *(iv)* Y.
4b Common AQL is at 1%.

Chapter 7

3a Typical rating 86 points, but it will depend on the assumptions made.
3b AQL is 0.65%, also depending on assumptions.

Chapter 11

1b 59.84 mm.
1c *(i)* 1.64%) *(ii)* 8.08%.
2a The data is Normal because the plot on probability paper gives a straight line.
2b Mean = 10.02 ohms; standard deviation = 0.148 ohms.
2c *(i)* 9.43 to 10.62 ohms; *(ii)* 9.58 to 10.47 ohms.
2d C_p = 1.8 approx, which is very capable.

Chapter 13

1 Control limits: average chart = 10.71 and 11.29 ohms; range chart = 1.03 ohms.

Chapter 14

1a Control limits: average chart = 9.034, 9.039, 9.055, 9.060 mm; range chart = 0.040, 0.051 mm.

2b Control limits: average chart = 12.064, 12.069, 12.088, 12.094 mm; range chart = 0.039, 0.051 mm.

2c Conventional limits do not allow for drift.

2d ±0.045 mm.

(Answers will be slightly different if the American constants in Section 14.5 are used)

Chapter 15

1b *(i)* Control limits 0.41, 1.10, 3.90, 4.59%;
   (ii) Control limits 2.03, 5.52, 19.48, 22.97

Chapter 16

1a Control limits 0.6, 9.4, 11.5. (The lowest control limit is below zero.)

Chapter 27

1b *(i)* Mean = 120g, standard deviation = 1.15g;
   (ii) $t = 3.01$ which is significant.

2b $y = 2.9x - 20.0$.

Chapter 28

1b *(i)* 906 hr; *(ii)* 0.0011 failures per hour; *(iii)* 89.6%.

1c 71.8%.

INDEX OF SYMBOLS

LCL	Lower control limit on a chart	Not used in book
LTPD	Lot tolerance percentage defective	48
m	expected or average number defective in a sample $= n\bar{p}$	43
MTBF	mean time between failures	318
MTTF	mean time to failure	318
n	number of items in a sample	45
N	number of items in a batch or lot	69
p	percentage or fraction of defectives in a sample or batch	42
$\bar{p}$	average percentage or fraction of defectives over a number of samples or batches	217
ppm	parts per million	60
q	percentage or fraction good in a sample or batch	42
$\bar{q}$	average percentage or fraction good over a number of samples or batches	220
r	cost of repairs, retest etc., when one defective item is fed into production	69
R	alternative symbol for w, the range of a sample	–
R(t)	reliability after time t on test or in service	317
RQL	rejectable quality level	48
RV	reference value for a cusum chart	207
s	standard deviation of a sample	138
S	scrap and rework cost over a set period	179
t	constant used in Student's t test	307
t	time so far, in a reliability life test	
u	number of defects per unit	228
$\bar{u}$	average number of defects per unit over a number of samples or batches	
U	upper specification or drawing limit	143
UCL	upper control limit on a chart	Not used in book
w	range within a sample	173
$\bar{w}$	mean range	173
x	any measurement, e.g. 20·34mm	138
$x_1, x_2, x_3, ---x_i ---x_n$		
	measurements in order on a sample of n items, where x_i represents any term in the sequence	138
$\bar{x}$	average of a set of measurements	138
z	number of standard deviations a sample mean is displaced from the process mean, or maybe another sample mean	307
z(t)	failure rate	317

α	significance expressed as a probability	306
θ	MTBF	325
2θ	angle of a V mask for a cusum chart	210
λ	constant failure rate	317
v	degrees of freedom	308
σ	standard deviation of a process	138
σ̂	best estimate of the process standard deviation, made from a sample. Pronounced "sigma cap".	138
$\sum\limits_{1}^{n} x_i$	summation: total all values from x_1 to x_n	138

INDEX